NORTHWEST DISASTER:

Avalanche and Fire

BY RUBY EL HULT

Here for the first time is a complete and true account of two of the worst disasters ever to occur in the Pacific Northwest: one a thundering, murdering avalanche of ice and snow, the other a huge inferno of rampaging forest fire— both told with all the swift impact with which these catastrophes smashed into people's lives. The place was the Cascades and the Bitter Roots; the time, 1910.

The weather had been strange that year. Suddenly powerful natural forces tore out of control. Men and towns were hurled deep into icy graves. Later that same year they were trapped in a raging maelstrom of fire.

Ruby El Hult is a master storyteller. Here she writes unforgettably of each person who lived to tell of snow burial high in the Cascades, of a fire that darkened much of the world. We learn who the people were, something of their friends and families, their business and hobbies, their hopes and dreams and joys, their reactions to approaching danger, their behaviour in crisis ... and how they met death.

NORTHWEST DISASTER:

Avalanche and Fire

BOOKS BY RUBY EL HULT

LOST MINES AND TREASURES OF THE PACIFIC NORTHWEST

Long-accepted treasure stories of Oregon, Washington, and Idaho are thoroughly investigated.

TREASURE HUNTING NORTHWEST

A sequel to Lost Mines and Treasures, *along with many new tales for treasure hunters.*

UNTAMED OLYMPICS: The Story of a Peninsula

True account of one of the wildest, strangest, most fascinating wilderness regions in America.

NORTHWEST DISASTER: Fire and Avalanche

First complete narrative of two of the worst disasters ever to occur in the Pacific Northwest.

STEAMBOATS IN THE TIMBER

Early steamboat days in Idaho, with many tales of the colorful characters who manned the boats.

Northwest Disaster:

Avalanche and Fire

by

RUBY EL HULT

BINFORDS & MORT, *Publishers*

Portland　　·　　Oregon　　·　　97242

DEDICATED
TO THOSE WHO LOST THEIR LIVES
in the
WELLINGTON AVALANCHE
and the
GREAT IDAHO FIRE

ACKNOWLEDGMENTS

Wellington Avalanche

Although Pacific Northwest newspapers gave uncounted pages of space to the Wellington disaster at the time of its happening, newspaper accounts tend to contain many conflicting and confusing elements, and without two other main sources of information I should have been unable to put together a coherent and cohesive, as well as accurate, account of the week-long ordeal suffered by the people detained on the two snow-bound Great Northern trains which were overwhelmed by the avalanche at Wellington, Washington, on the night of March 1, 1910. My two other main sources have been:

(1) People still alive, who, because they were near-victims, inhabitants of Wellington, or rescue workers, possess direct knowledge of the tragedy. A list of the people interviewed concerning the avalanche is given in Appendix I, "Those Who Remember."

(2) The 900 pages of certified trial testimony, *Topping vs. Great Northern Railway Company,* on file in the office of the Clerk of the Supreme Court of Washington, Olympia. See Appendix I, heading "Legal and Public Documents."

I thank Benjamin T. Hart and his friend James McCabe, both retired railroad men living in Seattle, for reading my manuscript and making helpful suggestions and corrections concerning railroad terms. Mr. and Mrs. Raymond Starrett, Olympia, also read a portion of the manuscript.

1910 Fire

The collecting of the 1910 fire material gave me an opportunity to revisit Spokane, the Coeur d'Alene mining country and the St. Joe Valley. For their hospitality during my various trips I thank Eleanor Garst, Cordie Averitt, Bonnie and Stan Kreshel, Ruth and Herman West, Hazel and Vance Corbeill, Elizabeth and Gene Saunders, Mr. and Mrs. Roy Peterson, the Chris Nelson family, and the Dale C. and Lyle (Red) Hult families.

Particularly helpful were interviews and correspondence with Walter Hanson (now deceased), who was mayor of Wallace in 1910; with Joe B. Halm of Missoula, a forest ranger believed lost during the 1910 fire; and with William G. Weigle of Pasadena, California, who was Supervisor of the Coeur d'Alene Natonal Forest in 1910. Other people whose reminiscences supplied additional details are listed in Appendix II.

I am indebted to Mrs. Bertha Kottkey, Mrs. Elsie Pulaski Pabst, and Mrs. Walter Hanson, all of Wallace, and to Mr. Weigle, for loans of pictures; and to Mrs. Pabst for making available a manuscript written by her mother, Emma Pulaski.

I thank Dr. Donald H. Clark and Professor Walter Schaeffer of the University of Washington School of Forestry, who read the complete fire manuscript and made helpful suggestions and corrections. Hazel Corbeill of Kellogg, Idaho, and Harry McLeod of Wallace, read portions of the manuscript.

I also thank John Penny, Kellogg, for a most pleasant drive across the old burn area from Wallace to Avery.

* * *

I wish to add that this book is in no way to be regarded as fiction. Disasters such as the two whose complete stories are told here for the first time, present themselves to the people involved, first as threatening, worrisome situations; and, in the end, as dramatic, tragic forces smashing into their lives. I believe that history as truth is added to, rather than detracted from, if the "feel" of an event—its impact at the time of happening—can be projected along with the historic facts. In attempting an on-the-scene reconstruction, I have carefully refrained from adding to the information revealed by my research, or departing from it; even the conversation is based on details known to have happened and what was reported said at the time.

RUBY EL HULT

CONTENTS

WHITE DEATH
IN THE CASCADES

1

In a hotel room in Spokane, Washington, jolly Nellie Sharp said to her companion, Mrs. Herbert Tweedie, "I'll tell you what we'll do. We'll draw for it. The one who gets the short straw goes east to Montana, the one who gets the long, west to Seattle."

In that year of 1910 women had not yet won the vote or the undisputed right to project their talents on the world. So these two were daring adventurers—women journalists from the East, traveling through what they considered "the Wild West," gathering materials for an article for *McClure's Magazine*. What Mr. Tweedie,, if one existed, thought of this project is not known, but Miss Sharp, in pursuing her literary career had parted from a husband named McGirl and resumed her maiden name. Journeying together to Spokane, the two women decided to divide the research territory between them.

Nellie, short, broad and irrepressible, took two bristle-like straws from a hat trimming, arranged them in her palm and closed her chunky fist around them. "You draw," she said, and her friend did, with a laugh and no presentiment that this was a game deadlier than Russian roulette—two chances, one to mean Life, the other—*Death*.

Mrs. Tweedie displayed the short straw. "You get the cowboys of Montana," said Nellie. "I go west to the loggers and fishermen."

"And I expect to have fun," she added. "I always dreamed of visiting Seattle and the Coast."

That evening, Tuesday, February 22, 1910, Mrs. Tweedie kissed her companion goodbye as the younger woman stepped onto a westbound train. She herself would take a later train to Montana. According to plan they would meet again in Spokane in a few weeks ready to write their article on the Pacific Northwest. They would set the exact date of their reunion later, when they saw how long their research took them.

Great Northern Railway's Local No. 25, which Nellie boarded, was made up of two day coaches, two sleepers (the Winnipeg and the Similkameen), a mail car, a baggage car, and an observation car or smoker. It served Spokane, Wenatchee, Everett, Seattle, Tacoma and way points, a run of about 375 miles.

Right behind it Train No. 27 pulled out. This was a four-car fast mail from St. Paul whose usual crack trip had been slowed by snow in the Bitter Root Mountains of Idaho.

Because No. 27 was running late, the two trains traveled practically together for the 200 miles across the Washington plains, making No. 25's scheduled stops at little wheat and orchard towns along the way. Together they approached the Cascades, the mountain chain which forms a dramatic barrier north and south across the state of Washington.

The Cascade Range is, geological speaking, a relatively new mountain pile, seven hundred miles long, built partly through volcanic action. It has not yet existed through the eons needed to erode its more spectacular features, and its northern reaches in particular are rugged in outline, with deep clefts and jagged peaks.

Because the mountains thrust their mass five to eight thousand feet into the air currents sweeping west to east from the Pacific Ocean, they cause the clouds to give up much of their moisture, and the western slope of the range is subject to heavy snow and rain.

But on this night it was not merely the Cascade peaks which were enveloped in storm; it was the whole of the Pacific Northwest. All the way from Spokane it snowed thickly and steadily.

"A night for Eskimos in igloos," said the fireman as he peered into the storm from the tender. "A helluva night," said the engineer, watching wild snow streak by his locomotive headlamp.

All that season Old Man Winter had outdone himself whipping up bad weather. For months incessant storms had raged over Europe and the American continent. With the New Year things had got worse instead of better.

In the Cascades the height of the snow pack had built up and up, grimly, until drifts twenty to thirty feet high lay along the mountain backs and from ten to twenty feet high at Stevens Pass where the Great Northern tracks went through. Such a winter, the G.N. officials had convinced themselves, could never occur; yet that possibility had haunted their dreams. For Stevens Pass was, as a G.N. official admitted later, "the weakest link in our transportation chain."

"A night to be home toasting your shins by the fire," said Brakeman Ross Phillips as he came swinging his lantern on board, stamping snow clogs from his boots.

Inside the train the storm was shut securely out. In the coaches, dimly lighted, the air hung warm and heavy, carrying a murmur of talk which increased in volume as passengers began to get acquainted.

Nellie Sharp was a naturally friendly and open personality who meant to miss no opportunity to learn about these western people and this western country. Soon she was conversing with Catherine O'Reilly, the pretty, vivacious nurse from Spokane who was caring for a sick sheepherder confined to a sleeping car berth; with young Mrs. Latsch who had been visiting her traveling salesman husband in Spokane; with sweet old Mrs. Covington, on her way home to husband and grown children in Seattle;

with the Reverend James H. Thomson, Seattle-bound to take over new church duties there.

An elderly couple traveled with a sad, black-garbed woman and her three children. They were Mr. and Mrs. William May and their daughter, Mrs. Ida Starrett, whose husband William had been killed just before Christmas in a G. N. yard accident at Hillyard, near Spokane. The Mays were now taking her with them to their home in Chemainus, British Columbia. "Oh, how sad!" murmurred Nellie. For the youngest Starrett child was still a baby in his mother's arms. The other two were a dark-eyed boy of seven and a girl of nine.

There were other personal sorrows on board. George Davis, a street car motorman with the Seattle, Renton line, was returning from Spokane where he had just buried his wife. With him was his pretty, three-year-old daughter Thelma, an obviously pampered child, at once his problem and his consolation. He was now taking Thelma to live with her grandparents.

John Gray of Nooksack, Washington, was traveling in a sleeper berth with a broken leg. Anna, his wife, had to cope with their fat, golden-haired baby, eighteen-month-old Varden Gray, besides waiting on John.

Another passenger who was not well was slender, anxious-eyed Mrs. Ada Lemman. She retired to her berth almost immediately. Ada had a nervous condition, her distinguished looking lawyer husband, Edgar Lemman, explained. They were on their way from Hunters, Washington, to the Coast to seek medical aid for her. At home in the little wheat town they had left their fifteen-year-old daughter.

A family of five on board were Mr. and Mrs. G. L. Beck and their three children. Two years ago they had come to try life in the little town of Marcus, Washington, but the winters were too tough for them, especially this one. They were returning to their old home town of Pleasanton, California.

Back in the smoker men were swapping yarns and facts about themselves. Some of the younger ones kept apart

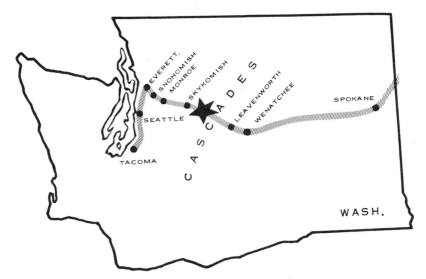

Route of the Great Northern Mainline. Star indicates the scene of disaster.

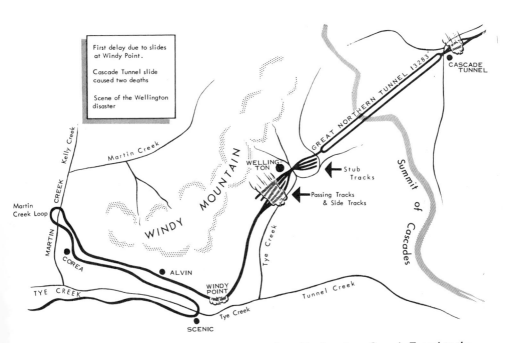

First delay due to slides at Windy Point.

Cascade Tunnel slide caused two deaths

Scene of the Wellington disaster

Closeup of the disaster area, showing route of the Great Northern from Cascade Tunnel to the town of Scenic, Washington.

Desolate little railroad town of Wellington, Washington, after the avalanche poured down off Windy Mountain slope.

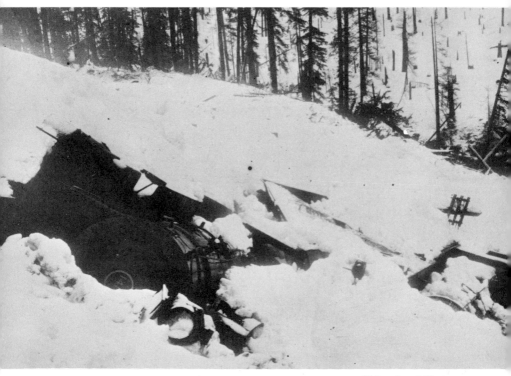

Even locomotives were tossed like toys to the bottom of the ravine and covered by wildly cascading snow when Wellington's avalanche struck.

and talked among themselves: the three friends from Ireland, who had been working in Canada and now planned to visit an Irish friend in Seattle; the two trampy-looking Boles brothers and Samuel Field, a musher from Alaska; Frank Ritter of Bellingham and Milton Horn of Wenatchee, each only eighteen years old; Ed Rea and the ex-sailor Sam Lee.

As for Ed Chisholm and Ben Thompson, two old miners from Rossland, B. C., they spoke of nothing but pay streaks and gold-bearing quartz.

The others making up the fifty-five passengers were middle-aged business and professional men traveling on business trips. They played cards, passed their bottles and told stories till midnight, when everyone began to settle down.

With no sense of trouble ahead all were asleep by the time the train stopped at Leavenworth around 1 a.m.

2

Leavenworth is a small Great Northern division point located on the eastern slope of the Cascade Mountains at an elevation of 1100 feet. Ahead gloomy, snow-draped peaks rise to six and eight thousand feet. Into these mountain fastnesses the G.N. main line penetrates, following the Wenatchee River, then its tributary Nason Creek.

In 1910 the line rose up and up, clinging to steep canyon walls, crossing dark ravines over streams that in summer tumbled down whitely but now in February were frozen solid and covered over with snow.

At 3340 feet the peaks were by-passed by the Cascade Tunnel, bored two-and-a-half miles through the mountainside and coming out at 3105 feet. Westbound trains entered the tunnel at the east portal railroad yard of Cascade Tunnel; they emerged on the western end at another yard called Wellington.

Below Wellington the tracks made a gradual descent by means of a long narrow loop around the mountain which included a snake-coil turn-around. More than half of this loop was mere detour to lose elevation. It took nine miles to reach Scenic Hot Springs, only four miles away as the bluejay flies but 1000 feet lower on the mountainside.

The mountain stretch of fifty-seven miles between Leavenworth and Skykomish, fifteen miles beyond Scenic, was the big headache. Here winter staged an annual contest for superiority with the warders of the railroad. Over the years the Great Northern had improved its strategic position by building a mile and a half of snowsheds, but the enemy could still defeat railroad crews by huge drifts and avalanching snow.

Head of the railroad forces was James H. O'Neill, Superintendent of the Cascade Division. He was thirty-eight years old, slender, of medium height, with a well-moulded, intelligent face. In times of relaxation he dressed well and enjoyed the better things of life, but confronted by work he applied himself with intense concentration and forgot all in the emergency of the moment.

Ordinarily, section men along the Great Northern main line liked to lean on their shovels as they watched the private car of the division superintendent go by. "There's a plush job for you!" they'd say. "How I'd like to have a soft spot like that." But during this present winter of 1909-10 you couldn't have handed any one of these boys the job of Superintendent O'Neill—no, not on a silver platter. For the "Super" was deep in trouble—snow trouble.

Conditions had been particularly tough since the first of the year. O'Neill had ridden continually up and down the line, shunting crews to trouble spots, sending requests for additional laborers, ironing out kinks so trainmasters and rotary conductors could keep the snowplows always turning. Slides were cleared in one place only to come down in another, but all were licked somehow and in spite of delays the line was kept open.

Crews were exhausted. With the month of February drawing to a close and spring approaching, Division Superintendent O'Neill prayed for better weather.

Instead, a siege of storms moved in which in the next fortnight put down one of the heaviest snowfalls ever to arrive in the Cascades so late in the season. Fresh snow piled inch by inch and foot by foot above the crust of the already top-heavy pack. Nature, in malevolent mood, was building up to the most disastrous avalanche America has ever known—the most disastrous avalanche in all railroading history.

3

The siege began on February 21 with a new and sweeping storm which blanketed the whole state of Washington and laid down snow at the rate of a foot an hour in the Cascade passes. The storm kept up all night and into the next day—the day Nellie Sharp took the gamble which headed her west on the evening train; the day the other passenger were impelled by their personal stars—by reasons of family, health, pleasure, business, or private tragedy—to board Local 25 and so link their fate with Nellie's.

On the afternoon of February 22, Superintendent O'Neill, responding to the seriousness of the storm situation, ordered his private car hooked onto an eastbound train and set out at Wellington, at the top of the pass.

The little hamlet of Wellington, hanging on the mountainside like a Swiss village in the Alps, served as headquarters for tunnel work, for passing and meeting emergencies, and since the past summer when the tunnel had been electrified, for electric motor work.

Three stub or spur tracks splayed across the edge of a flat near the tunnel mouth. A few hundred feet west, where a shelf had been gouged from the sheer hillside, lay two passing tracks and a couple side tracks, serviced by a close-crowding coal shed and chute, a water tank and an engine pit.

Before reaching this narrow ledge, the main line, coming west from the tunnel and stub track area, curved slowly past a motormen's bunkhouse, a roadmaster's office, a section house and a small depot.

Crowded against the hillside back of the depot lay the town of Wellington—if town it could be called. Mostly it consisted of the Hotel Bailets—three attached wooden structures which served as hostelry, general store, post office, dining room, tavern and card room. A half dozen cabins for workers lay to the east of the hotel, and a few other shacks had been squeezed in where room could be found on the steep terrain.

On the winter's day O'Neill's private car arrived, the place presented one long vista of snowdrifts, snowbanks and snowcaps. Snowbanks where the main line and other tracks had been plowed. Snowbanks where paths had been shoveled. Snowdrifts leaning against porches. Snowdrifts peeping in murky windows. Fat snow layers padding every roof. Snowcaps overhanging every eave.

The division superintendent had brought with him his nineteen-year-old private secretary, Earl R. Longcoy, and his colored cook and steward, Lewis Walker. To Walker with his long experience on the road Wellington seemed no more dismal than any other little railroad town, but to young Longcoy it looked horribly desolate and forbidding. As for O'Neill, he scarcely saw the place as he faced the emergency.

Already at Wellington he found William Harrington, trainmaster in charge of snow removal for the division. Harrington, popularly known as "the Snow King," was "featured like a Roman gladiator, thewed like an ox, with a chest like a cider barrel."

O'Neill and Trainmaster Harrington coordinated efforts. They directed the movements of the four rotary snowplows at their disposal, as well as the efforts of all the section men and track laborers they could summon. Working with a vigor borne of desperation, they managed to keep the track open all through the snowy day of the 22nd and into the wind-tossed night.

The early morning hours of February 23 arrived with the storm still raging. Trains No. 25 and 27 awaited orders at Leavenworth, passengers and mail clerks asleep, crews aware of the vast storm but taking it as a matter of course.

Great Northern trains were as yet only a little behind schedule. Both the Oriental Limited and No. 26, eastbound, had followed a rotary to the top of the pass and now, between 1 and 2 a.m., were descending the eastern slope without encountering trouble. A westbound freight, which had met these two trains on the hill, had just reached Scenic to report heavy snow and blizzard conditions but no slides of consequence.

O'Neill had no reason to believe the two trains at Leavenworth could not get over the hump with dispatch, no reason to suspect an evil genie was busy laying a snowy snare. Around 1:30 a.m. he ordered Trains No. 25 and 27 to move on.

Trains doubleheaded over the pass—that is, were given an extra engine, added eastbound at Skykomish and westbound at Leavenworth. At 2 a.m. a helper backed up and coupled on to Train No. 25, the passenger train. Half an hour later it started west behind Rotary X802, in charge of Conductor M. O. White. The mail train, also with helper, followed at 4 a.m.

At Chiwaukum, eleven miles west of Leavenworth, passengers were awakened briefly when No. 25 ran onto a passing track and the Oriental Limited, coming down off the mountain, roared by. At Merritt, another ten miles west, the passenger train again sidetracked to let No. 26 rattle by. Then it began the dizzy climb to the tunnel, with No. 27 not far behind.

The passengers were lulled back to sleep and remained snugly unsuspecting of danger ahead as the trains toiled upward into the heart of the Cascade Mountains—to a rendezvous with sliding hell.

4

At about the same time that Train No. 25 left Leavenworth, a rotary snowplow started west from Wellington. It was in charge of Conductor Homer E. Purcell and its routine schedule was to clear tracks as far as Sky, then return ahead of an eastbound mail.

In his three winters on the hill Purcell had never seen a storm such as the one he now encountered on the west slope. Snow was falling heavily, blowing in such blinding sheets that the crew of X807 traveled in nightmare blur. All along the tracks, banks were sloughing—a name the men gave to the caving-in of the snow walls built high by constant plowing. A mile west the machine was stopped by a small slide but soon bucked through it.

Two miles farther west lay Windy Point, a treacherous place where for a half-mile the tracks turned on a narrow ledge around the rocky face of Windy Mountain. This was the devil's own place for slides. An early part of the turn had been protected by Snowshed 3.3, but before the machine could reach that shelter, the headlights, penetrating the crazy patterns of blowing snow, picked up a slide ahead. It had filled the snowbanks to the brim, completely obliterating the tracks for some distance. It must have come from quite far up the ravine, for the snow was balled and hard-packed.

This would be a tough one to lick, Purcell thought as he signalled the machine to the attack and the rotary blades began to knife in. The "bite" of the rotary was only about a dozen feet and this pile loomed higher than the rotary hood. For a time a geyser-like stream of white rose from the ejection chute, described a great wavering arc and fell along the outer reaches of the right-of-way. Then the rotary blades jammed and the machine jarred to a stop. Engineer William Courtney, needing to back away from the barrier for a new start found the nose of the plow stuck fast in the bank and his front truck wheels clogged with snow, so he couldn't take the slack.

They were in real trouble, Purcell realized. Without shovelers to whittle the snow pile down to size and dig out the front end of the rotary they weren't going any place.

* * *

All through the night Superintendent O'Neill worked at the side of the telegrapher in the Wellington depot. Keeping in touch with all the little stations on the hill and in the mountain vicinity he formed a picture of the storm. It was from the west and striking with greatest force on the west slope. On the east, snow was heavy but not coming down with the same blizzard-like intensity.

He was alarmed by the strengthening of the storm on the west slope. He groaned, visualizing that trouble spot, Windy Point. If any place were apt to slide, that was it. Probably it already had. Where was Purcell? If he weren't hung up along the way he should have already reported in from Alvin, the little station a half-mile beyond Windy Point. Even allowing for a snail-pace trip and minor slides he was late.

In his anxiety O'Neill rose to pace the floor. If Windy Point should be blocked, what then? For even at this moment he had two trains laboring up the east slope. He would have to do something about them. Neither had a diner. If stall they must, it had better be where he could get the people out to eat—or pack food in to them. Those people were his responsibility. He should have to bring the trains up to Cascade or Wellington, the only two places on the mountain where food was available.

Wearily he slumped to a seat and leaned his head on his hands. Four a.m. Four-thirty. No word from Purcell. That could mean only one thing. The way west was blocked, at least temporarily.

Since the storm was less intense on the east side, Cascade Tunnel seemed the safest haven at the moment. He dispatched an order for the trains to run in on the passing track at the Cascade yard, there to await further instructions. Before long he would know whether the way west was open and was safe.

5

To their dismay, the passengers discovered on awakening that they were not nearing the Coast as scheduled. Instead they were at a standstill in a high mountain world in a blinding snow storm.

"I've been awake for hours," complained Mrs. Latsch. "Whatever is the matter? Why are we stalled here?"

"We've been here since six, ma'am," said Lucius Anderson, porter of the sleeper Winnipeg. "There's trouble somewhere."

"In this weather it could mean anything," said George Davis, dourly. He went off in search of information and returned a short time later to announce, "We're up at the east portal of the tunnel, at Cascade. We have to stay here till they clear a slide ahead."

Outside, the snow came down in feathery concentrations. "See, that's what I mean!" exclaimed excitable Mrs. Beck. "It's weather like this we can't take. The summers in this part of the country are wonderful, I'll grant you that, but the winters—ferocious! Wait till we get back to California—we'll never leave."

Conductor J. L. Pettit, entering the sleeper a little later, was met by a chorus of voices: "What's the trouble?" "When do we get going?" "When do we get to Seattle?"

This was to be but the first of a hundred times in the next many days when he would be importuned by such questions, when he would be turned to eagerly for reassurance. On this morning the stop at Cascade represented to him nothing but a slight, even routine, delay, and his task was easy. A smile spread over his broad, kindly face as he held up a silencing hand.

"All I can tell you is there's a little trouble ahead. It's being cleared up and we'll be on our way before long. In the meantime we're going to give you a treat. How'd you like to get out and have breakfast at the railroad cook shack? Have a chance to stretch your legs? Besides, we've got to show Miss Sharp this country out here. I'm sure she's never eaten in a railroad beanery."

Neither had most of the others, for that matter, and put like that it seemed an adventure. Even those who ordinarily would have grumbled about getting out into the storm acted pleased with the diversion, and all who were out of their berths started to get ready. The children, of course, were elated, and dived into coats and hurried to pull on caps, mittens and boots.

George Davis dressed Thelma in her fancy bonnet and velvet coat, put her hands into her white fur muff. In the night she had cried a good deal missing her mother, but now she seemed aware she looked fetching and even managed a shy smile.

The fat Gray baby, being too heavy for Mrs. Gray to carry, was shouldered by Albert Mahler, a real estate man from Seattle who was missing his own wife and boy.

Only the sick ones and the late risers remained on the train—they and Mrs. Covington, who was nearly 70, and grieving Mrs. Starrett. The Becks offered to bring the old lady back something, and the Mays would do the same for their daughter. The rest descended on Cascade.

A dozen years before, at the time the tunnel was being built, Cascade had gained the title of "wickedest town on earth." But the roaring construction workers and their camp followers had long since departed, leaving on the south hill above Nason Creek but a minor railroad yard—a little depot, some side tracks, a water tank and a turntable. The tunnel electrification had added an electric sub-station and a three-stall house for electric motors. These scattered railroad installations and the few workers cabins were mostly hidden in drifts and by the plowed snowbanks which stood wall-like on either side of the tracks.

Fast falling flakes enveloped the passengers in thick swirls. Passing single file between train and uphill embankment they followed a partly beaten path to the cook shack door. It was one big formless room thrown together out of raw lumber. A dozen or fifteen rude tables were spaced about the board floor, flanked on either side by equally rude benches. Tables lay ready for service, being set with white enamelware and tin cups turned upside down.

At one end of the room a great pot-bellied stove sent out warmth, nourished from a nearby bin of railroad coal. At the other end of the room was the kitchen, where reigned a mammoth, flat-top cook stove. Big pans and kettles hung from spikes on the wall, and on rough, board work tables lay other pans and kettles, knives and cleavers, and opened tins. Sacks and barrels of foodstuff sat about on the floor.

Conductor Pettit, who had accompanied his charges, called Miss Sharp over and introduced her to the fat cook John Olson and his shy, taller helper, Henry Elliker. "I want you to tell Miss Sharp all about cooking for railroad crews," he said.

He left the passengers sitting down to a breakfast at which, for the ravenous, there were flapjacks and eggs, and for those of more delicate appetite, cooked cereal and tinned fruit.

Train No. 27 had run in behind No. 25 on the passing track at 6:40, and later the crews from both trains filed in for their breakfast—engineers, conductors, brakemen, firemen, porters, express messengers, mail clerks and weighers.

"Hey, Martin," said Conductor Walter Vogel of the mail train, addressing the engineer of the passenger train, "if you'd get that lousy string of cars out of the way we'd get going."

Answered Francis Martin, "With a hog head like Ed Sweeney you ought to be able to go right around us."

"Or over the top," said Sweeney as he cut his flapjacks, three-deep and swimming with syrup. "If you don't get your hind-end out of there, I'm liable to do just that."

During this same breakfast hour Purcell's brakeman walked into Wellington. He went directly to O'Neill to deliver a message from the rotary conductor. "We're hung up in a pretty bad one at Windy Point. Making little progress. Need shovelers badly. Send 10 or 15 if you can."

The line ahead was blocked, then. Yet O'Neill heard the confirmation of his fears without too great alarm. Late in the season like this snow flurries were usually of short duration, and this storm had already lasted 40 hours, something of a record. It would have to let up soon, and one slide, even a fairly big one, wasn't too serious. With enough shovelers, the rotary would be able to cope with it in a few hours, and he could still have the trains off the mountain before the day was over.

Such were his thoughts as he dispatched a dozen laborers to Purcell and watched them wade off through the drifts in the direction of Windy Point.

6

And all day the delayed passengers fretted and stewed. All day they groused to each other, comparing notes as to why they were on this particular train and wishing to God they were elsewhere.

"It's all right with you, Nellie," chided lively, personable Libby Latsch. "This way you get more to write about. But I need to get home to my little boy, Kean. He's only four and does miss his Mama."

"How come he's not with you?"

"I left him with my housekeeper in Seattle so I could go over and have this weekend with my husband. Now I won't be back when I promised."

With a nod toward the end of the car where the harrassed mothers and Grandmother May were trying to keep the children quiet, she added, "If Kean were here, would he add to the mischief!"

Even without him, the six children and two babies managed plenty of mischief and personality expression all their own. They jumped about, whooped, cooed and cried, all with a vitality that made impossible the thought that they could ever die.

Raymond Starrett, seven years old, bounced on the green plush seats and tapped the window panes. He helped the three-year-old Beck boy push his toy train about the floor, and sometimes they argued about whose turn it was, and there were squeals of rage. His sister Lillian giggled with Marian Beck, who was also nine. Emma Beck, three years older, displayed more maturity; she comforted and cared for Thelma Davis when she howled over disputes with ths other children or just because she felt lost and motherless.

Varden Gray hardly knew what he wanted and was so restless he was wearing his mother out. The eight-month-old Starrett baby, Francis, was a lively armful, too, and though he brightened his mother's grief, he also helped to tire her.

Reverting to her own problems, Mrs. Latsch said, "No, it just doesn't work out with me in business in Seattle and my husband traveling out of Spokane."

"What kind of business?" For Miss Sharp was always interested in the emancipated female.

"I'm head of Northwestern Sales in Seattle. We manufacture what I call 'Always-in-Place' hair supporters."

"If they're as good as their name, sell me a few," said Nellie, pointing with a laugh to her own heavy brown hair with its persistent inclination to stray.

"Yes, as good as their name and a good item," conceded Mrs. Latsch. "Even so, I've about made up my mind to sell out and move to Spokane, where I can see more of my husband. By the way, did you know Mrs. Covington is going home for her *golden wedding* anniversary?"

They looked over to where that little old-fashioned lady sat talking to the Reverend Thomson. She was dressed in a pleated shirtwaist overlaid with a white lace collar and hung with a small cameo on a tiny gold chain. Her gray hair was parted in the middle and drawn back, but a few locks had escaped and hung softly about her face.

She and Thomson were discussing family concerns, too. They had much in common, they had discovered, for one of Mrs. Covington's sons was a minister, and both had illness at home. "Husband's been sick most all winter," she explained now. "I stayed in Spokane at our son's nursing him. In January he seemed some better and went to Seattle to be with another son there. I stayed on to visit friends. Now our anniversary is next Thursday and I must be home for that. But husband isn't well," she added fretfully, "and my being late this way, he'll worry and may get worse."

"We must ask God for patience," said the minister.

He was thinking of his own wife, who lay seriously ill in Bellingham. With her so sick, the state church work he had been handling had seemed hard because he had to travel so much. Now he was taking over the Seattle department and was thankful, for it meant he could be home more. "If it only be God's will that my wife's health improve," he breathed.

"I will pray for her," said Sarah Jane Covington simply.

When the minister moved away, Mrs. Covington rummaged in her bag for her pen and the papers on which she was keeping anxious notes about the day's delay, and also writing letters to her husband and married children. Penning her thoughts passed time and eased her mind. "Many on the train drink and play cards," she wrote now, "but others are nice."

The Reverend Thomson was one she termed nice. Others were H. D. Chantrell, U. S. Customs Collector at Blaine, returning from a visit to a brother in Spokane; Edgar Lemman, worried about his wife's condition; R. M. Barnhard, a prominent lawyer of Spokane, who in high white collar was traveling to Olympia to argue a land case before the State Supreme Court; wealthy Charles S. Eltinge, treasurer of the Pacific Coast Pipe Company of Seattle, whose family still lived in Spokane, where he had important banking connections. These men did not hang out in the rear-end smoker; those who did gained Mrs. Covington's disapproval.

7

There was far less of drinking back in the smoker than the old lady imagined. This was not due to any particular virtue. Bottles brought on board had already been emptied, leaving the men with nothing to do but smoke, play cards, tell stories, and indulge in their own brand of grousing.

"I been pegging away farming for forty years," said John Brockman, a middle-aged bachelor rancher from Waterville, Washington, who wore a mustache and heavy beard streaked with gray. "Never did take a vacation. This year I decided I'd go south and get a little sunshine. But if I'm going to travel I want to travel; I don't like this being stopped all day. I'd just as lief stayed home on the ranch as this."

"Travel's always hell in winter," rejoined Henry H. White, a salesman for the American Paper Company, from Minneapolis. "About this time of year I start thinking about getting me a desk job in the Cities. Wouldn't take my feet off the desk all winter!"

Two other traveling men laughed and nodded their agreement with this sentiment. They were Bert Matthews of Cincinnati and Edward W. Topping of Ashland, Ohio. The latter represented the Safety Door Hanger Company, which he owned with his father. His private life was like that of George Davis, for his wife had died recently, leaving him a two-year-old son, William, to raise.

Ponderous Albert Mahler sighed, "I expected to be home three weeks ago. When I left for Quincy, I told the wife and boy I'd be back in a few days. Went over to file on a desert mining claim. But the weather was so bad I had nothing but trouble and couldn't get the business finished up. Sure wish I'd managed to get a train a few days ago. I'd be home now."

"We've been out on mining business, too—to Soap Lake," said Judge James McNeny, an old-time Seattle lawyer wearing a pointed beard. "Why didn't we put this trip off till spring—eh John?"— John M. Rogers being his client with whom he was traveling.

"Well, nobody told me it was going to snow like this," said Rogers, a Seattle real estate man.

"And why couldn't they put off court till spring?" asked John Merritt of Lewis Jesseph. They were two more lawyers, Merritt from Spokane, Jesseph from Colville, on their way to appear before the State Supreme Court at Olympia. "Looks like our eloquence is to be snowed under!"

"The worst of my business," said George Loveberry, "is it won't wait till spring." He was the proprietor of a livery stable and feed store in Georgetown, a Seattle suburb, and was returning from a horse-buying trip through eastern Washington. "I ought to get back even if I have to hoof it through the snow."

"My trouble is the opposite," said R. M. LaVille, an unemployed electrician from Missoula, Montana. "I have more time than money. Let it snow!"

"Believe me, it's done nothing else up in Idaho where I've been," said Solomon Cohn of Everett. "High as a house." He was plainly a man of easy companionship, across whose ample chest hung a heavy gold chain for his big gold watch. To White and the other traveling men he added, "Being a mining man's no better than being a drummer"—drummer being his former occupation. Now he was developing the Eureka Mine near Wallace, Idaho.

"This trip of mine—I'd meant to get it over with a week ago," said R. H. Bethel, a tall man with a white goatee. He was a contracting and consulting engineer returning from Wenatchee on business for his firm ot Bethel & Downey of Seattle. "Things came up and I couldn't make it earlier. Wouldn't care, but my wife usually goes along on trips and she'll be mighty worried."

The hours wore on with snow falling relentlessly. A few sought the depot to send wires to families or business associates to explain the delay and give assurances of safety. But for most the monotony of the seemingly endless day was broken chiefly by trips to the cook shack for meals.

For lunch Cook Olson ladled out a big savory stew, served with many thick slices of his own, home-made bread. For dinner there was roast beef, lots of potatoes, and more slices of bread.

"When I write my life's adventures," Nellie Sharp declared to Olson, "I'll name you the best cook in all the west."

8

On Train No. 27 that afternoon, the eight postal employees were catching up on their work, their sleep, their letter writing, their sewing on of buttons, and any other chores they could think of.

Four of the older men had now settled down to a rather

silent, abstracted game of pinochle. John D. Fox, the man in charge, was a serious fellow by nature; his mind kept straying to Seattle where his wife and three children waited and watched for his return. George Hoefer and John C. Tucker had worrying, waiting wives, too, theirs living in Spokane. Richard C. Bogart was not married, but was a naturally steady type, a most trusted employee. All had been a number of years in the mail service— Bogart for nine—and they knew that in winter or in any other railroad emergency you got home when you got there, and no use fretting.

Alfred B. Hensel, a dapper type with hair parted in the middle and a snappy mustache, lay in his bunk reading a magazine. He, too, had learned fortitude.

It was Charles S. LaDu, a sub of only 10 weeks' service who could not seem to settle down to anything. "Sure, I wanted an appointment," he grumbled, "but when does the thing come through—the middle of the winter, of course!"

The express messenger, H. J. Drehl, a big man about 40 with thinning gray hair, said, "Oh, cheer up, the first thousand runs are the hardest."

Tucker, looking up from the game, remarked, "If you think you got it tough, what about the new weigher on 25. One week in the service and he gets into a ball-up like this!"

Fred Bohn, the young mail weigher on 27, turned to LaDu. "What say, Charlie, let's go up to No. 25 and commiserate with the poor bastard. As one mail weigher to another I gotta help keep his spirits up."

Putting on coats they made their way along snow-trampled paths to No. 25's mail car. Here they found not only Lee Ahern, the 24-year-old mail weigher who had struck such rough luck on his first trip out, but also Grover Begle, the express messenger, and big Hiram Towslee, in charge of the car. The five men chinned for quite awhile.

As the visitors departed they noticed that a rotary, not in evidence earlier, was working its way down the passing track, while section workers were digging snow away from the trains.

"Must be orders to get out of town," they said to each other, and hurried back to their train with a lifting of spirits.

"No such luck," said Conductor Vogel. "But we'll probably go out first thing in the morning. At least we're supposed to. That means we've got to take water. To get us up to the tank they'll have to get No. 25 out of the way. I think Sweeney's going to take 'er into the tunnel."

It was dusk by the time both trains had been dug from their snow-bound positions. The passenger train then pulled ahead and stayed for a half hour inside the east portal of the tunnel while the mail train moved up and filled its water tank. By dark both trains were back in their original positions.

These movements proved a diversion for the people on board, but the temporary excitement was over all too soon. The trains again came to a standstill and left the passengers with nothing to do but wonder when the slide would be cleared and they could get going. Glum and irritated, nearly everyone went to bed and to sleep early, in the hope that when they awoke the trains would be in motion.

9

For the snow-fighting crews there was no sleep. It was a night of ferocious battle with the elements.

Rotary X802, the machine which had run ahead of the passenger train into the mountain, had been given the helper off the mail train that morning at Cascade Tunnel. With this extra pusher it had gone on to Wellington, where it took on coal and water and spent the day plowing out tracks.

Meantime, the rotary which had preceded the Oriental Limited to Leavenworth, No. X800, had turned around and returned to the pass. It had reached Cascade about 2:30 in the afternoon and was the machine the postal employee saw plowing out the passing track.

Toward evening Rotary X802 came back to Cascade from Wellington and Trainmaster Harrington decided to combine the two machines into a more powerful piece of snow-fighting equipment—a double rotary; in fact, nearly a triple, since X802 already had two pusher engines. The rotaries coupled up rear-end to rear-end so the resultant train could fight drifts or take slack coming or going. It then moved through the tunnel to the Wellington water tank and coal chute to take on supplies for the night's labor.

The need for refueling and rewatering was the fatal flaw in the machines. Men could go without sleep and without food in the emergency but the mechanical demands of engines and rotaries must be met promptly or the machines stopped cold. Water tanks ran low every four hours, though this supply could be supplemented by shoving snow into the tanks and running the steam line in. Coal was another matter. If the going were easy, the amount carried could last as long as 20 hours, but in tough conditions like these, it was more apt to run out in 12 to 15. Emergency supplies were maintained in a few of the snowsheds, but refueling usually meant getting back to Wellington, the main supply point.

The storm grew worse at nightfall. The wind blew in vicious gusts. Snow swirled, it pelted, it swept in sheets. It struck so hard and thick it plastered the double rotary to the tracks almost as fast as shovelers could dig it out. As there were three different water tanks and three tenders to fill, numerous small moves were necessary to bring the train into just the right positions at tank and chute. For each of these moves, freshly formed drifts and ice wedges had to be removed. A job that should have taken an hour or more became an almost hopeless task. Long after midnight the double rotary was still groping its way through the storm front in the Wellington yard.

Down at Windy Point that day Rotary X807 had continued to fight the blizzard and the slide. It had been forced to run back into Wellington for coal in the afternoon, which it did in a temporary abatement of the storm. For a time after it returned to the scene of battle, the breather continued. Then as darkness came on the fury of the storm increased and wild accumulations of blowing snow interfered with progress.

To Conductor Purcell their task began to seem as insurmountable as hacking at a mountain with a teaspoon. He felt weary, bewhiskered and desperate. He knew that the fourth rotary of the division, X801, had come from Sky up the hill as far as Alvin, where he had been slated to meet it. It was now side-tracked, awaiting his coming.

Fairly early in the evening, he clambered over the icy reaches of the slide ahead and made his way into Snowshed 3.3, where a telephone station was maintained. He called Alvin and got through to Irving J. Tegtmeier, the traveling engineer with Rotary X801. "We need help, Teg," he said. "Could you come on up the hill to meet us? If you can buck this slide from one end, and us from the other, that might help. Otherwise we'll never get through it till doomsday."

With Tegtmeier was 33-year-old Trainmaster Arthur Reed Blackburn, on his way to assist his chief, O'Neill. The sixteen hours that Rotary X801 had been stopped at Alvin had seemed interminable to him. His wife had given birth to their first baby the day before he was called away from Everett.

The whole crew was sick of the delay and Tegtmeier was glad to accede to Purcell's request. Rotary X801 ran on up, and the two machines fought the slide, one from the uphill side, one from the downhill. Around 8 p. m., some 18 hours after X807 first left Wellington, they broke through and met.

It was decided to return to the sidetrack at Alvin to couple up. This done, the new double rotary started back to Wellington to plow out any places which in the continuing storm might have slid again.

The machines had a heavy time of it. Snow was drifting and sloughing off the sides of the banks, blowing around and under the wheels of locomotives and snowplows. Bucking and chewing, pausing only to melt snow water for the boilers, they made about a mile an hour. Fortunately no new slide had come down, and the double rotary reached Wellington in the early morning hours of February 24.

The crews, bone weary and in need of sleep, prayed the tracks would stay open behind them.

10

At Cascade on Thursday morning, the second morning of the passengers' ordeal, cheering news came through shortly after another breakfast in the cook shack. The trains were to be dug from the snow and move to Wellington; with luck they would be off the mountain that day.

In the smoker the three Irish boys threw their caps in the air and shouted, "Bully!"

In the Similkameen, Mrs. Starrett, who had endured so much, sighed to her mother, "Thank God. I don't feel I could stand any more of this."

"We ought to sue the railroad for the time we've spent here," Mrs. Gray said crossly.

"But think of all the free meals," Bethel countered, a twinkle in his eyes. "Why, we've near eaten poor Cook Olson out of his cook house." And it was true that with a hundred unexpected mouths to feed all the eatables had been fast cleaned out of Cascade.

Superintendent O'Neill, who had ordered the move to Wellington, remained disturbed. Sleepless and harried, he saw the storm continuing, even if in somewhat gentler mood this morning. More snow could only mean more trouble, and he ordered double rotary X801-X807 back west to patrol the critical stretch around Windy Point and keep it open if humanly and mechanically possible.

The other double rotary O'Neill ordered east through the tunnel to help break the trains from the drifts in the Cascade yard. When it left he and Harrington hopped aboard and went along to supervise operations, taking with them a crew of section men.

Soon there was a concentration of activity around the

trains. The double rotary plowed out tracks as close to the cars as it could get, and a large squad of men, including the two big bosses themselves, wielded shovels.

An awful havoc had been wrought in the night. Another foot and a half of the white stuff had fallen, making a total of more than three feet while the trains had been held up at Cascade. That depth, piled upon the snow already on the ground, was enough to half bury the trains. The cars all wore heavy white caps, drifts were up to the windows, and, worst of all, slamming winds had driven hummocks and hardened wedges between rails and under wheels. Engines themselves were stalled, and even if free could never have budged the entrapped trains.

Tracks had to be cleared down to the train—wheels freed one by one—cars rolled forward by the electric motors—ice dug from between flanges of the rails.

All day the storm continued. All day there was cursing, trouble and delay. By late afternoon not all the cars had yet been loosened. At 5 o'clock a power line snapped and the electric motors went out of commission.

Shovelers had to dig out the steam engines then, and after complicated switching maneuvers, they stood ready to complete the job. The double snowplow was uncoupled. Rotary X800 went ahead to prepare tracks at Wellington; X802 remained to help with the trains.

After dark the passenger train finally stood free with full traction under its wheels. The power was still out, but from Cascade to Wellington electric motors were not used anyway, for downgrade the steam engines could "drift" through, throttle cracked, keeping smoke and fumes at a minimum.

About 8 p.m. No. 25 entered the tunnel westbound and drifted down. Inside the west portal it was flagged to a stop. For again at nightfall a fierce wind had risen and drifts were forming with wild abandon. The rotary still struggled to clear the way, while shovelers were busy digging out switches.

In an hour all was ready and the train signaled on. Passing the depot and the few other glimmering lights of the town, it ran in on the No. 1 passing track, next to the main line.

Around 10:30 the mail train followed. It came right through the tunnel but paused briefly in front of the depot while a switch ahead was being thawed out. In those few minutes so much snow was driven beneath the wheels that Engineer Sweeney had to take the slack three times before he crunched through the drift and got the train in motion again. He ran it in on the No. 2 passing track nearest the downhill embankment.

Thus were the two trains with their freight of human beings moved inside the loop of the laid snare.

11

The meager facilities of Wellington had been greatly overtaxed by the influx of rotary men, shovelers and other assorted snow diggers. Many of the railroad workers now sought any extra room to be found on the two trains. A contingent of laborers were assigned the rear end coach on the mail train. Extra firemen, brakemen, engineers and rotary conductors bedded down in the mail cars or took over unoccupied berths and coach seats. The Snow King himself found a berth on the Similkameen.

February 24 was all but over. The hopes of the morning had been frittered away in the heart-rending delays of the day. And, through an unfortunate thrust of fate, no one knew at this late hour if the way west from Wellington was still open.

For as the double rotary had run toward Alvin that morning, it had experienced an accident. It had come upon a small slide, and in attempting to clear it, had rammed a stump embedded in the debris. The front truck wheels of the head end rotary, X807, had been thrown off center. Disabled, the double rotary had been forced to return to Wellington to seek a replacement for X807.

But both other machines had been busy all day at Cascade. Only now that the two trains had been safely moved to the Wellington yard could a new rotary line-up be considered. O'Neill and his two trainmasters went into a huddle.

The most urgent thing, they realized, was to find out if the line was still open west. O'Neill, tired as he was, decided to order two rotaries coupled up. He and Blackburn would then ride this double rotary down as far as Alvin to observe conditions of the road. In the morning Harrington would take the third machine and go east to keep the tracks open in the direction of Leavenworth.

The double rotary got away around midnight. O'Neill, riding the head end machine beside the pilot, kept anxious eyes ahead. He saw many sloughed banks, lots of bad drifts, and overhead slopes hung with ominous walls of snow. There were even a few small slides, but nothing the rotary couldn't buck through.

Then came Windy Point, that damnable danger spot. And sure enough, before they reached Snowshed 3.3, a slide loomed ahead across the tracks. It lay in the exact spot where Purcell and his crew had worked 18 hours clearing the last one.

The rotary ground to a stop. O'Neill stepped into the storm, Blackburn at his side. The two climbed to the edge of the snow barrier to survey the scene. An avalanche some 900 feet wide barred the way, covering the tracks to a depth of 25 feet.

This was colossal ill luck, and O'Neill knew it. But back at the rotary he said only, "It's a big one, boys. But I guess there's nothing to do but tackle it. You ready?"

The front end of the double rotary nosed ahead, and all night the rotary blades knifed at the great obstacle in its path. The snow was not hard packed and contained little debris. By dawn the machine had cut a way one-third through.

12

The railroad yard at Wellington sat high on the side of a narrow V canyon. The gouged-out shelf where the passing tracks lay was but fifty feet wide. Below the standing trains was a steep drop-off where the mountainside

plunged down to Tye Creek, now frozen over and covered with snow. Above the trains a great snowfield rose
without a break 2000 feet to the top of the northeast
summit of Windy Mountain. This slope had been burned
over and tall snags showed black and ugly above the snow.
Nearer at hand, along the right-of-way, the tops of telegraph poles barely protruded from drifts.

Passengers, opening their eyes on Friday morning,
February 25, their third day of waiting and hoping, saw
snow still coming down. Even as they took in the look of
the ravine below and the vast snowfield overhead, an
awful piece of news ran through the cars. At Cascade during the night an avalanche fifty feet wide had burst loose
from the upper bank, hurled itself across the tracks, swept
the cook shack into the ravine and demolished it. Harry
Olson and Henry Elliker had been crushed under the
debris.

Passengers and crew members alike gasped in disbelief,
then looked at each other with horror-stricken eyes. Not
only because the friendly cook and his helper, so alive
only yesterday, so responsive to everyone's needs, now lay
dead, but because they felt the brush of sinister wings
across their own faces. If the trains had not pulled forward to Wellington last night, they too might be dead
under the snow pile.

At Cascade only the most nervous ones had talked of
avalanches, and the others had made light of their fears.
Now all were shaken. "Aren't we in danger here, too?"
they demanded of Pettit. "Look at that mountain up
there—it's practically straight up and down! Isn't it liable
to slide. Can't you put us somewhere safer than this? If
the way to Scenic is blocked, why can't we go back to
Leavenworth?"

After two days and two nights of delay, the conductor
had lost his smile and his easy assurance. Such a long wait
was inconveniencing for all, he knew, and nerve-wracking
to many, and he felt truly concerned and sorry. But this
talk of danger was to him silly, and he replied with conviction, "Now, calm down—you needn't have any worries

about this train. We're safe here, absolutely safe. There's never been a slide off this hill and it is not the kind of place that slides.

"It's a terrible thing about ·Olson and Elliker—terrible," he went on. "But if you'll remember there was a ravine above the cook shack. It's down ravines and draws slides come—not down off slopes like this one. Besides, there's a hogback up high on the hill that would shunt the snow the other way if it did start to move. As for going back to Leavenworth, the slide at Cascade blocked the track in that direction."

"Then how long are we going to be here?" people cried.

He went on to explain the situation patiently and in detail: There had been a second slide at Windy Point. O'Neill himself was down there with a crew of picked men and a double rotary. They had worked all night and this morning had come back to the coal chute to refuel. They had gone out again now and O'Neill expected to have the rest of the slide out of the way in a few hours.

Pettit added diplomatically, "You'll all feel more cheerful when you've had some breakfast. All the arrangements are made. You're to eat in the Bailets Hotel dining room. The hotel's right back of the depot. You can't miss it. even in this blizzard."

All bundled up warmly before they ventured out into the storm. Rotary X807, the disabled machine, sat mute and cold behind the passenger train, but Harrington's rotary had come down to plow out the passing track and was now headed back for the main line. Crouching behind it for protection they ran along and found it left a smoothed-out path between the rails.

The hotel, with annex building on one side and false-fronted saloon on the other, was an unpretentious affair. But passengers coming in out of the storm found the high-ceilinged, wall-papered dining room warm and pleasant—even elegant after the rude cook shack at Cascade. Long tables, covered with blue and red checked table clothes, were flanked by individual chairs. Windows were hung with lace curtains. On little tables covered with crocheted and embroidered scarves sat pots holding green-growing plants.

These feminine touches were supplied by the dining room manager, cook and dishwasher, hardworking Mrs. Bailets. She was a small, thin-faced, old-fashioned woman who with her husband had come as a pioneer to Wellington. She cured her own ham and bacon, canned fruits and vegetables, baked her own bread, clerked in the store and post office, made beds in the hotel, and did laundry for the place by hand.

She had managed to cope with the extra numbers of railroad men and snow shovelers, but was swamped by the influx of so many passengers. Catherine O'Reilly, whose patient was left under the watchful eye of Porter Adolph Smith, pitched in with Nellie Sharp and Libby Latsch to help with the serving. Miss O'Reilly donned a white, enveloping apron she found hanging on a nail in Mrs. Bailets' big kitchen. As she came in carrying a platter of ham and eggs, her Irish eyes sparkled. "I've turned in my nurse's pin and have joined the waitress brigade," she laughed.

13

As the passengers came struggling out from breakfast (in more cheerful mood as Pettit had said they would be) they looked southeast from the hotel porch to the blind end of the canyon where the railroad disappeared inside the tunnel portal. The main line track, plowed only last night, was already badly blocked by blown snow; while the stub tracks, unplowed since the beginning of the storm, were lost in such a sea of tumbled drifts that only the corners of work-train cars and boxcars poked through.

Harrington's Rotary X801, slated for the job of clearing the slide at Cascade and working on east, labored up the slight main line grade toward the tunnel. Plainly the going was heavy, and the watchers on the hotel porch saw the machine buck into a big drift and come to a halt. Shovelers swarmed around it.

On their way back to the train a few of the passengers stopped at the depot to send messages. Albert Mahler wired his family, "Am all right, plenty to eat, good bed. How are you?" Bethel sent word to his wife that he was well and safe, would be home soon.

Shortly after the late breakfasters returned to the train, the rotary came backing down the main line and onto the passing track. "We thought the machine was on its way to Cascade," people remarked in perplexity. "How come Harrington's brought it back here?"

"Just too much snow, too many drifts," explained Brakeman Ross Phillips. "He couldn't get the machine up the grade with only one engine. His crew's going to dig out our helper engine, and use that as an extra pusher. We won't need it on the downgrade anyway."

The digging-out took some doing, but at last the helper engine was coupled up to the rotary, which then made its way back up the main line. Some of the men accompanied it to watch its progress. Around noon they returned to say it had got through this time and had disappeared into the tunnel.

The trains were left alone in the wilderness world of white—the mail train standing at the outer edge of the shelf above the yawning ravine, the passenger train next to it, and across the main line on another track, the superintendent's car, some boxcars and electric motors—all enveloped together in the immobilizing snowstorm. Passengers, crew members, mail clerks and O'Neil's two aides passed the time as best they could and prayed for good news from Windy Point. In the smoker, men roundly cursed the railroad company.

If the waiting was hard for the well ones, to the sick it was almost beyond human endurance. Mrs. Lemman, who boarded the train in a state of nerves, was now near collapse. Mr. Vail, the sheepherder, in pain from the carbuncles that were his ailment, moaned only to be taken to the Seattle hospital where he hoped to find relief. Mr. Gray, whose broken leg was in a cast which gave him much discomfort, was wild with helplessness and frustration.

Only the ministrations of Miss O'Reilly kept these three in control of themselves. She, a veritable angel of grace and good cheer, had extended her nursing care to all who needed it. The smile of this winsome colleen was at once serene and merry, her ways confident and even jaunty. She was an inspiration to all, and for the ill and distraught she could adjust a pillow just so, pat them with her strong, ringed hand, and say, "Now, there, everything's just right, isn't it?" —and, sure enough, things did seem brighter,

The children, cooped up now for the third day, were getting restive and plaintive, and mothers were at wits' end. Other passengers did what they could to help. They sacrificed books and magazines for reading and picture cutting, trinkets for playthings. Lu Anderson, porter of the Winnipeg, and William Duncan, day coach porter, tap danced, all white-toothed and laughing. Others sang songs, told stories, and thought up games.

Adults, too, tried to cheer themselves by acting a gayety they did not feel. They twitted Miss Sharp, "Now we bet you wish you'd stayed in the East all nice and cozy. This will prove to you the West is really wild."

"Oh, I wouldn't have missed this for anything," insisted the imperturable Nellie. "I'll have enough to write a book about."

"Now, that's the true Wild West spirit," said Ed Topping, and after that they called her "the Wild West girl."

Bestowing nicknames was diverting. They told Mrs. Latsch she seemed to be doing remarkably well without her husband and called her "the Merry Widow." In Bethel they discovered a likeness to Buffalo Bill and dubbed him "Colonel Cody."

But these attempts at merriment were strained and all echoed the sentiments of Lu Anderson, when he said in his deep Alabaman tones, "When I get off this mountain, no more of this northern country for me. No, suh, me for a place where there's 'possum and 'simmons every day for supper."

14

Late in the afternoon the double rotary came back into Wellington from Windy Point. No, the blockade wasn't completely cleared away yet, Superintendent O'Neill reported. While the machines were being coaled and watered, the men would grab a bite to eat at the Hotel. Then they'd be on their way back there. They would have the slide out of the way by morning, he felt sure, and the trains could go out then—definitely.

This was the word brought back to the train by the men passengers who had walked up to the coal chute to see what was going on.

"By morning!" people protested. "But it was only last night the snow came avalanching down to kill Olson and Elliker. No telling what will happen tonight. By morning we could all be dead!"

When Pettit appeared later and reluctantly corroborated the fact that they would be detained here another night, there was a great clamor for him to have the train moved to some other place. "Run it into the tunnel," Mrs. Beck pleaded. But others were horrified at this idea and turned on her demanding, "Then what if a slide came down over the tunnel mouth? We'd be trapped for sure!" And they asked Pettit if he couldn't have the train run down on one of the spur tracks instead.

The conductor remained patient and emphatic, stating that the train was now in the safest place on the mountain and was not in any danger. "Just quit worrying and tomorrow morning we'll be on our way out."

Then he added as an afterthought, "If you think things are tough up here now, you should have been through this way in the old switchback days."

To distract them he told stories of how, a little more than a decade ago, the trains used to go clear over the 4000-foot hump of the pass by switchbacks. "Somebody called it 'an eccentric piece of railroading,' and that's what it was for sure. There were six zigzags on this side of the mountain, four on the other—most of it at four per cent grade, mind you. The trains had one engine in front for pulling, one in back for pushing, and when they came to the end of a leg, they ran out onto a spur, then started up the next leg in reversed direction. At the top on this side you could look down on all six tracks below, and it was a wild ride getting down, I can tell you!

"No," he concluded, "since they built the tunnel, things are pretty tame through here, at least by comparison."

The passengers derived no particular comfort from the comparison. Still haunted by what had happened at Cascade, they lay down that night depressed and apprehensive. Among those whom sleep evaded, some turned their thoughts to that old switchback system, and asked: Why would any company resort to such a piece of railroading? Why had the G. N. used this pass anyhow? Was there none better?

Only Engineer John Stevens, surveyor of the route, could have answered their questions and told them the whole story.

In the early 1890's that dynamo Jim Hill was busy hurling his parallel lines of steel westward like a spider throwing out the main spokes of its web. Westward ran the tracks through the Dakotas, Montana, north Idaho, and into Spokane, Washington. From there Hill was determined to tap the wheat and apple lands of the Wenatchee Valley. But from Wenatchee how was he to get the line over the Cascade Mountain barrier to a terminus on Puget Sound?

Engineer Stevens was sent ahead to solve the problem. From the east he found a good approach to the mountain backbone by way of the Wenatchee River and Nason Creek; from the west, a good approach up Tye Creek, a tributary to the Skykomish River, which flowed to Puget Sound. Between lay a 4000-foot gap to which the name Stevens Pass was given.

At first this seemed an ideal set-up. Then preliminary surveys dashed Stevens' enthusiasm. The escarpment, especially on the western side, was abrupt and precipitous. There would be trouble getting trains up to the hump; worse, there would be hell's own problem in getting them down again.

But Jim Hill's passion for progress and Jim Hill's railroad were at Stevens' heels. The railroad was on its way west, and it must be rammed through the mountains. There was no time for further exploration, study, consideration. That one pass, named for himself, was all Engineer Stevens had, and all during the winter of 1890-91 he worried how he was to get the line over. In spring, as soon as the snow melted, he went into the mountains and standing on the ground, mapped out the fantastic switchback system and a horseshoe curve, later known as the Martin Creek Loop, where the tracks turned through an angle of 180 degrees.

"Death Mountain," the train crews called the old switchback maze where runaways were a constant threat and avalanches a commonplace. Stevens had conceived the arrangement merely as a temporary expedient, and it proved even more hazardous than he had foreseen. Within three years the railroad company began construction of the Cascade Tunnel which went into operation in 1900.

The new route eliminated the worst of the trouble but still left two-score miles of snow-sliding mountain terrain. The tunnel itself was fumey, smoky, wet, dripping and dangerous. Even after its electrification in 1909 it had many disadvantages.

Not until 1929 when the Great Northern relocated 43 miles of track and bored an eight-mile tunnel at lower elevation through the Cascade Mountains did it fully lick Mr. Stevens' abrupt escarpment. Which was 20 years too late to help the passengers, crew members and mail clerks marooned this night on the trains at Wellington.

15

The people, awakening on Saturday morning, February 26, many of them after a bad night, knew little, if any, of this past history. Blessedly they could not foresee the future. All that concerned them was the present, and as they gazed again at the white walls which bound their world, their hearts sank to see snow still coming down.

"Did the rotary get through the slide?" they asked anxiously. "Do we leave this morning?" For this was the beginning of their fourth day on the mountain.

Pettit was happy to answer the first question in the affirmative. "Yes, the rotary got through all right. O'Neill then wanted to go on around Windy Point to see if the way were open to Alvin. But they were so near out of coal they had to come in to the coal chute first. That was early this morning. They've gone on west again now, and if everything's all right as far as Alvin, O'Neill's going to bring us on down."

In the meantime he urged everyone to get his breakfast and be ready to leave when the order came through. This the passengers hurried to do, but on trying to leave the train found no trail existed to the hotel. Another foot of snow had fallen, old snow had drifted with it, and this morning there had been no rotary at hand to plow the track.

Instead crew members, aided by male passengers, turned to with shovels, cut steps up the snowbank and made a shortcut path across of the old drifts to the hotel.

Raymond Starrett and his sister Lillian giggled delightedly when Nellie Sharp stumbled off the path and floundered in the deep snow. Laughing herself, she sprawled helpless as a bug on its back until a couple of the men pulled her to her feet.

They bolted their breakfasts and were soon back on the train buttonholing all the trainmen they could find. "How soon can the rotary get out to Alvin? How long before we should be underway?"

If the rotary were plowing ordinary snow it could get through in less than an hour, they were told. If it were bucking drifts and sloughed banks, longer, depending on conditions. O'Neill had left with the double rotary quite

Pressed into service as an emergency hospital was this motormen's bunkhouse. A shed is to the right.

Sledding bodies of avalanche victims at Wellington. The hospital is in the background.

Superintendent James H. O'Neill grimly inspects the splintered wreckage of a railroad car in the Wellington ravine.

Crisscrossed tree trunks hide cars of Mail Trail No. 27, flung to the bottom of the heap when the avalanche tore loose.

early. That meant he should have reached Alvin by now. but no word had come through.

While they continued to wait tensely, Pettit visited the coaches to make a short speech. "It seems that Wellington is running low on food," he said. "After all, with crews and passengers we're a hundred extra mouths to feed. Now, don't worry, no one's going hungry, but we think it best to ration what there is. So there'll be only two meals a day as long as we're here, or until extra supplies can be brought in."

"I thought we were leaving in a little while!" people cried protestingly.

"Yes, I expect we will get away soon," the conductor maintained. "This rationing is merely a precautionary measure."

But his announcement created consternation, and as he went on, a new note of pessimism and blame cropped up in comments. "If they really thought we were going to get out today they wouldn't be thinking about food rationing." "If food's that scarce—and with all these slides around—they better be doing something to get us out of here!"

Another hour passed and still no message came through from the rotary. Most of the passengers gave up their air of tense waiting and slumped into despondency.

Mahler, meeting Pettit in a vestibule, said heavily, "Doesn't look good, does it?"

"Oh, it's too early to tell. Let's not borrow trouble—yet."

"Well, I might tell you, Mr. Pettit, I don't think this train is safe here. I think we ought to be moved."

"I'm sorry you feel that way, sir. But there would be no point in moving now. We'll be out of here yet today, I feel sure."

But the big real estate man was beyond believing any such assurances, and he sputtered, "I object to your leaving us here another night!"

Pettit's answer was on the sharp side. "Well, as I said, I don't think we'll be here tonight."

Around noon the rotary itself reappeared and brought bad tidings. It had not been able to get through to Alvin but only down to that same spot at Windy Point. Yes, there was a new slide there—a third one! But it wasn't such a huge one this time, and as soon as they filled water tanks, they'd go back and should be able to buck through it.

Like Mahler, most of the passengers had passed beyond taking such optimistic estimates at face value. They were frankly discouraged, and remained sunk in attitudes of defeat and despondency.

16

O'Neill, deadened with fatigue as he was, worked all afternoon with the rotary train. It was with the dourest of thoughts that he saw the white veil continue to envelop the mountainside. The storm, or series of storms, was now more than 100 hours old, and such a thing *just couldn't be!* Even in midwinter he had never seen a siege of such fantastic duration, and this wasn't midwinter, this was the end of February, almost March and spring.

Every hour that snow fell meant a greater depth to fight. Every added inch meant more weight—more danger. It simply *had* to stop now. Then somehow they could cope with the terrific amount that had already fallen. If it continued then nothing was of any use, for the whole Cascade world would be drowned in the stuff.

The rotary battled on. The snow spiraled down in wet, heavy accumulating flakes.

Late in the afternoon the head end rotary ran low on coal and he ordered the rotary train back to Wellington It had not traveled far when it was stopped hard by a big slide, a new one, not far from Snowshed 3.

As he got out to look the scene over, his despair hit a new low. For this was no trifling slide—it was fully 800 feet long and 35 feet deep. Worst of all, it lay between the double rotary and its coal supply at Wellington. And without coal . . . .

Still, some coal remained in the east-end rotary, the one headed into the new slide. They would not give up yet.

He ordered the machine into the snow bank. But it was no use. For this avalanche had brought down with it an overhead forest of green timber. The packed snow was full of tree trunks and other debris no rotary could touch.

O'Neill was licked, and he knew it.

He dispatched the double rotary back to the safest spot between the two slides, left four men with it to keep steam up. Then at the head of the rest of the crew, he crawled disconsolately over the slide and walked toward Wellington.

* * *

On the trains there had been hope. Even the grumblers had hoped their prognostications would prove ill-founded, that the new slide would be cleared sooner than they thought and that they would find themselves underway. This enforced stay, first for two days at Cascade, and now for two days at this untenable, precipitous spot, had seemed always a temporary emergency, one which might end at any moment.

News of the defeat of the double rotary train changed all that. Now all the rotaries were out of commission—the one disabled, the two stalled between slides, the fourth held up somewhere east of the tunnel. No further efforts toward freeing them could be made. They weren't going anywhere — not today — not tomorrow — only God knew when.

"We may sit here till spring!" Mrs. Beck cried bitterly.

Albert Mahler again sought out Pettit. "You'll remember, sir, that I protested having the train left in this spot another night. What do you propose to do now?"

The conductor was beginning to feel badgered, and two bright spots appeared in his cheeks. "There's nothing to be done," he snapped. "I've told you and others repeatedly—we're in the safest spot up here."

But he was besieged on all sides—by those who begged him to take the train into the tunnel—by those who insisted the spur tracks would be safer — by those who thought one of the snowsheds down the main line might afford protection.

To all he answered testily, "No, it's not possible. The tunnel is cold and damp, and you couldn't stand the smoke fumes. The spur tracks haven't been plowed out since the beginning of the storm, and we have no rotary to plow them with. None of the snowsheds is long enough to cover the train. Besides, not one of those places is as safe as this one right here."

And then, in final weary desperation, "Besides, I have no authority to move the train even if it could be done."

17

Back in the smoker, men who had managed to appear unperturbed through the whole delay, now gave up their card playing and got down to a serious discussion of the situation.

"I have to admit it—with the rotaries stopped, this is upsetting," said Judge McNeny. "Not that I'm one of the alarmists. I don't think this hillside is going to slide and I believe we're safe enough. But a predicament like this is pretty tough for the women with children and those with sick ones to care for. Besides, the rest of us ought to be getting home to our businesses and families. Perhaps we should all get together in a protest meeting—try to force the railroad company to some kind of action."

"According to Pettit, there isn't much they can do," put in John Rogers.

"He's a prince of a fellow, is Pettit," admitted Merritt. "He'd get us out of here if there was any way to do it, I feel sure of that. But we all know he's got his orders. What we need to do is talk to someone with some real authority."

"Well, we certainly ought to do something," the judge insisted, "and a meeting of discussion couldn't hurt anything. We might get some ideas. Anything is preferable to sitting and worrying fruitlessly."

Rogers and Topping volunteered to go through the cars to ask all who were interested in such a meeting to assemble in the smoker. As opinions were now in a ferment, nearly everyone was eager to give voice and vent to his grievances and anxieties, and before long the smoker was jam-packed.

The judge called the meeting to order, recounted the talk which had led to the calling of the assembly, then invited suggestions and comments.

"Maybe we could wire the Seattle *Times,*" said Bethel, looking very Buffalo Bill-ish, with white goatee protruding. "The Seattle Chamber of Commerce, too. They could get publicity and bring pressure on the railroad company—make them take some action to get us out of here."

"If they can't get the tracks open," cried Mrs. Gray, who held bouncy Varden on her lap, "the least they could do is bring in a doctor. Surely they can't let those who are sick just lay here and die!"

"Is drinking snow water healthy?" someone asked, and that brought up all sorts of complaints about sanitary conditions, which had been deteriorating rapidly.

"The first thing to do is make them get us out from under this cliff," insisted Beck. His wife had stayed with the children, but he was as nervous as she about the situation and they were of one mind about what should be done. "Why, this is the worst spot up here! Let's all sign a petition demanding they run the train into the tunnel."

But a number of others had claustrophobic feelings or fears of entrapment, and they violently opposed this idea. "If we insist on being moved, the spur tracks are the best place," argued John Merritt. "They're on level ground and don't have a hillside towering over them like the tracks here."

John Rogers spoke up. "I've talked to Mr. Bailets, who has lived up here for 20 years, and he swears it has never slid down across here where the trains are standing, and we have nothing to worry about."

"Has he ever seen snow like this?" demanded Matthews.

"He claims he's seen it deeper. Besides, Pettit says they couldn't get the train up onto the spur tracks or into the tunnel without a rotary."

"That's a good excuse when they don't want to!" countered Beck. "They've put us here, and here we're expected to stay—and keep our mouths shut!"

"Pettit really seems to believe we're safest here," Rogers noted.

"I have lodged my protest with him," said Albert Mahler.

Edgar Lemman then rose. "My friends, may I say a few words? The suggestion about wiring the *Times* or Chamber of Commerce has merit, I believe, but should not be done hastily. None of us has talked to Mr. O'Neill, and I think we owe it to him to find out just how serious he regards the situation and what his plans are. I suggest a committee be formed to talk to him. We ought to tell him, too, about our concerns for the safety of the train. As I understand it, if the train were to be moved, it would have to be on his orders. But, quite obviously, we're not in agreement about what should be done. Probably we should ask O'Neill his opinion about the safety of the tunnel. A man of his caliber and experience knows far more about that than we do.

"As for Mr. Vail and the others who are sick, what they need is to get to Seattle where they can receive proper medical care. What is worst for Mrs. Lemman, I know, is the strain of delay and waiting. I doubt that bringing in a doctor would help materially. Miss O'Reilly is very competent, and it seems to me that she is doing as much as can be done while we remain here."

This, suddenly, made order out of the chaos of their conflicting views. R. M. Barnhart rose and said, "I move that a committee be appointed to talk to Mr. O'Neill, and that Mr. Lemman be made its chairman." The motion was quickly seconded and passed. Sol Cohn and Henry White were named to serve with him.

18

The superintendent had reached Wellington at five that afternoon and had gone to his private car, where his cook, Lewis Walker, had fed him. He knew he needed rest and sleep but the predicament he was in was too extreme for that. Even more he needed to send messages, reports and SOS's to his head office, to Everett, and to other places, and he trudged away to the depot.

William Flannery, the station agent, broke the bad news. "Sorry, Mr. O'Neill, I hate to tell you this, but the line's got knocked out some place this afternoon. Or maybe more than one place. We've got no communications either east or west."

No rotaries turning, no telegraph service east or west . ..

He walked over and slumped down at the desk of Sperlock, the night operator. As he sat there, he reached down benumbed and unlaced his soaked boots. Pulling them off he set them at his side and put his wet sock feet on the floor. It was the first time in a week he'd had his shoes off. In the past 36 hours he had had no sleep at all, and in that time only two full meals and a scanty lunch. His eyes were red-rimmed and glazed; his face, where it showed above a murk of whiskers, was creased with fatigue.

James Henry O'Neill had become a track laborer for the Great Northern Railway when he was a boy only 14 years old. He had been with the company for a quarter of a century, minus one year. He had risen through the ranks from brakeman, to conductor, to yardmaster to trainmaster, and now for eight years had been a division superintendent, first with the Montana Division, now for three years with the Cascade. In those three years he had run 4000 trains through Stevens Pass under winter storm conditions and had never before had one delayed more than 24 hours.

Yet for five days now he and his crews had worked to

the point of collapse—and to what avail? The line was tied up tighter than ever. A great transcontinental railroad stood paralyzed, completely blocked in his division.

He was dead beat.

In this position and in this mood Lemman and the passenger committee came upon him. He listened wearily to their grievances.

"Believe me," he replied, pulling himself more erect, "I've never forgotten the situation of the passengers, even for a moment. That is the message I want you to take back to the others. I have worked with only one thought in mind—of opening the line and getting the trains off the mountain. No one is more concerned about the inconvenience and delay than I, but I don't know what I can do that I haven't been doing. No one has ever seen such a storm as this, not even the old-timers. Five days of it! We've cleared parts of the track three times, and slides are coming down now where they've never come down before! I've never had a train stalled this long on my division before, and believe me, this is as distressing to me as it is to you."

Sol Cohn cried out, "Then you admit slides are coming down where they never did before? Pettit and everyone has tried to tell us we're safe just because that hill has never slid. But places are sliding for the first time!"

"Wouldn't we be better off in the tunnel?" pursued Lemman. "Or at least up on one of those spur tracks, where there's no hill overhead?"

"The tunnel is absolutely out of the question," said the superintendent with a squaring of his jaw. "I wouldn't put a dog in that black hole. It's cold and damp and dripping with moisture. If we tried to keep the steam up, you'd all be suffocated by smoke and fumes. If we didn't you'd all freeze. Besides, we couldn't get food in there from the hotel, and people couldn't get out, because there's a stream of water on either side of the track."

"Then how about the spur tracks?" asked White.

"Who said there was no hill above them?" countered O'Neill. "If you'll take a good look you'll see those spurs end near the hill above the tunnel, and that hill is steeper than the one you're complaining about. Part of that hillside avalanches every winter and some of the snow hits the spurs. No, those spurs are in far more danger of slides than where the trains stand now."

"What about the snowsheds?" asked Cohn. "Wouldn't they afford us protection?"

"For a few cars, maybe, but not for the whole train. And those snowsheds are built at draws where slides are most apt to come down, so the exposed cars would be in real danger. No, you must believe me—the trains are in the safest possible place up here."

He went on to explain what he planned to do next. A couple days ago he had wired for more rotary assistance. One plow was coming out from the Rockies, and another was on its way from Seattle to Scenic—in fact, had no doubt already arrived. "Early tomorrow morning I'm going to try to hike out to Scenic. Now that telegraph service has been knocked out here, I need to get down there to send some wires. Then I personally will direct the work of the rotary up the hill."

He turned to them earnestly. "I shall do everything I can to get the line open at the earliest possible moment. Beyond that, there's nothing I can do."

It was impossible not to realize he spoke the truth. Walking back to the train the committee members agreed there was no doubting the superintendent's personal sincerity and his great personal efforts. Yet the facts stood out starkly—facts they hated to take back to their fellow prisoners on the train:

O'Neill would not consider moving the train.

He simply didn't know when he could get the line open.

"I am afraid we will be snowed in here a long time," Mrs. Covington wrote in her notes that night. "The people are very blue."

19

The sabbath day, February 27, dawned to the same

blurred outlines that haunted each morning in this high mountain world. Snow still fell. Now it came in larger flakes, now in smaller, now it came straight down, now it scattered in crazy patterns ahead of capricious canyon winds—but always it continued relentlessly, inexorably as though it meant to bury them alive in its soft, smothering depths.

After the last wind-blown passenger had returned from breakfast at Bailets, the Reverend Thomson announced he would hold a church service in one of the coaches. H. D. Chantrell, the customs man, went over to invite the crew and clerks from the mail train to attend.

Earlier that morning, when Engineer Ed Sweeney checked over his engine as he usually did, he couldn't get the injectors to work to put water into the boiler. His supply must be too low in the tank, he decided, and called in some laborers to shovel snow in. But after melting the snow he still couldn't draw water and his engine was about to die. Engineer Francis Martin of the passenger train came over to help. The two located a length of fire hose in a railroad shed and were trying to set up a syphoning system.

Chantrell appeared to tell them of the Sunday service on the passenger train. "We'd be pleased to have you come, he said, "but you two look pretty busy,"

"I'm having trouble with my engine and can't get away," replied Sweeney. "Sorry."

As Chantrell started to leave, Engineer Martin said drily, "You'd better have them pray we get some water into this boiler!"

The crew of No. 27 stayed by their engineer, but the mail clerks all combed their hair and went over to the service. By the time they arrived the passengers had assembled and a rough-looking man was singing "The Holy City" in a deep bass voice.

In the white gloom the minister opened his Bible and invited this congregation of strangers to repeat after him the verses of the 17th Psalm.

Hear a just cause, O Lord, attend to my cry;
     give ear to my prayer.
If thou triest my heart, if thou visitest me by
     night, thou wilt find no wickedness in me . . .
My steps have held fast to my path, my feet have
     not slipped.
I call upon thee, for thou wilt answer me, O God.
Incline thy ear to me, hear my words . . .
Keep me as the apple of thine eye, hide me in
     the shadow of thy wing.

Here where the quivering snow field towered overhead and the ravine yawned below, the words fell from
impassioned, pleading lips.

The Reverend Thomson's sermon was on patience,
faith, and the power of prayer in times of trouble. Mrs.
Covington sat piously, hands folded in her lap. All the
children except the smallest remained quiet while their
mothers drank in the words of inspiration. The older
men leaned forward seriously like elders of the church.
Even the salesmen and some of the more motley passengers from the smoker listened attentively, as did the mail
clerks, crew members and section men standing at the
back of the coach.

The service ended with their reciting together the optimistic, comforting words of the 27th Psalm:

The Lord is my light and my salvation; whom
     shall I fear?
The Lord is the stronghold of my life; of
     whom shall I be afraid? . . .
Though a host encamp against me, my heart
     shall not fear.
Though war arise against me, yet I will be
     confident . . .
For he will hide me in his shelter in the
     day of trouble,
He will conceal me in the cover of his tent,
     he will set me on a rock.

Not long after the final "Amen," the group working on the mail train engine got the injectors to functioning. Martin, with a sly wink at Sweeney, said, "Well, Ed, I guess prayer does work!"

20

O'Neill had started for Scenic. With him were two brakemen, Big Jerry Wickam and J. S. Churchill, to break trail.

That news filtered through the passenger train later in the morning. And back in the smoker John Merritt looked at Lew Jesseph and Lew at John, and they said, "If he can make it, why can't we?"

Over the days the passengers had heard a great deal about the road to Scenic. Only three-and-a-half miles away, on the west side of Windy Point, the tracks came out on a shelf above the little railroad town, but the drop-off at that point was 800 feet and there was no way down. To follow the railroad line the whole way while it lost the elevation of the drop-off was to walk five extra, desperate miles—a long swing into the mountains beyond the town and back. All the trainmen who knew the country had insisted that it would be foolhardy for passengers to attempt to walk out.

Yet O'Neill was going now, and as the two lawyer friends discussed the situation, they felt they could do whatever he could do. George Loveberry said he wanted to throw in with them if they decided to go, but all the other men tried to talk them out of the idea.

"You're a lot safer here than out in that blizzard," argued Judge McNeny. "Do you want to end up lost, caught in a slide, or frozen to death?"

"I'm not one of those who's worried about the safety of this train," Merritt replied. "But I've got urgent business in Olympia. I'd like to get it over with and start back home. The same is true of Lew. If we follow O'Neill's trail I don't see why we should get into any trouble."

Field, the Alaska man, advised them against setting out

unless they had snowshoes and a guide who knew the
country. "What about that old trapper, Schwartz, who
hangs out at Bailets?" asked Loveberry. "He claims to be
an old Alaska musher and has been around Wellington a
dozen years." They decided he would make an acceptable
guide.

Up at the hotel they located the trapper—bewhiskered
and tobacco stained, the very picture of an old mountain-
eer. But when they offered him $20 to lead the way to
Scenic, he looked them up and down—at their business
suits, their wool overcoats, their shoes with low rubbers
meant for city wear—then spat contemptuously. "Nope,
don't care to," he said. "I could get down easy enough.
Nothing to it. But I don't mean to be responsible for
any city dudes."

Walking away, they choked with anger. "*He* can get
down! Then we can, too. We'll show the old coot!" They
decided to go, guide or no guide, snowshoes or no snowshoes.

They went back to the train and gathered up a few
things. As they shook hands around and bade the others
goodbye, they found some of the men acting as though
they were going out to sure death, but others seemed
tempted to join them.

"If you get there all right, try to get word back to us,"
commanded Bethel. "Someone may be coming up this
way, or maybe telegraph service will be restored. Let us
know how the trail is, what kind of a trip you have. If the
way isn't too tough, some of the rest of us will follow."

The going *was* tough. Not far west of Wellington a
slide 200 yards wide covered the tracks to a depth of 20
feet. This snow was treacherous and uneven, and they
found themselves sinking in to knees, to thighs, to arm-
pits. Floundering, falling, crawling, they knew what Field
meant when he said they'd need snowshoes.

Beyond the slide, they found an easier track with only
drifts and deep snow. They were wading along when they
were hailed from behind, and turning saw two figures
climbing down off the slide. Young Milton Horn and Ed

Rea caught up with them. "We've decided we're fed up with that train," Rea said. "Can we go out with you?"

Jesseph said, "Well, you look young and able-bodied. You'll probably make it better than we will."

The group of five came to another slide, which they clambered over. On its other side was the double rotary, stalled between that and the next slide—like some monster caught helplessly in a pitfall of snow. They stopped to talk for a few minutes with the men standing by the machines, then went on.

By the time they had conquered the next slide they were exhausted. That hateful prison, the stalled train, now began to seem a haven, warm, dry and comfortable, and they wished they had never left it.

Near Snowshed 3.3 they found men dressed in heavy clothes and hung with paraphernalia. They were linemen working on the telegraph line, trying hard to get service restored. "You're damn fools if you go on," they warned. "The only way down to Scenic is to slide, and if you try that you'll probably kill yourselves."

But they were too weary to turn back; their only salvation lay ahead. They staggered on, crawling through the top of the snowshed, which was partly broken down and filled with snow and ice.

All the way around Windy Point the tracks followed the sheer mountain edge where a rolling fall or an entanglement in sliding snow could easily take them into the cavernous ravine. They picked their way along as gingerly as mountain climbers on an icy peak. Presently they rounded a turn and came out at the vantage point where far below, off at the bottom of a steep and fearsome slope, they could see the big resort building, which, at this height, marked the location of Scenic Hot Springs.

The trainmen and linemen who had warned them about the way down had not exaggerated. The telegraph right-of-way descended here and that had been cleared of trees. But there was no track nor trail and no way to pick their way down. It was slide or nothing! Pulling their overcoats over their buttocks and their coat tails up between their legs they sat down. Downward along the telegraph line the snow-quilted way looked smooth and soft.

"God save us from jutting trees and rocks," said Jesseph, and letting go they were off on a wild, 800-foot ride. It was a long way to be without air, and yet they were unable to catch their breaths all the way down.

They ended up in flying heaps at last, and to their amazement picked themselves up snow-clogged and shaken, but unhurt.

As they hurried on toward the buildings of Scenic, they overtook Superintendent O'Neill and his two men. Big Jerry Wickham was torn and tattered, with bleeding face and scratched arms, and he was limping badly. "What on earth happened to you?" they demanded.

"Oh, I tangled with a snowslide."

"He went down nearly a thousand feet into the ravine!" said O'Neill. "It's a miracle he wasn't killed."

When they reached the inn, all the passengers, even the two young men, collapsed, their strength gone. Lew Jesseph looked at John Merritt and both at Loveberry. "No, it's too dangerous and rough. We couldn't advise the others to try it. The older men—the women and children—they just couldn't make it!"

They composed a telegram which read: "Col. Cody: Arrived safely. Do not come. Our regards." Horn and Rea revived enough to take it down to the depot but found the telegraph line was still out of order. They gave the message to O'Neill instead, on the off chance that he could send it later, either by wire or by someone walking in.

21

All that anxious, snowy afternoon aboard the gloomy dungeon that was the train the talk turned to those who had made their bid for freedom. Had they reached Scenic safely? How dangerous had the trip been? Had O'Neill got there to send his reports and wires? How long would it be before the superintendent could get up the hill with the rotary?

But of course no one could give any answers. Instead, the stranded people became aware of further disquieting developments here in Wellington.

For one thing the engines were running low on coal to keep their steam up and the coaches heated. There was still some coal at the coal chute, but without a rotary to clear the track, it was out of reach. There was a coal car on the spur tracks, too, but it was heaped with drifts and entirely inaccessible. Fortunately, however, the mail train engine still had a fair supply, and it was broken out of the drifts, moved up near the passenger train engine, and a transfer of coal made. If worst came to worst, the mail train engine could be let die and the coaches heated with Baker stoves.

For another thing, the laborers were quitting the town. Most of the afternoon people saw shovelers straggling by the train windows, carrying packs and bedrolls and making their way on down the tracks. Perhaps the men were going down to report to O'Neill and shovel snow on the uphill fight, the passengers speculated. But, no— George Davis came back with a rumor of a darker tinge. "The men have demanded higher wages, and their bosses have refused to listen to such a thing. The men are quitting in bunches."

Stalled as they were, shrouded in an ominous snow blanket—were they to be utterly abandoned as well?

*   *   *

Late in the afternoon Bill Harrington and the rotary crew which had left with him on Friday appeared out of the tunnel and tramped into Wellington. Harrington no longer merited his Snow King title, for the white stuff he was supposed to rule had routed him. He had been forced to abandon Rotary X801 near Gaynor, out of coal and trapped between two slides.

Taking turns at breaking trail, and climbing over slide after slide, he and the crew of 14 had hiked the eight miles to Cascade, reaching there last night. Now he had come over to report to O'Neill.

But O'Neill had been defeated, too, he learned, and had gone out to Scenic to rally forces and begin a new attack from there. Trainmaster Blackburn was supervising work at Windy Point. The double rotary trapped there had run completely out of coal and Blackburn had assembled a crew which was cutting wood for fuel to keep steam up. Harrington walked down to join Blackburn.

As the people on the train repeated this latest news they found talk of so many slides to the east chilling. Worse, as the afternoon wore on, they heard strange roars in the valley around them. This, the alarmists claimed, was the noise of avalanches coming nearer.

All that day John Rogers had been hypnotized by the white panorama of the mountainside overhead. It seemed he could not pass a snow-drifted window without pausing to gaze upward. On the first morning the train had stood at Wellington, the snowfield had been strewn with dark stumps and snags. Since that time, so much depth had been added that blemishes and disfigurements had been covered over. Now it was one immense quilt of pure white snow—so beautiful, so awesome that he could not help viewing it with admiration. Could it actually be as dangerous as some of those on board believed?

The waiting, now that they had nothing immediate to wait for, was intolerable. Rogers, discovering he was running low on tobacco, was glad of the excuse to get away from the train. Putting on his coat, he tramped the snowy path to Bailets to replenish his supply.

Just east of Bailets Hotel a half-dozen workers' cabins sat at the base of a gulch. Beyond, to the northeast, other gulches came down to the side of the triangular flat at whose outer edge lay the spur tracks. As he approached the tavern porch Rogers jerked his head around quickly at a sound which sprang from the mountain reaches in that direction. With eyes of utter amazement he saw a part of a hillside in that area simply fold up and start sliding down with a roar. Snow-draped evergreens which stood on the hillside splintered with loud, snapping noises, and the whole mass descended, a white river of movement on the otherwise solid mountainside. Rumbling and grinding, it spread out on the flat below.

During these last days on the train, when in spite of all the anxiety generated, they had continued to live safe and unharmed, Rogers had found it difficult to worry over an avalanche. In his mind he had never been able to imagine one demolishing anything as stable as a warm, lighted, seven-car train full of men, women and children —men with their business preoccupations and smoker stories, women with their compassionate hearts, children with their laughter and cries, and Miss O'Reilly with her merry Irish eyes.

The demonstration before him shook him. He knew now beyond any doubt the source of those roars they had been hearing around them in the valley. As he went on into the tavern, he found himself trembling.

22

The nights were the worst for everyone, and this night, the sixth since leaving Spokane, was the worst of all.

Daytime they had their sense of togetherness, their mingling in the cars, their deliberate joking and making light of the situation, their endless speculations about what would happen next, their attempts to cheer the sick people and to amuse the children. All these things were bulwarks against grimness.

But at night alone in their berths or coach seats, all the horrible possibilities rose up to haunt them: hunger, cold, even death. Hunger if the food at Wellington ran out. Cold if all the coal were exhausted. Death if the mountain snowfield above them should slip. Too tense to sleep, they lay with fear gripping them, or if they dozed, started wildly awake at the least noise.

John Rogers had not been one of the nervous ones, but Sunday night he did not sleep either. He quaked as two or three times he heard avalanches let go in the surrounding canyons. By dawn he resolved that at all costs he would flee the train and chance the walk out to Scenic.

In the morning he immediately began canvassing among the others for men willing to make the trip out with him. Many looked as baggy-eyed and weary as he felt, and a half-dozen others decided with him that the rigors of the trail could be no worse than this sitting day and night in suspense. Among those who wished to go were Sam Field, the Alaska man, and one of the Boles brothers. The other brother, less adventurous, elected to remain where he was.

Rogers, thoroughly alarmed now, urged Judge McNeny to join the group. "I beg of you to come! I'm convinced it is very dangerous here, and I'll feel guilty if I leave you behind."

"No, I'm all right," insisted the judge. "I'm too old to go floundering around in blizzards. Besides, I think you've gone a bit snow-daft. This train is safe!"

The men in the party were anxious to find some railroad man who knew the way to guide them. To Rogers' disappointment he learned that Conductor Vogel, Engineer Sweeney and two electric motormen had already started for Scenic earlier that morning, Vogel to wire authorities about his delayed mail, Sweeney and the others to look the situation over and report to O'Neill.

But Pettit, it seemed, also needed to take the trip out, to try to make arrangements to have supplies packed in.

Many of the passengers, especially the women, felt consternation to see Pettit leave. Through the days his concern and kindliness had proved a great comfort; even when he had been impatient or sharp it had been only to convince them of their safety. He was the good father who had watched over them and kept them from harm.

"Oh, I'll be right back," he assured them. "I hope to send some wires, get some things on the way up here, then turn around and start back."

Mrs. Latsch hurriedly wrote a letter of business instructions to the manager of her hairpin firm and asked Rogers to mail it for her in Scenic.

The party of 11 got away around noon. Those left on board felt a new sense of desertion and despair.

The children became whinier, more quarrelsome and noisy. Happily, Nellie Sharp hit upon an idea with which others cooperated. A number of passengers dug into suitcases and found clothing they could dispense with—at this juncture clothes mattered little anyway—and they started the children playing "dress-up." This new game took their fancy and they stayed with it for hours. So they kept busy and giggly most of the afternoon while around them adults gave way to panic.

For at last the weather was showing signs of change— for a horrible worse. After all these days of snow—with a new depth of five or six feet laid down—now the storm front was beginning to bring rain. And rain could mean nothing but havoc.

That havoc was not long in making itself apparent. Slides began letting go in batches. Quiveringly, the passengers would hear one start, the avalanche roar low at first but growing to frightening proportions, accompanied by the explosive sounds of trees breaking off like match sticks; then the roar would dwindle to a rumble and die away. Another would start, seemingly closer than the last.

It was a war of nerves, and at last Edgar Lemman, whom they all regarded as their leader, jumped to his feet. "The tunnel can't possibly be more dangerous than this! They'll have to put us in there. Or else take us out to Scenic somehow. We'll have to make them do something!"

Even those who had been most afraid of the tunnel were ready to agree with him now.

Pettit came dragging himself on board. He had not gone the whole way to Scenic, for things were so tough he was afraid he couldn't get back if he did. So he had imparted instructions to another of the railroad men regarding what he had hoped to accomplish in Scenic, and he had turned back. It had been a terrible trip, for track conditions were awful, there were lots of slides along the way and he had to dodge others, and footing was getting impossible in the rain. Exhausted, plainly dispirited, he was for the first time himself alarmed about avalanche conditions. But when various passengers importuned him to move the train he only shook his head wearily and said, "I have no authority."

Lemman knew that this was true. He and his committee hastily organized another protest meeting, with a demand that someone representing O'Neill attend it. This time they meant to get action—or blood.

23

Never in the ambitions of Earl Longcoy to secure a position as a railroad stenographer had he foreseen as one of its hazards being stranded on a mountainside for a week in a blizzard. Being snowed-in left him strained and apprehensive. Besides, he was anxiously intent on getting back to Everett, headquarters of the division. There a most happy event awaited him. His mother and sister were arriving from Wisconsin to make their home with him. As he had been away from them six months, and this for the first time in his life, he was waiting hard for the reunion.

Yet he had to try to keep his mind on his work, for the superintendent had kept him busy with reports and messages, and even after O'Neill left for Scenic, there was work to be done for Blackburn and Harrington, as well as catching up on correspondence and filing.

Most of the detained trainmen cursed the weather vehemently, with proficient vocabulary. But Longcoy was a member in good standing of the Everett YMCA and did not swear. Instead he paced the car restlessly. "Isn't it *ever* going to stop snowing?" he demanded of Lewis Walker, O'Neill's colored steward, who sat playing solitaire.

During Walker's long years with the railroad his hair had turned to gray and he had taken on a thick coating of stoicism and resignation. No reaction of his to white men's foibles ever appeared even fleetingly on his face. "Looks like it's not," he answered, barely glancing up from his game.

"I'm so frustrated not getting to Everett to meet Mother and Mettie," Longcoy fretted.

Walker thought of his own wife in Everett, and of his ancient grandmother, 107 years old and a former slave, who lived with them, and how these two would be worrying and waiting for him. But because of his color, others did not consider his emotions valid, he felt, or those of his family, and he kept silent.

Longcoy walked back to the window. Above the steep snow slope he could see into the higher Cascade peaks, wrapped in clouds and mist. Young and impressionable, he had recently been much taken with a quotation from Byron that he had run across in a G.N. pamphlet describing the beauties of the trip west. Now as he gazed upward into the snowy castlements he repeated aloud:

Above me are the Alps,
The palaces of nature, whose vast walls
Have pinnacled in clouds their snowy scalps
And throned Eternity in icy halls
Of cold sublimity, where forms and falls
The avalanche, the thunderbolt of snows.

"You know," he exclaimed, turning to Walker, "they used those very lines to describe the Cascades through here. It gives me the shudders!"

"A mighty nice verse," said Walker.

This was not the point to Longcoy, and the steward's lack of understanding depressed him with an acute sense of isolation. Disconsolately he stood by the window—alone with Byron and Byron's awesome lines.

Later when Trainmasters Harrington and Blackburn came in from Windy Point, Blackburn was plainly worn out and in impatient mood. "The passengers are holding a meeting tonight and have asked someone to attend representing the railroad. I have a hundred things to do, and can hardly take time out to go. What about you, Bill?"

Harrington felt the same way but suggested, "What about Earl? Surely he could represent O'Neill."

The two turned to the young secretary and said, "Earl, how about your attending a meeting on the passenger train tonight? Make notes of any complaints and refer them back to us. We'll take them up with O'Neill as soon as we're in touch with him."

Longcoy felt ill-equipped to stand in O'Neill's shoes even for an hour, but he knew a command from superiors when he heard one. He nodded his assent.

24

Well might the young stenographer, Earl Longcoy, have felt trepidation. The mood of the passenger committee and of the passengers around them had changed drastically from what it had been on Saturday.

Then Lemman had been the objective arbiter who mainly sought knowledge of the situation. He had given the passengers' complaints, then listened to O'Neill's rebuttal and willingly if unhappily accepted the superintendent's estimate and vague reassurances.

Today Lemman's role had changed. Now he was the gimlet-eyed prosecutor intent upon wringing emergency action from the scene.

From the beginning he minced no words. "The railroad is placing our lives in jeopardy unnecessarily," he accused. "The rotaries are all stopped. The workers have quit—whether for justified or unjustified reasons I don't know. No fighting force is left up here. Nothing at all is being done to get us out. In the last 12 hours the avalanche situation has worsened in a truly alarming way."

Turning directly to Longcoy, he shouted, "We refuse to be left on this train exposed to danger this way. Order the train taken into the tunnel. Or else get fifty workers to rope off a trail and assemble what equipment they need to carry out the children, the sick people, and the others who can't negotiate the trail. We demand this be done, and done *now!*"

The secretary, utterly unprepared for such an ultimatum, faltered, "There aren't that many workers up here."

"How many are there?"

"I—I couldn't say."

"Well, we understand there are 125 at Scenic. Fifty of those could be ordered up here to our rescue, bringing ropes, sledges, stretchers, and whatever else is needed."

"I don't think Mr. O'Neill would authorize anything like—"

"O'Neill be dammed!" Henry White broke in. "You're O'Neill's representative here. *You* order those men up here to get us out!"

Longcoy gasped, "I'm afraid I couldn't do that."

"You refuse?"

"I'm afraid I must."

"Then put it in writing!" Lemman, court room dramatist that he was, shoved pen and paper toward the young man. "If that is your answer, write it down in black and white and sign your name. We'll show the world that the railroad has refused, refused in cold blood, to provide the men and equipment to take women, children and sick people to safety."

Longcoy shrank back, "I have no authority to do that."

"No authority? Then who has the authority?"

"Mr. Blackburn, I think, sir."

"Then get Blackburn. Let's see *him* put his refusal in writing!"

25

Trainmaster Arthur Reed Blackburn, when he appeared, showed plainly he was angry ·to have been summoned and was in no mood to be trifled with. But Lemman quailed not at all. Ringingly he repeated his demands, then added, "If you are in authority in Mr. O'Neill's absence, then we want the answer direct from you."

"Yes, I am in authority, and I am here to tell you what you ask is as impossible as it is absurd. There is no cause for this hysteria. There's never been a slide down across here and there never will be."

"How can you say that? Slides are coming down all over where they never came before. So why can't it slide here? The only protected place up here is the tunnel, and we demand you run the train in there before all of us are killed."

"Even if I thought it a safer place, which I don't," said Blackburn, "I couldn't put the train in there."

"Why not?"

"The tender is almost empty of coal. If we used what little there is to get up the grade, there'd be none left to heat the coaches."

"The engine will burn wood to keep up steam, won't it?"

"Well, yes."

"Then run the train into the tunnel, and we'll turn to, every man on board, and cut enough wood to keep the coaches warm."

"It took the rotary two pusher engines and its plowing equipment to get up the grade into the tunnel," Blackburn pointed out, wearily. "That was three days ago. The way it's snowed and drifted since then, we couldn't possibly get there with only one engine and no rotary to plow the track. Besides, that tunnel is a miserable, dangerous hole. It's entirely out of the question."

"Then order men up here from Scenic to get us out!"

"Mr. Lemman, if I actually thought you were in danger here I would do that. But I see no cause for all this commotion. This train is in a safe place, and our workers are needed where they are."

"Have you looked at that snow cap up there?" Lemmen demanded, waving his hand overhead. "It teeters—on the verge. If you refuse us help in getting out from under it before it descends—then put that statement in writing and sign it." The lawyer shoved pen and paper forward as he had with Longcoy.

That gave even the formidable Blackburn pause. To refuse was one thing, but the thought of having to answer later to officials higher up for a signed refusal was something else again. He ignored the writing material and changed his tack.

"If you are so afraid for your safety, why can't you walk out as others have done? Why should I provide help for able-bodied men?"

"I've never asked help for any able-bodied men, and you know it. But there are sick people on board, and women and children, and it is for them I ask help. The only way we can get them out is with workers to break trail, string ropes and carry stretchers."

"But you must be insane!" exclaimed Blackburn. "You mean you would take the women, children and sick people from the warmth and safety of this train—out along that terrible trail where slides are apt to sweep down at any moment? Then you just don't know what you are doing! You haven't seen the track around Windy Point or that hill down to Scenic. If you had you wouldn't even consider anything so dangerous—so foolish.

"I'll tell you what I'll do—I'll provide ten men to break trail for any of the men who wish to go out. But, believe me, no woman, child or sick person is going to leave this train with the permission of the Great Northern Railway!"

"Then we'll go without your permission and without your help. If anything happens, the railroad will be responsible. Don't forget that—the railroad will be responsible. Here, put your refusal in writing. I want it in writing!"

Blackburn flung paper and pen aside with an angry motion. "No one is going to take any women and children off this train!"

"How can you stop us?"

"I'll use force if necessary!" And, red of face, the trainmaster stalked from the smoker.

26

For a long moment there was stunned silence. Then a pandemonium of indignation broke out. "Stop us—what does he mean, stop us!" "I'd like to see him try it!" "We're not railroad property!" "Does he think he can herd us around like sheep?"

Mrs. Latsch, a business woman who thought she knew her own rights, announced grimly, "He'll have a chance to show his force in the morning. I've had my fill of this, and if any of the men decide to go out, I'm going with them."

"Count me in," cried Nellie. "If he tries to put me back on the train, I'll bite him!"

But as the excitement died away, sober reality set in. The threat he had made in the heat of argument, Edgar Lemman realized, was one they had no way of carrying out. From what he knew about that precipitous hill down to Scenic, they would have to have ropes, stretchers or sleds, and a crew of men to help lower the ones who could not walk or slide.

So, without cooperation of the railroad, many of the people on the train were going nowhere—not the Becks with their three children; nor the Mays with Mrs. Starrett and her three; nor Mrs. Gray and her two immobile charges; nor George Davis and his armload Thelma; nor Catherine O'Reilly and her patient, Vail; nor Lemman himself with his nervously sick wife; nor old Mrs. Covington or the older ones among the men.

Only the unencumbered and the stout of limbs were free to go. Among the nine women aboard, only Nellie Sharp and Libby Latsch were in this category, and they stuck to their decision to make the try.

Libby looked down at their dark skirts which nearly swept the floor and shook her head. "We can't hike out dressed like this, Nell. Let's see if we can borrow trousers from any of the men."

Judge McNeny, the Reverend Thomson, and R. M. LaVille were among those who believed there was least risk in remaining on the train. As members of the passenger committee, Henry White and Sol Cohn felt it their duty to stay. A number of others, including Eltinge, Barnhard, Bethel, Mahler, Matthews, and Topping, were determined to leave in the morning. The three Irish friends still debated the question, as did Sam Lee and Albert Boles. H. D. Chantrell, John Brockman and the two Canadian miners, Chisholm and Thompson said they were too old and lazy to make the trip; they'd take their chances where they were.

"Oh, don't feel so bad!" cried Nellie to Mrs. Beck, embracing her. "The minute we get there we'll get help for you."

"We'll get all kinds of publicity," Mrs. Latsch echoed. "We'll force them to action!"

"We'll go to the highest railroad authorities in Seattle, wire the head office if we have to," Bethel promised. "We'll *make* them send men to bring you down."

This cheered those who must stay and while the mood was momentarily brighter, Nellie said, "Since we want to get an early start, Libby and I will cook breakfast. You see, I've got a meat grinder—"

"A meat grinder!" they chorused. "Do you travel around with a meat grinder?"

"Where I got it I refuse to answer." Then, trying to rouse Lemman, who was sunk in gloom, she added, "I won't put it in writing either! Anyhow, instead of getting Mrs. Bailets up, Libby and I are going to cook breakfast, and it's going to be a real treat—roast beef hash!"

"Hooray for the Wild West Girl! Hooray for the Merry Widow!" shouted the men.

Henry White, hoping to further sustain this lighter mood, said, "Now that everything's settled, let's quit being so gloomy. Those who are leaving have promised to get action, and I believe they will. Everything's going to turn out all right. So why don't we have a little entertainment now to chase our blues. Who can do a stunt or sing a song?"

All were relieved to forget their predicament in the camaraderie of the moment. Those who could told stories, gave recitations, performed tricks or stunts, and then they joined in group singing until 10:30. At that time "the smoker," as they called it, broke up. A few men stayed on to talk another hour, then they too went off to bed.

As midnight ushered in March 1 at Wellington, all was quiet on passenger train No. 25. On Mail train No. 27, mail clerks slept and dreamed of sorting mail. On both trains tired trainmen slumbered, and in the extra mail coach laborers sprawled at rest. In O'Neill's private car, Longcoy had forgotten his impatience to see his mother, Blackburn his quarrel with the passengers, and Walker his isolation in a white man's world. All slept.

Even at Bailets the last desultory poker game had folded up. Silence, if not repose, settled down on all the troubled souls imprisoned together on the snow-piled mountainside.

27

Overhead a flash of light stabbed the night. A rolling sound echoed in its wake.

A moment of darkness and silence. Then again a forked tongue of flame writhed in the sky. For one long vivid moment the wilderness lay revealed in all its savage, snowy grandeur. Then darkness again, with the rumbling cannons of thunder ricocheting their iron balls of sound off the mountainsides and dropping them reverberatingly into canyons.

The time was a little after 1 a. m. Tired as he was, the noise of this winter electrical storm penetrated the consciousness of Charlie Andrews, an electrical engineer asleep in one of the little cabins for workers not far from Bailets Hotel. He had worked down at Windy Point all day helping cut wood to keep the rotaries alive. Weary and soaked to the skin, he had taken off his wet clothes, hung them near the stove and dropped into bed like a stone.

Like many of the railroad men, Andrews believed the fear of the passengers was silly and hysterical. That hillside above the tracks would never slide, he felt sure. The real danger lay in the gulches behind the hotel and the workers' cabins where he lived. The nearby slide on Sunday had proved that.

Now as he heard the thunder he jumped from his bed in alarm, fearing the vibrations would bring down the snow behind his cabin and he would be engulfed. His clothes were still wet but he hastily donned them and dashed outside. It was raining in torrents—a perilous sign. He went about pounding on other cabin doors, putting his head in to shout to fellow workers, "Big storm—liable to bring down a slide. Better get out and down to safety."

The other men groaned and rasped back, "You've got slides on the brain. Go away and shut up!" They turned over and went back to sleep.

Shivering and disgruntled, he walked down to the depot, wondering what to do. Maybe he was jittery, he admitted, but he had such horrid pictures of getting trapped in his cabin, he didn't mean to go back there.

From the depot platform he could see the back end of the passenger train a short way down the track. He was cold in his wet clothes, and the escaping steam from the valve on the rear-end car looked warm and inviting. He considered walking down and climbing on board. But the train was full, he knew, and he probably wouldn't find a spot to bed down.

He turned east instead, heading for the section men's bunkhouse. There was a big stove there, where he could huddle for warmth and maybe even find a place to stretch out. The rain pelted down, and overhead another stroke of lightning was followed by the batteries of thunder.

Just as he reached the bunkhouse, a new sound sprang into being behind him. He wheeled, and in another vivid lightning flash saw White Death moving down the mountainside above the trains. Relentlessly it advanced, exploding, roaring, rumbling, grinding, snapping—a crescendo of sound that might have been the crashing of ten thousand freight trains. Colossal it was—in the manner the world might end. Onward it rolled in a majestic wave, crumbling the whole canyon wall before it. It descended to the ledge where the side tracks lay, picked up cars and equipment as though they were so many snow-draped toys, and swallowing them up, disappeared like a white, broad monster into the ravine below.

For a moment longer Andrews stood mesmerized— helplessly immobilized by the awful scene. Then acti- vated by horror he rushed to the bunkhouse and burst in upon the sleeping men.

"My God, boys, get up! The hillside's torn loose. The trains are gone!"

Andrews dashed off to waken the men in the cabins above for the second time and to rouse the sleepers in the Bailets Hotel. By the time he ran back down to the bunk- house, he could hear moans and shrieks, like the voices of tortured souls, coming out of the depth of the canyon below. Peering down, he could see but one coach end sticking out; all else seemed buried beneath tons of cascaded snow.

Silent and as though moving in nightmare, he and the other men began to light railroad lanterns and button on coats for the descent into that valley of hell.

28

The following morning John Wentzel, a member of the section crew at Wellington, limped into Scenic. Numb with shock, he hardly knew how he got over the slides and down the hill from Windy Point. About 7 a. m. he burst into the Hot Springs Hotel gasping, "All wiped out. Tracks gone. Trains dumped into the canyon." Then he collapsed.

On reaching Scenic on Sunday, O'Neill had learned that the rotary from Seattle was working near Corea, the next little station east. After completing his business at the depot, he joined it there. The machine, in charge of Master Mechanic J. J. Dowling, had run back into Scenic both Sunday and Monday nights for coal and water. Now again on Tuesday it was ready to head for the hill, the superintendent with it.

A worker ran for O'Neill at once — O'Neill, the man on whose shoulders rested the responsibility for the many decisions made in the last few days, decisions which no matter how sound they had seemed at the time they were made, had now proved tragic beyond immediate comprehension.

He whitened but said nothing, and hurried to the hotel, where he obtained what details he could from the incoherent Wentzel. Then he strode to the depot to send the news by coded message to his Everett headquarters and to order a relief train. The Everett office, later that day, released the news to the world.

For nearly a week now families and friends had sought word about passengers on Local No. 25, about mail clerks on No. 27, or about crew men on one train or the other. Only a few had received wires from Cascade Tunnel or Wellington; the others scanned the daily papers eagerly yet fearfully.

The newspapers contained long columns about the weather crisis. A great storm was sweeping the whole northern hemisphere, with blizzard conditions prevailing from the North Pacific to the North Atlantic. On February 22 snow fell at a foot an hour in the Cascade passes, the Seattle *Times* reported. Northern Pacific trains were delayed one to four hours, while the Milwaukee Railroad was forced to suspend operations altogether.

By the next day ALL railroads were blocked through the Cascades. N. P. trains with 200 on board were stalled near the Stampede Tunnel, and six trains on the G. N. line at Skykomish and Leavenworth.

In the next few days all newspapers reported terrible conditions. TEN MILE SNOW SLIDE BLOCKS GN TRACKS, said one headline. The accompanying story told how snowplows, rotaries and 300 men were battling the elements between Scenic and Wellington. Stalled passengers from G. N. trains were either taken care of at Scenic or taken back to Spokane.

On February 26 the Seattle *Times* reported that passengers and mail delayed at Scenic had been brought to Seattle. This was doubtless true concerning passengers and mail from eastbound trains brought to a stop at

Scenic when the pass became closed. But still the waited for passengers, mail clerks and crew members of Trains No. 25 and 27 failed to materialize—nor was any news of them forthcoming.

During that whole week no newspaper hinted that two G. N. trains were stalled on the mountain in a place of danger. Not until Sunday when O'Neill and his men and the Merritt Jesseph party hiked to Scenic did the fact become public knowledge. On Monday, February 28— only after the trains had already been stalled for six days—the story broke.

HUNGRY PASSENGERS MAROONED IN THE CASCADES, headlined the Seattle *Times*.

"Sixty passengers on a westbound train have been marooned on the blizzard-swept summit of the Cascade Mountains at Wellington," read the accompanying story. "The beleagured and hungry passengers begged Division Superintendent J. H. O'Neill of Everett to take the cars back into the tunnel, as at Wellington there was scarcely more than a half mile of clear tracks and within a few hundred feet immense snowfields carrying boulders and immense trees from the steep mountain would become loose and slide down the mountain creating a horrible groaning noise and forming a spectacle at once awe-inspiring and terrible to look on. By Saturday rations were short, which may result in acute suffering in a day or two."

All families personally concerned found this strangely delayed news disturbing and ominous. They slept on it uneasily that night, hoping for reassurance the next day. Instead, they picked up their newspapers on March 1 to be stunned by great black headlines:

AVALANCHE
BURIES TRAIN AT WELLINGTON
Two Killed and Several Injured
NO WORD AS TO SAFETY OF
OTHERS
Rescue Parties Rush to Scene

In Seattle the old husband of Mrs. Covington wept, as did Mrs. McNeny, who had been married to the judge for 23 years, and Mrs. Bethel, who had followed her husband to many spots on the globe. In Spokane, Mrs. Victoria Barnhard took her son Richard, age 5, into her arms and hugged him tightly while she prayed. Mrs. Eltinge and scores of other wives in other places paced the floor like trapped animals. Little Kean Latsch kept asking, "Why doesn't Mama come?" Older children tried to comprehend why Mother cried and feared something had happened to Daddy.

Wherever they could, male relatives and friends made ready to go into the mountains to learn the worst or help with rescue work. In Canada, the news reached other daughters of the Mays (sisters of Mrs. Starrett) ; their husbands, Sam Turpel and Pete Pearson, headed for the scene. From Spokane, L. M. Latsch, husband of Libby, started west.

From Bellingham came a minister friend of the Reverend Thomson, and later a son from Yakima. From Seattle came Bethel's partner, Downey; a member of Eltinge's firm, the two sons of Mrs. Covington; and a lone woman, Carrie Phillips, wife of Ross Phillips, brakeman on No. 25. Brothers of several trainmen left their homes. From Scenic Edward Boles and his friend Field turned back to learn what they could of Boles' brother Albert.

Soon that fearsome, impossible, snowbound incline up to Windy Point bore a distinct resemblance to Chilkoot Pass at the time of the Alaska gold rush. But these antlike figures who toiled upwards were filled with no lust for gold. Within them was a dull, sick incomprehension of the errand of horror and mercy on which they were bound.

29

O'Neill had decided he must wait in Scenic for the relief train, to take charge of workers and supplies that it would bring, but he rounded up 50 men and sent them forth in charge of Engineer Dowling. With Dowling were

Roadmaster Thomas McIntyre and Engineer Ed Sweeney. Also in the party was J. L. Godby, an attendant at the Hot Springs inn baths and a nurse of sorts, who had grabbed up what first aid supplies and medicines he could find at Scenic.

This group, hurriedly dispatched, was first up the harrowing incline. And once up, they found conditions along the track incredible. In the night the electrical storm had brought down the whole mountain of snow, and now there was almost one continuous slide all the way from Windy Point to Wellington.

Six hours after Wentzel reached Scenic, and nearly 12 hours after the accident, the party floundered across the last slide area and came within sight of the Wellington yard. They all stopped aghast.

It was a particularly hard moment for Ed Sweeney. Yesterday morning—could it be only *yesterday?*—when he had decided to walk down to see if he could help O'Neill, he had said to Francis Martin, "Look after my engine for me while I'm gone, will you, Frank?"

"Sure enough," said Martin. "I'll keep 'er going, and don't hurry back on my account." Then gripping Sweeney's hand and no doubt thinking of the avalanche danger along the track, he said gravely, "I hate to see you go, Ed."

And where was Frank Martin now?

For the entire passenger train had disappeared, the mail train, the disabled rotary, O'Neill's private car, the electric motors, the boxcars—all that had stood upon the sidetracks. The sidetracks themselves and also the water tank from alongside them were gone. From the coal chute east nearly to the depot, a distance of 1400 feet, or more than one fourth of a mile, the whole canyon side had been swept bare of everything but remnants of clinging snow.

Above, along a line that extended upward a thousand feet, snowbanks stood distinct, cut off sharp as though a knife had ripped out the colossal, thirty-acre—or even forty-acre—chunk which had fallen.

In the ravine 150 feet below, dark figures moved

against the snow. These were the people of Wellington intent upon rescue work, yet almost nothing down there
marked the wreck. One coach end showed, here and
there a splintered bit of hardwood or a twisted piece of
iron protruded, and the side and blades of the rotary
were visible—but out of 15 cars and coaches and a half-
dozen locomotives and engines that was all. The roof of a
worker's shack, knocked out by the avalanche, had ridden
the crest of the wave to the bottom of the ravine, but
nearly all else had been covered over by the fluid snow
which had poured over the lot like cake batter.

A knot of men detached themselves and ascended the
icy path from the ravine, slipping and sliding as they
tugged upward at a laden sled behind them. Silently
the caravan approached the freight shed at the side of the
depot. No word was spoken but all knew the sad contents
of that muffled parcel swathed in a blanket. The body was
laid beside a dozen others in the improvised morgue.

Dowling led his men across the slide area to the motormen's bunkhouse, which had been pressed into service as
an emergency hospital. Here the injured had been
brought, and here Mrs. Sperlock, wife of the night operator; Mrs. Flannery, the station agent's wife; and Mrs.
Bob Miles, an electric motorman's wife, had been giving
what first aid they could. With prayers of thanks they
welcomed Nurse Godby with whatever modest skills he
possessed and the medical supplies he brought.

The relief train reached Scenic late that same day. It
carried doctors and nurses from Everett, plus extra doctors picked up along the line at Skykomish and Monroe.
It brought coroners, undertakers, sheriffs and detectives.
It carried, too, a contingent of workers to pack up medical, surgical and other needed supplies and do rescue
work when they got there.

Andy Pascoe of Skykomish helped guide Dr. E. C.
Gleason, also of Skykomish, up that snowy, windy hill in
the inky darkness. A husky logger, he loaded himself with
75 pounds of food, the doctor's bag, a bundle of splints
and a shovel, then gave the doctor the coal oil lantern to
carry to light the way. Ahead were other men and other

lanterns, and as they neared the top of "Chilkoot," Pascoe saw those other lanterns blink out one by one. This puzzled him until he and the doctor reached the same spot and were nearly knocked flat by a gale that came out of the canyon below. Their lantern was snuffed out too. In trying to relight it in the dark they nearly stepped off the precipice into eternity.

The next day in daylight the first two professional nurses, Annabelle Lee and Lenora Todhunter, clad in trousers and hip boots, walked in. That day, too, came the news reporters and photographers, a plethora of additional undertakers, as well as wild-eyed relatives and friends.

Who had survived and by what miracle? That was the question of all who sought friends or loved ones.

It was the newsmen who put the story together—the newsmen with their professional prying, their unflinching questioning of those who had just known shock and tragedy. It was they who reconstructed all that will ever be known of that awful moment of finality, the zero hour when the Wellington avalanche struck.

30

On the trains there had been sleep—and then people woke (all who were ever to waken) to the sound of that unearthly roar. Henry White, the salesman from Minneapolis heard it and knew immediately it was the slide of which they had lived in fear. "This is it!" he whispered as the car lifted and went hurtling through the air. He seemed to have plenty of time to think and he wondered where the killing blow would strike. He closed his eyes to protect them and held his breath expecting a shock. There were many grinding noises and he kept falling—falling so long that the thought flashed, "I'm not dead yet—maybe I've escaped!" As the grinding ceased he was catapulted forward and found himself lying in his pajamas in the snow. As he rose to his feet he saw lightning rend the sky — "like an old-fashioned Minnesota thunderstorm," he thought in surprise.

"Snow King" Bill Harrington did not rouse until he was being hurled through space. He heard alarming crackings of timber, then blacked out. Coming to, he like White was stretched out in ice and snow in his night clothes. As he picked himself up, he knew he must go for help, but when he tried to climb the slippery side of the ravine he discovered he was barefoot and injured.

"It's the end of the world!" muttered Ray Forsyth. He was a section worker who had feared the bunkhouse might be swept by rolling snow and had crawled aboard the passenger train for protection. Now he heard a commotion worse than anything he had imagined. He lost consciousness, and reviving later found he was imprisoned in an overturned coach. Breaking a window he started tunneling through packed snow.

Lucius Anderson remembered nothing of the avalanche impact itself. He was aware of trouble, however, as he woke to hear someone complaining of the cold. Always the amiable porter, he murmured, "Yessir, I'll get right up and turn on the steam, sir." Opening his eyes he saw that his sleeper was crushed, twisted, filled with snow. Fireman Ross, standing naked nearby, kept repeating. "Jeez, I'm freezing." The two started fighting their way through the snow that blocked their exit.

Henry White had risen from his icy bed and was staggering about in dazed condition. Seeing strange movements in the snow he went over to investigate and found a man trying to dig himself out. Lending a hand he pulled forth the still-naked Ross. Behind him came a dark object—Lu Anderson. By some fortunate forethought, the porter had grabbed up a couple of blankets. They wrapped Ross in one, put the other around White's bare feet. The salesman began to realize he had been hurt in the wreck and felt unwell.

In the second-class mail car a number of men had been sleeping—Conductor Homer Purcell, his friend Ira Clary, Brakeman E. S. Duncan, the mail clerk Alfred Hensel, and others. All started awake to the sound of slipping snow, but before they could figure out what was happening the thing hit. The car was tossed up as though it were a juggler's ball, turning over and over. They were slapped to the top, to bottom and back again, being banged viciously each time. Then the coach seemed to strike something in its path and burst open like an eggshell. From above came the sound of sliding snow.

Feeling suffocated, Clary tried to move and breathe but found himself encased in snow. Panicked, he clawed at the icy stuff until his fingers ached. He paused in despair,, then thought he saw a faint light and cried out, "Help! For God's sake, help!"

"Is that you, Clary?" It was Purcell's voice, not far away. "Where are you?"

"In here, walled up like a mummy! For God's sake, get me out!" Frantically he tore at the spot where the light had come. Outside he could hear Purcell digging too. A hole formed and in a lightning flash he saw a hand extended. He grabbed it and Purcell jerked him from his snowy cave. His shoes and socks fell out with him. Discovering they were both barefoot, he slipped on the shoes, handed Purcell the socks.

The two of them then hurried off to answer a nearby call for help and found Brakeman Duncan trying to burrow his way out through splintered timbers and packed snow, They had just helped him out when through another splintered opening Alfred Hensel emerged; he was gripping his shoulder and seemed to be hurt.

Close by, a steam locomotive had been overturned and cries came from beneath it. They rushed toward the spot but as they approached, Purcell let out a yell and started to fall, but Clary grabbed him and pulled him back. Steam from the engine had escaped and created a cauldron under the snow, into which the conductor had partly fallen and burned his leg. He was able to go on, however, and skirting the danger spot, they found two men pinned down. Charlie Smart was halfway out of the snow and they were able to free him by digging with their hands. But Brakeman J. L. Kerlee, known as Curley, was trapped between engine and snow, and it would take greater efforts than theirs to release him. Brakeman Duncan hurried to fetch the men who had by now arrived from the hotel and bunkhouse bringing lanterns and tools of rescue.

While some of the men started to dig around Curley, others went roving the snow searching for other victims. W. R. Bailets found little Raymond Starrett lying unconscious in the snow, his forehead laid open by a great gash. The hotel man tenderly carried him up to Wellington.

31

Ida Starrett, Raymond's mother, had occupied a lower berth across the aisle from her two older children. When the disaster struck she was sleeping fitfully with her baby in her arms. Although she lay down haunted by Lemman's talk about "the quivering snowcap, ready to descend," the sound which roused her seemed too stupendous even for the talked-of avalanche. "The whole mountain has slipped!" was her terrorized thought as the train was struck with awful violence.

The sleeper soared upward. It struck another object. It seemed to veer and whirl. Then its motion stabilized, and it began to fall down . . . down . . .

Ida Starrett landed with a jolt that knocked her momentarily senseless. When she recovered she was lying face downward in the snow, her hand under her head and her face in the crook of her elbow. A heavy object of some kind pressed into her back. Beneath her body the baby lay against her abdomen. By holding her own breath she determined it still breathed. But when she tried to gather it closer she found she could not move, except to wiggle the fingers of one hand.

The nightmare of pain began. On her back the weight of the thing which held her down kept increasing steadily, and she knew she was being slowly crushed. For an hour or two she could still feel the baby's warmth and its rhythm of respiration; then, as in a kind of living death, she felt it shudder slightly, give a gasp—and she knew it breathed no more.

After that she was sometimes conscious, worrying about her other children, often unconscious, yet aware always of the back-breaking weight as it settled heavier— at last not caring whether she lived or died, hardly knowing which she did except for a dim perception that proved she still breathed and suffered.

She had no sense of time now, knew only that eternities of agony had passed. Then, with dazed disbelief, she heard voices and the chink of shovels somewhere above her head. She could not move. She was all but flattened by the weight upon her. She had nothing of strength left. Yet those sounds from the world of life stirred her. They revived in her some almost snuffed-out will to live, some basic urge to be saved. Summoning all the courage and breath in her she called a weak and feeble "Help!"

On the surface of the snow in that ravine of death and near death the bitter dawn had long since come and gone. Many morning hours had passed. All around, men worked desperately, plied frantic shovels, axes and crowbars. For only four people—White, Harrington, Purcell, and the Starrett boy—had been flung clear of wreckage and snow. Only a half-dozen others—Lu Anderson, Ross, Duncan, Hensel, Clary and Smart—had dug their way out quickly or been freed almost immediately by others, and of these Ross had died of injuries and exposure. All the others on the two trains and the private car—seventy-five people, perhaps a hundred, no one knew for sure— were pinned in the wreckage or buried in snow. Many were dead, no doubt, but any who were alive must be got out at once.

Overhead the precipitous slopes of Windy Mountain towered upwards in the continuing rain. The threat of further avalanche hung like a poised and unpredictable weight—yet the men of Wellington labored on, cold, wet, hungry and half-dressed. They found and released Mrs. May, held down and injured by some sleeping car timbers. They disinterred R. M. LaVille from a snow pit, and helped Ray Forsyth to make his way to daylight. They discovered baby Varden Gray unconscious beneath the snow surface, and deeper down, the two Grays, alive and conscious, but held down by a log.

They got Brakeman Kerlee out alive, after six hours' digging. They heard the cries of Fireman Samuel Bates, who for long hours had been trying to claw his way out from under his engine, and they dug him out too. They rescued Porter Adolph Smith, pinned down but protected by some sleeping car berth screens. They found bodies, too, those of Bethel, Sam Cohn, Mr. and Mrs. Lemman, and of several firemen and brakemen.

Seven hours after the accident, a shovel crew, answering faint tapping noises, uncovered the end of the popped-open mail car. From a corner which had somehow not been crushed by the tons of snow which had poured down on it, they carried out Conductor M. O. White, Fireman George (Bat) Nelson, Brakeman Ross Phillips, and Engineer Irving Tegtmeier; all were injured but none seriously.

After that they took out only bodies—those of Barnhard, Judge McNeny, Chisholm, Chantrell, and yes, of Nellie Sharp. The straw she had drawn from her friend in Spokane had proved the fatal one; her adventures in the Wild West were over; she would never write the planned article or the laughingly proposed book; her irrepressible spirit had met the final repressant, and her once vibrant hair now spread limply and damply over the snow . . .

The rescuers believed that no one else lived among the wreckage until a few men, working in one spot, picked up a faint sound, hardly louder than the mewing of a far-off cat. They answered it and it came again. Someone must still be alive down under the snow! They followed the sound as best they could, and arriving where it seemed loudest started to dig. They struck a big tree trunk, two feet in diameter, and shaking their heads uncomprehendingly were about to give up. Once again they heard it, this time an unmistakable faint "Help" from beneath the tree bole. "Someone *is* alive down there!" cried Charlie Andrews and summoned men with larger tools.

They sawed the tree trunk away and uncovered Mrs. Starrett and her baby. The child had been dead for hours, and the mother herself lost consciousness as they worked to clear the snow from around her. After an eleven-hour ordeal in her icy tomb, she was carried up to the bunkhouse more dead than alive.

32

Not long after that, the digging took a particularly gruesome turn. A crew with shovels came upon a log which held down a half-dozen crushed and mangled bodies. Retrieving these grisly remains was such nauseating work that more than one man walked away and was sick in the snow. One fellow came over to Engineer Sweeney working nearby and asked, "Do you have any authority around here? Could you for God's sake get us some whiskey?"

Sweeney was no drinking man but if there was ever justification for alcohol, this was it. "I don't have any particular authority," he answered, "but I'll get you some whiskey." He started up the path to Bailets Tavern.

The hotel man was down among the diggers, and it was Mrs. Bailets who came to the bar. Her face was white and stricken. "I need some whiskey for those fellows down there," he told her.

Without a word she reached for it. He took two quarts. "Just charge it to the G. N. Want me to sign for it?"

She shook her head. "If you need more—come and get it—anything in the hotel."

He never knew whether the G. N. paid the bill or if the Bailets stood the cost, but he did know that those white and shakey men were deeply appreciative as he passed those quarts around.

Jack Scott, an electric motorman, came up. "My shack was knocked clean to hell, with my partner, Ed Campbell, in it. Don Gilman and Andy Stohmier are gone, too, in their shack. Give me a drink—I think I need it. It's funny, but I'd be down under there myself if I hadn't got sore at Ed last night."

He told how he and his brother Neil Scott, together with Joe Beuzer of the section crew and some others had been drinking at Bailets the night before. They had all planned to go down and play poker on the mail train. Instead they had a few too many, and some of the most hilarious ones fell to teasing an old track-walker from Windy Point. He, Scott, had objected to this, and when Campbell set fire to the old fellow's coat tails, he got really sore.

"You and me are through, Ed," he had said. "I wouldn't live one more day with a bastard like you." And he refused to go home with Campbell to the shack. Instead he had turned in with John Finn up at the hotel.

Now he shook his head wonderingly. "That's all that saved me. I sure do wish I could find Ed alive, though. Gilman and Andy, too, if I could only figure where those cabins got knocked to."

"What about the roof down below?" asked Sweeney.

"Not another splinter of the cabin anywhere around. I've looked. If I knew they were flattened out, dead, it wouldn't be so bad. What gets me is that they might be alive somewhere."

He took a second draw at a quart, then hurried away on his quest.

That haunting thought—that someone might be alive under the snow—kept the searchers going even after dark. The night digging proved inexpressibly weird and eerie. Twinkling lanterns gleamed over the tangled masses of snow, mere specks in the white-spread desolation, below the massive, shadowy peaks which held the possibility of new slides. The work was uncanny, unreal. Men moved mutely and mechanically, trying not to disturb with voice or sudden movement the silence and awe of the majestic mausoleum.

33

The motormen's bunkhouse, which had been pressed

into service as an emergency hospital, was a squarish building, its interior divided by one rough partition. As victims had been brought up from the ravine, women and children had been placed in one room, men in the other. When bunks had overflowed, the injured were given beds of blankets on the floor.

Throughout the afternoon Nurse Godby and his help-ers gave what first aid they could, but doctors were badly needed, and it was with great relief that they saw the contingent of medical men come tramping into the strick-en village that evening.

They took over—Dr. W. C. Cox. a G. N. physician, Dr. H. P. Howard, Dr. James Chisholm, all of Everett; Dr. J. A. Gherkin and Dr. A. W. Stockwell, of Monroe; and Dr. Gleason, of Skykomish.

Anna Gray lay moaning, her nose bashed back into her face, a gash across her cheek, one side of her body badly bruised. Her baby had a sharp cut clear across the top of his skull and down to his ears; he was partially para-lyzed and on the verge of pneumonia.

John Gray, oddly enough, had only a leg fracture—the same one he went into the slide with. After it was reset he was in pretty good shape, except for a few bruises.

Mrs. May had incurred some broken ribs. The doctors taped them and patched up her cuts and scratches. She had been conscious when brought up the hill and had whispered to Mrs. Flannery, "My husband?" but that lady could only shake her head. Later Mr. May's body was found.

In giving first aid that day, one of the amateur nurses had pared away some of the flesh and skin that hung from the great gash on Raymond Starrett's forehead. Now as the doctors tried to sew it up properly, they had to pull the scanty remains together as best they could. They shook their heads dourly over the results.

Alfred Hensel, the doctors found, had sustained a brok-en collarbone, as well as cuts and bruises; Henry White cracked ribs and contusions; Bill Harrington, severe bruises and shock; Irving Tegtmeier, a sprained hip and internal injuries; Ross Phillips, a crushed foot and scalded leg; Adolph Smith, cut tendons in one hand, a badly bumped head; Lu Anderson, a lacerated head. A number of other trainmen had received bruises and minor cuts.

Some of these injuries were painful but none was critical. Only Ida Starrett lay like death. She had been so near to freezing that she was still more icicle than human being. All afternoon they rubbed her, piled hot bricks around her, and swathed her in wool blankets—all without much effect. Now the doctors injected stimulants,and worked to patch up her back and legs where flesh had been mutilated and pressed to a lifeless jelly.

By morning—the morning of March 2—all patients had been treated and were resting comfortably. The Gray baby's lungs were clearing and his paralysis leaving. Even Mrs. Starrett seemed to be sleeping more normally.

No new victims were brought from the ravine, and when the professional nurses, Annabelle Lee and Lenora Todhunter arrived, there was more nursing and medical staff on hand than needed. Five of the doctors departed, leaving big, cheerful, young Dr. Stockwell in charge. "Yep, everybody will recover," he said. "All doing fine. A great lot of patients and corking good nurses."

On reaching Wellington, Carrie Phillips found her husband, Ross, in the emergency hospital with bandaged feet and legs. Sam Turpel and Pete Pearson, coming from Canada in search of the Mays and Starretts, were not so fortunate, for they found in the hospital only three of the six they sought; in the morgue they claimed the bodies of Mr. May, Lillian Starrett and the Starrett baby.

Downey identified the body of Bethel, and a member of his firm the body of Eltinge. Mr. Latsch broke down when he learned that Libby was still missing and presumed dead. A minister friend claimed the body of the Reverend Thomson, who on that past snowy Sunday had preached his last earthly sermon. Mrs. Covington's two sons reached the scene before their mother's body was found. They returned to Scenic near collapse. Edward Boles and others who arrived with a like mission joined

the diggers and eventually helped to locate the bodies
of the brothers they sought.

34

Enough snow had fallen in the Cascades to last a few
lifetimes. Or so it seemed to everyone at Wellington.
Yet the day following the accident the rain changed to
snow. Again it snowed intently, maddeningly, frighten-
ingly, day after day. The storm made life harrowing for
the "grub runners"—the packers who toiled up the hill
from Scenic with food and supplies. One man slipped over
an icy cliff, fell 800 feet and was nearly killed. The storm
made increased difficulties for the diggers in the ravine,
and some said that not all bodies would be recovered
until the spring run-off.

O'Neill arrived on March 2, bringing more rescue
workers. At that time 27 bodies lay in the morgue. Yet
only shattered pieces of the sleeper Winnipeg had as yet
been found. Only Porter Anderson had come out of it
alive, the passengers sleeping aboard it were all still missing. No trace had been discovered of O'Neill's private car
with its three occupants, nor of the workers' cabins with
their three dwellers. Of the 11 postal employees on both
trains, only Alfred Hensel had been accounted for; the
rest were presumed dead. None of the laborers sleeping
in the rear-end mail car—no one knew how many—had
been located. Also missing were Conductor Pettit, Engineer Martin, Fireman McDonald, and a score or more
other G. N. employees, most of them sleeping on the
mail train. Some fifty people were still listed as missing,
and there might be more.

With set face the superintendent descended into the
ravine to inspect the wreckage. There wasn't much to be
seen: a car truck here, a portion of an engine there, the
blades of the rotary, some splintered panels that had once
been a part of the Winnipeg.

O'Neill took over direction of the 150 diggers. As they
plied their shovels, they found the whole slide one big
hasty pudding. Suitcases had been ripped apart, contents

sprinkled along for yards and mixed with every con-
ceivable item from the trains. One small square revealed a
part of a car lamp, a sack of mail, a whisk broom, a hunk
of coal, a woman's shoe, a drummer's sample shirt, a railroad report, and a crushed baby carriage.

Another square of debris also yielded a gruesome object—a detached hand. It proved to be that once capable,
once comforting hand of pretty nurse Catherine O'Reilly,
as identified by her rings. Her body, found not far away,
was badly mangled.

And so in the improvised morgue the windrows of
draped parcels lengthened. When it was discovered that
one worker had lifted the gold watch off Sam Cohn's body
and others were stealing clothes from smashed
trunks, the thief was arrested and the looters run out of
Wellington at gun point,

Workers became numb with horror. They learned to
follow up blood trails in the snow, for at the source they
were sure to locate bodies. Yet even the most stoical were
sickened when a band of diggers came upon the rods of
the Winnipeg bent like so many pipe cleaners and holding in their twisted embrace a half-dozen victims who
were literally lashed to a big stump. Among the dead
was George Davis, with little Thelma in his arms.

<h2 style="text-align:center">35</h2>

For a week the disaster was the big news in the Pacific
Northwest. In Seattle, the *Times,* the *Post-Intelligencer*
and the *Star* were filled with zero-hour accounts, human
interest stories, interviews with survivors, and daily bul-
letins about the progress of rescue operations. Photo-
graphs of Wellington, the wreckage in the ravine, the
sledding of bodies, were blown up to half-page size.
Long, chilling lists of dead, injured and missing, both of
passengers and trainmen, were revised daily and carried
in black-bordered columns.

A false story reported the occupants of O'Neill's private car dead before the car was located. A number of
trainmen, first reported as injured, were later found to

be among the dead. Names included as those of passengers missing turned out to be names of laborers, some of whom were not even missing. But for the most part the lists were accurate and carried the final, grim truth to readers, and it was here that many people first learned the fate of family members, relatives or friends.

Newspapers vied with each other for coverage. On March 3, the Seattle *Times*, in a boxed item under the heading TIMES FIRST ON SPOT, reported, "J. J. Underwood, the *Times* Staff Correspondent sent to Wellington after the first report of the fatal snowslide, is the only newspaper man at the scene of the terrible accident. He wired, 'I am the only newspaper man here. The others quit at Scenic.' Enough said."

Too much said, according to the rival Seattle *Post-Intelligencer*. The following day it published a claim that its staff photographer, F. A. Jacobs, together with J. A. Juleen, an Everett photographer, hired by the *P.I.*, was first at the scene.

Which claim was true is not known, but one thing is sure: The subsequent reporting of the *P-I*. was at times far from reliable. According to a *P.-I* account, Charlie Andrews, the eye-witness, was fast asleep on the passenger train and was awakened by a mysterious dream voice warning him to flee for his life, which he did just in time to save himself and to turn and see the trains tumble into the canyon. Andrews himself protested this distortion of truth, but no correction appeared in the *P.-I*. columns.

The *P.-I*. also reported what it called "a most miraculous occurrence." A child about a year and a half old, it said, had been found "on top of the snow unharmed and unconcerned, babbling and playfully tossing the snow about." The mother had been swept into the ravine and horribly mutilated, while the father was so badly wounded on the head "he rose an insane man and dropped dead soon afterwards." The child, cooing contentedly and in innocence of its orphaned state, had become the pet of the hospital.

Yet the only child this age rescued was Varden Gray,

and he was both unconscious and injured, and he did not lose his parents. Still, the story was in all probability inspired by the Gray child. In that camp of death, his golden curls, his chubby face all full of smiles as he recovered, epitomized life. He was given the nickname "Duke," and was certainly the pet of the place.

On March 4 the *P.-I.* bannered a headline: TEN PERSONS TAKEN ALIVE FROM EXCAVATED CAR. This was cruelly misleading, for the last person rescued alive from the wreckage was Mrs. Starrett three days earlier. And all those who had had loved ones killed on the mountain must have shuddered to read in the same edition that at Wellington in the fatal ravine, "the wailing of the mountain lions and the doleful barking of wolves add to the weight of gloom."

These two things were so far from the truth that the Seattle *Times* felt called on to take the *P.-I.* to task for sensationalism. In its next edition, below a headline, ACCURATE NEWS OF WELLINGTON DISASTER FOUND ONLY IN TIMES, it said:

"A high official of the Great Northern today made the following statement to the *Times* for publication: 'The *Times* is the only newspaper which has published accurate, conservative and truthful accounts of the Wellington disaster and the events following it. Certain sensational stories in other newspapers should be promptly denied. There have been no living persons rescued from the wreckage. There has been no howling of wolves—no gathering of cougars. Such stories are both willfully and unnecessarily false.' "

Yet the *Times* made its own misstep. While on the whole its reports were well-tempered and reliable, in one notable instance it failed in conservatism. On March 3, after tallying its reports of dead and missing, naturally and correctly presuming the missing now to be dead, and adding 30 laborers thought to have been sleeping on the mail train, it rocked its readers with a great ebony headline four inches tall:

118 VICTIMS

That figure the *Times* regarded as conclusive and did not budge from it until on March 10 when the Great Northern in an official report estimated only 95 dead (which, in the final count, was within one number of being correct).

To this day the erroneous figure of 118 dead often crops up in stories of the Wellington wreck, obviously traceable to the *Times'* aggressive use of it.

36

At Wellington the work of recovering bodies went on. As facts were pieced together it was discovered that, with two or three exceptions, all who had come alive from the passenger train had been sleeping aboard the Similkameen, which had broken open in its fall and strewn its occupants into the snow. Now as day coaches and passenger mail car were dug out, the bodies of Conductor Pettit and other trainmen were found, as well as those of No. 25's three postal employees, Ahern, Towslee and Begle. Among passengers dead in the day coaches were Sam Lee and the three Irish boys.

Not till the last smashed splinters and twisted irons of the sleeper Winnipeg had been unearthed were all passengers accounted for.

On the day before her golden wedding anniversary the remains of Mrs. Covington were recovered. In her ripped bag were her notes, now water-stained and crumpled, in which she had written, "I trust in God to save us."

In Seattle Mrs. Latsch's letter to her business manager had come through—a voice from the dead. For diggers found Libby's body at last; she would never return to her hairpin business, to her beloved husband or to little Kean.

The bodies of all five members of the Beck family were discovered. Beck was badly mutilated but his wife and children seemingly had been encased in smothering snow while still asleep.

Vail's body was found; he would suffer no more from his carbuncles. Topping was dead, his little boy in Ohio left an orphan. And Mahler would never return home to the wife and boy he had loved so much.

On March 4 O'Neill's private car was at last located. It had not been swept so far from the tracks as searchers had thought, but lay rather high on the side of the ravine. Its top had been lifted off and its interior jammed with snow. Young Longcoy would never meet his sister and mother, Trainmaster Blackburn never again see his newborn child, and Lewis Walker never arrive comfortingly home to his wife and ancient grandmother—for all three men had died in their sleep.

The wrecked cabins were uncovered the same day, not far from their foundations; for, like the private car, they had not been moved as far as searchers had believed. And the uneasiness Jack Scott had felt that first day that one of his friends might be alive under the snow proved not without foundation. For, according to Dr. Stockwell, Donald Cameron Gilman and Ed Campbell had died instantly, but Andy Stohmier had lived a long time under the snow and could have been saved if rescuers had reached him in time.

Now only the men from No. 27 were missing. The mail train had stood on the outer bank, and its cars had been tossed to the bottom of the heap, with coaches, engines, rotary, and electric motors all slamming down on top, the whole pile being further crushed by countless tons of snow and trees. The only survivors had come from that one car which miraculously had bounced aside and popped open.

Extra workmen were added to saw and hack a way down through the debris. On March 6 and 7 the flattened mail cars were reached, and from then on for several days, diggers searched among the wreckage, revealing "the last secrets of the death chamber." One by one the bodies of still-missing firemen and brakemen, of the seven postal employees, and of a dozen laborers, came forth. The body of Engineer Frank Martin was one of the last to be recovered.

Thus the morgue remained full, even though bodies were being hauled out to Scenic as rapidly as conditions would permit. Fifteen Yukon sleds had been hoisted up the Scenic incline and dragged into Wellington on March 3 for the purpose. On the trip out, each laden sled was accompanied by six men, and all six were needed to pull their burden along the hard trail and to lower it down a life-line which had been rigged at the point of the big drop-off. "Dead Man's Slide," they called the arrangement.

Relief trains were running as far as Scenic, and there the bodies were trundled on board. On March 7, thirty victims went out in the first big shipment. Eight of the dead were Everett men, and at the Everett depot families and relatives gathered to claim the last remains of their loved ones.

Earlier, at Wellington hard feelings had developed between undertakers from Everett and from Seattle. Wellington was nearer Everett than Seattle on the G. N. line, and the majority of the trainmen killed lived at division headquarters, Everett, in Snohomish County. Yet the accident had happened within the boundaries of King County. The King County coroner, J. C. Snyder, had hurried to the scene, bringing with him a number of undertakers from Butterworth & Sons of Seattle. As King County morticians, Butterworth & Sons believed it was their prerogative to prepare *all* bodies for burial. They at once relegated to the background the undertakers from Jerread's of Everett, who had arrived first at the scene. Embalming materials that Jerread's men had struggled to carry up the hill to Wellington went unused.

But the farthest thing from the minds of bereaved families was county lines or division of authority. Women sobbed and men stood with bare, bowed heads as the train pulled in. They waited patiently but saw no bodies forthcoming, and presently all understood something was wrong. Muttered word passed through the crowd that the

King County deputy coroner on board refused to release the bodies of the Everett men, insisting all bodies must go on to Seattle, where families could then claim them at Butterworth & Sons.

Anger and hysteria swept the gathering. Loudly weeping women besieged the conductor, while men made quick threats and some pulled off their coats to fight. But before riot could ensue, a clerk from O'Neill's office, himself an Everett man, settled the argument. Seizing the deputy coroner by the collar he hissed, "You release those bodies or I'll pitch you off this train!"

The officiousness of the coroner wilted, and he gave his reluctant consent to have the bodies unloaded.

"Greed," editorialized the Everett *Morning Tribune* next day, "is a stronger trait than reverence in the make-up of some of these dealers of the dead."

37

All this time, the transcontinental line of the Great Northern remained snowbound in the Cascade Division —"the most calamitous and greatest blockage of a railway system in all American railroad history," in the words of a G. N. official.

E. L. Brown, General Superintendent of the Great Northern, and J. M. Gruber, General Manager of the Western Division, arrived to assist in the emergency, and together with O'Neill surveyed the seriousness of the situation.

For 25 to 30 miles through Stevens Pass the tracks were covered by one almost continuous slide of great depths. At the worst place, near Berne, the pile was from 80 to 100 feet deep. Many of these slide areas were mixed with rock and crisscrossed with tree trunks.

Dowling had returned to his rotary at Scenic and was working night and day up the hill toward Wellington. The rotary from the Rockies had arrived and had tackled the job west from Merritt. At Gaynor when it reached Harrington's abandoned rotary the crew carried sacked coal over the snow and got X801 going again.

But rotaries were helpless in slides mixed with big rocks and logs. Gruber, Brown and O'Neill, putting their heads together, decided to try something revolutionary: to clear those mountains of snow off the tracks by the use of blasting powder.

A thousand kegs of black powder exploded, five hundred laborers digging constantly, the three rotaries turning—and still it was March 9 before the first train appeared in Wellington. It came not from Scenic but through the tunnel from the east. Irving Tegtmeier, ears trained by five years of locomotive driving, was first to hear it, and he managed to hobble to a window to see the monster machine coming down the track, devouring drifts as it came. '"Lord, look at that big chap eat up the snow! We'll be out of here in no time!" And sure enough, the next day, Gruber, who had come in on the rotary train, arranged for a special car to take the survivors away.

Over the preceding days a number of Stockwell's patients had become well enough to be discharged. Bates, LaVille, Forsyth, Clary had mainly been shaken up, and the burns on Purcell's leg had turned out to be minor. By March 6, Henry White, Bill Harrington, Conductor M. O. White, Brakeman Kerlee, Fireman George Nelson, and Porters Anderson and Smith were all well enough to walk out to Scenic as a group.

Only nine people still remained in the hospital. Of these, only Mrs. May and Mrs. Gray were able to walk to the train. Five others, Hensel, Tegtmeier, John Gray, Ross Phillips and Mrs. Starrett, were lifted on board by strong men. Husky Dr. Stockwell toted Varden Gray to his mother, then returned to take Raymond Starrett pickaback. Long years later Raymond remembered that ride through the tall drifts on the back of the doctor he had come to love.

The way to Scenic still being blocked, the train retreated through the tunnel. The white crystals still sifted down as the survivors gained their last glimpse of snow-beleagered Wellington. Then they traveled back toward Spokane, this pitiful remnant of the company which, two weeks earlier, had ridden west over these very tracks—to doom.

The rotaries and the men with blasting powder worked on, and on March 12 opened the way between Scenic and Wellington—briefly. For on the morning of the 13th, as the Oriental Limited sought to cross the pass westbound, a big slide came down not far ahead of it at Alvin, knocking a rotary train into the canyon below and killing one workman. Passengers walked to Scenic.

But in a couple of days the way was again cleared, this time for good. Operations got under way to salvage the $1,000,000 worth of railroad equipment at the bottom of the canyon. Workers built a spur track down to the wreckage, and cranes were brought in to hoist engines and electric motors.

The first through train took away all bodies that remained at Wellington. It took, too, all the mail salvaged from the wreck: nine pouches and four sacks of registered mail, and 25 pouches of ordinary letters. Most of the registered mail was in good condition with addresses intact. Ordinary mail pouches had not fared so well; some had been ripped open, and all were soaked. For days the Wellington depot had been strewn with soggy letters in the process of being dried out in the hope that addresses would prove decipherable. Newspapers and periodicals were ruined by wetting or had their labels soaked off. In the end, even though 10 of the 11 original couriers were dead, most of the mail went through, in accordance with the best tradition of the post office, "Neither rain, nor snow . . ."

In Seattle, at Butterworth & Sons the work of identifying and shipping bodies went on. The bodies of the Beck family went to their old home town in California. Mrs. Beck had been right: once they reached it they would never leave.

As it proved, John Brockman left a considerable estate, and several people turned up from Wenatchee and Waterville willing and eager to claim his body. One man identified the wrong body, and not until Brockman's brother arrived was the matter straightened out satisfactorily.

David Clark, himself a native of Ireland and a boyhood friend of the three Irish lads, identified them as George Heron, John Mackie and James Monroe. The three were buried far from their native land.

A brother and sister took the remains of Charles Dennison, a brakeman, back to Minnesota to his aged parents. The remains of Archie Dupy, also a brakeman, were sent to his family at Waynoka, Oklahoma. The body of Harry Partridge, a fireman, was shipped to his mother in Biloxi, Mississippi. Families far and near claimed the bodies of other trainmen.

Three of the laborers, Mike Guglielmo, Inigi Giammarusti and Giovanni Tosti, firm friends and working companions ever since leaving their native Italy, had met their end together. Their bodies were claimed by a brother of one of the men. But bodies of several other foreign laborers and two engine watchers remained unclaimed. They, together with six laborers never identified, were given burial in a common plot at Mount Pleasant Cemetery in Seattle.

One of the unidentified bodies had for a time worn the name tag of Joseph Benier, a timber cruiser—until he had walked in to stop his own funeral. The confusion had arisen because he had planned to take Local No. 25 out of the woods the night of February 22, but had somehow managed to miss the train and so save his life.

"My friends say you have me downstairs dead," he stormed to a Butterworth attendant. "I want you to know I'm the livest man in town!"

38

Not all these corpses had found a grave yet when on March 16, 1910, a coroner's jury convened in Seattle to fix the responsibility for the death of "John Brockman and 87 or more others."

The Pacific Northwest still reeled from this, the most disastrous avalanche and the second worst railroad accident the country had known up to that time. Even today, nearly fifty years later, there have been but two worse railroad wrecks in the entire United States, and no avalanche of near proportions as far as death toll is concerned.

The coroner's jury listened to 28 witnesses, made a trip to Wellington to the scene of the accident, then rendered its judgment four days after it convened.

The avalanche itself was beyond human control, according to the verdict, but the Great Northern was not blameless: It should have placed the trains on the stub tracks east of the depot; it should have had more coal at Wellington; it should have paid higher wages to retain its laborers.

For four years this charge of contributory negligence hung over the railroad company. Right after the accident the G. N. announced it would settle personal injury or death cliams on a fair basis, but over what constituted fairness there was soon difference of opinion and before long the railroad found itself confronted by a lawsuit which was considered a test case in the matter. It was brought on behalf of Edward Topping's small son, William, the complaint alleging general negligence.When the case same to trial, one of the chief arguments of plaintiff's attorneys, Fred M. Williams and L. F. Chester, was that the trains should have been placed on the stub tracks. To refute this, the G. N. attorneys, F. V. Brown and F. G. Dorety, called to the stand a dozen railroad men—O'Neill, Harrington, Tegtmeier, Dowling, Sweeney, Vogel, M. O. White, Purcell, Clary and others. All described their harrowing and harried work in the face of the invincible storm. All told why in their best judgment they had considered the sidetracks on the ledge safer than the spur tracks, and why in that hellish envelopment of snow it would have been impossible to move the trains to the stub tracks even if they had believed it wise.

The jury awarded little William Topping $20,000 damages. The Great Northern Railway then carried the case to the Supreme Court of the State of Washington.

In 1914 the Supreme Court reversed the decision of the lower court and ordered the cause dismissed.

In their written opinion the Supreme Court judges admitted that the avalanche was the primary cause of the accident but maintained that did not raise the presumption of negligence.

"At the time the train was placed on the passing track, where it was when it was finally destroyed, it was placed there by reason of the fact that this was considered the most convenient place for the passengers . . . and because this was apparently a safe place. No one at the time anticipated, nor at any other time could anticipate that a snowslide was about to occur at that place . . . These things are clearly beyond the knowledge of men," and it was plain, they said, "that this avalanche was what is known in law as an act of God."

(*Act of God?* No, surely this foul deed was cunningly planned and consciencelessly executed by that evil genie who had laid the snare, played with the caught prey for days, and then tiring of the game, tripped the taut, snowy cord and pulled the whole hillside down.)

The railroad was not only legally exonerated but its moral case was cogently stated and embodied in permanent form. A certified copy of the trial testimony, together with briefs and opinions, is preserved in the office of the Clerk of the Supreme Court of the State of Washington. No one could read those hundreds of pages of testimony without feeling sympathy and admiration for the snowfighters who struggled so valiantly day after day and night after stormy night only to see their best efforts engulfed in tragedy; without feeling an even greater pity—an almost unbearable empathy—for the marooned passengers waiting there day after day under the snowfield which was eventually to kill them. One is forced to admit that O'Neill and his aides made the wisest decisions possible in the face of an impossible situation, and that the labors of all these men verged on the superhuman. Puny man strove desperately against belligerent nature, with nature not

only holding the superior hand but also the trump card—
which in its own good time it brought slamming down.

Yet no railroad can feel that a major wreck is anything
but a blot on its record, and the Great Northern con-
tinues very sensitive on the subject. Not long after the accident it wiped out the very name of Wellington, changed
the little station and yard to Tye, and Tye it remained as
long as trains continued to operate on the fatal hillside.

During the spring run-off, melting snows revealed one
more body, that of Fireman Archibald McDonald. The
final death toll could then be tallied. The figure stood at
96.

At Eden, Colorado, in 1904 a rail accident had also
claimed 96 lives. In 1919 a wreck at Nashville, Tennessee,
killed 101 people, and in the same year 97 people lost
their lives in a disaster in New York on the Brooklyn
Rapid Transit line. The Wellington avalanche thus ties
for third place in any list of national rail disasters. Not
only that, but the three-week tie-up of its main Pacific
Coast artery cost the Great Northern Railway millions of
dollars.

James J. Hill immediately announced that measures
would be taken to prevent such a terrible and incapacitat-
ing thing from ever happening again. Before the next
winter the railroad spent a million and a half dollars
building more than a mile of additional snowsheds at 26
points through the pass area. At Wellington, the whole
ledge from which the trains had been swept down was
given fortress protection: a massive, double-tracked snowshed of reinforced concrete, 3900 feet long. And in the
following years Windy Point was tunneled through, and
snowsheds added until 60 per cent of the way between
Wellington and Scenic was covered.

Even so, Stevens Pass remained so unsatisfactory that in
the end the Great Northern was forced underground.
It spent $25,000,000 to bore an eight-mile tunnel 500
feet lower in the mountains and to relocate some 40 miles
of track.

The new route went into operation in 1929. Overhead

what had been Wellington—now Tye—fell into decay except for that colossal, indestructible concrete snowshed. Mossy and mildewed, impressive as some old Roman ruin, it stands to this day, plainly visible on the west side of Stevens Pass along U.S. Highway No. 2—the only monument to the Wellington dead.

THE END

FIRE BLITZ IN THE
BITTER ROOTS

1

THE manner in which the high-piling snow, cause of the Wellington disaster, arrived in the Pacific Northwest with total disregard for precedent or season, seemed to augur a wet summer ahead. Or a damp one, at least, with nature able to retain some of the extra supply of spring moisture. A mid-March check showed the snow-pack to be above normal in the mountains.

But weather patterns in that year 1910 had been knocked very much awry. In manufacturing that thick, post-seasonal onslaught of snow, the skies had apparently used up their last drop of available moisture. The storms stopped in late March, but the April rains failed to arrive. The hills barely got green that spring.

May and June broke existing heat records. Still no drop of rain fell. Farm lands all over the region burned up and farm workers were laid off because of crop failure. Searing winds blew out of the Columbia River Basin, scorching hills and mountains. Toward the end of June fires broke out in all the forests of the West, with those in Washington, north Idaho and western Montana being hardest hit of all. In July the heat wave intensified and lightning storms, sweeping the peaks, started batches of new fires.

The Far West was in the throes of the most drought-plagued summer it had ever known—a summer without rain, without mist or dew, when the greenery curled up, the moss dried out, and forest land across whole states became as though piled for a bonfire—complete with tinder and shavings.

The stage was set for holocaust.

2

With only a supervisor and a handful of rangers and

guards in each of the National Forests, how could you maintain adequate fire patrol and protection in a summer like this? You couldn't, of course. All you could do was act like a man whose house is on fire: not take time to wring your hands—just jump in and save what you could.

So thought William B. Greeley as he sat in his office in the U. S. Forest Service district headquarters in Missoula, Montana, one day early in August, 1910. Behind him on the wall hung a map of District One, the region of which as District Supervisor he was in charge—a region stretching all the way from the western corner of South Dakota across the great state of Montana, on across the Idaho panhandle and into the northeastern corner of Washington State.

Within that vast territory, the timberlands under his control were so immense as to seem staggering in the present emergency.

Forty million acres—64,000 *square miles*—an area the size of New York State with a few of the New England states thrown in for good measure — a territory so far-flung as to be organized into *twenty-two* separate forests.

In those forests one regularly employed man guarded, on the average, 250,000 to 400,000 acres. In an acreage of that size, one man was lost as a pea in a 40-acre plot. Such a meager permanent work force would be downright laughable if it weren't so alarmingly deficient.

Already in District One this summer they had dealt with 2500 small fires and at least 50 large ones. Already he had hired 300 temporary fire fighters, cleaning out the employment offices in Spokane, Butte, Missoula and Helena, and he had ordered camps and mines shut down so loggers and miners could join others on the fire lines.

In the past hectic weeks Greeley had found little time for office routine. He had traveled to the scene of the worst fires, superintending the movement of men and equipment to critical spots. Today he was just back from such a trip and was ready to leave again at a moment's notice, as attested by his heavy logging boots, "tin pants"

Smoke cloud from the great fire in the Bitter Root Range spread one-third of the way around the world. Map shows most heavily darkened areas.

The Great Fire wiped out all of the east end of Wallace, Idaho.

Ruins of the Coeur d'Alene Hotel and Depot. In 1910, this line was still the O. R. & N.

A $100,000 loss—what the fire left of the warehouse of the Coeur d'Alene Hardware Store at Wallace.

and work shirt. On his shirt was proudly pinned his two-inch Forest Service badge.

With his assistant, F. A. Silcox, Greeley was going over wires and reports received in his absence, with special attention to the forests of the Bitter Root Range along the Montana-Idaho line.

"At least what Koch tells me is encouraging," said Greeley. He referred to Elers Koch, Supervisor of the Lolo National Forest, whose borders began just west of Missoula. Koch had rangers and crews out battling a number of bad blazes but just that morning had informed district headquarters all fires were under at least temporary control.

"What do you think are the chances of the President's authorizing the use of troops?" asked Silcox. With the whole Far West in danger of going up in smoke, Major-General Leonard Wood, the Army Chief-of-Staff, a few days previously in Washington, D. C., had recommended the use of regular army troops on the fire lines. Permission for such use must come from William Howard Taft, President of the United States.

"I can only hope it goes through," replied Greeley. "Any bad luck at all and we'll need all the men we can get—and then some."

He hoisted his long, lanky form from his desk, walked to the wall map and stood eying the area of the Bitter Root Range with a worried, abstracted look.

The Bitter Root Mountains are the major chain lying between the Rockies and the Cascades. Beginning fifty miles south of the Canadian border near Idaho's Lake Pend Oreille, they extend south and a little east for two hundred miles, taking in such local ranges as the Cabinet, the Coeur d'Alene, the St. Joe and the Clearwater.

Greeley knew the area well, could see those two hundred miles of mountain in blue-green tiers running off to the horizon in every direction—a wilderness of bigness, most of it vertically inclined, where one seldom saw a high white peak, a gentle valley, or an appealing mountain meadow. Marching forests dipped into abrupt canyons, into blind gulches, down precipitous draws; reemerged on slope after slope, climbed ridge after ridge, to form a veritable sea of forest. Those close-packed mountain backs, no more than 5000 to 7000 feet high, carried in tremendous continuity trees of western white pine, western yellow pine, tamarack, cedar, white and alpine fir, white bark pine, lodgepole pine and Englemann spruce—some of it the District's most valuable saw timber.

The map did not indicate this uninterrupted expanse but was marked instead with the lines of the double tier of national forests set aside along the opposing slopes of the range. North to south on the Idaho side of the line lay the Kaniksu, the Pend Oreille, the Coeur d'Alene, the Clearwater and the Nezperce national forests; on the Montana side, the Kootenai, the Cabinet, the Lolo and the Bitter Root national forests.

Through the whole range the timber was at a pitch of dryness, with dozens of blazes burning—creating a situation which was sheer dynamite.

Placing a finger within the borders of the Lolo, Greeley said, "Well, anyhow, Koch is in pretty good shape at the moment, and—" shifting the finger over into the Coeur d'Alenes, "Weigle seems at least to be holding his own."

He took a deep breath. "If only he and Koch can hold! A couple more weeks without a big blow-up and maybe the fall rains will begin."

He walked to the window and gazed off to the west where the nearest mountains within the Lolo forest reared their timbered forms in the smoky haze. "What we can't stand now is wind, lightning, freaky breezes, storms of any kind."

And he added, part prayer and part groan, "God spare us those!"

3

In the rough terrain of the Coeur d'Alene mountain area which was his precinct, Forest Supervisor William G. Weigle had large fires burning on Pine Creek, up Lake Gulch, and on Placer Creek in the Coeur d'Alene River drainage; and on Big Creek, Slate Creek, Trout Creek and other spots in the St. Joe drainage. On all these blazes he had placed twenty-man crews, thirty-man crews, even fifty- and seventy-five-man crews, sending them out as fast as he could hire men locally, or as fast as Greeley could round up "temporaries" from employment offices and dispatch them to him.

Ten miles south of Wallace, Idaho, which was headquarters for the Coeur d'Alene National Forest, lay the top of the St. Joe ridge, dividing the two drainage systems. Deep in the St. Joe country, Ranger R. N. Debitt of Avery and Ranger Henry Kottkey of Falcon were in charge. The area was so inaccessible and with such poor communications that Weigle often knew little of what was going on there. And what made it really tough was that no trails or roads existed to places where fires started; men had to hack their own rough trails as they went, and little fires grew to big ones before crews arrived.

Along the top of the divide, Supervisor Weigle stationed one of his best rangers, Edward C. Pulaski, whose job it was to supervise different crews along a ten-mile stretch, distribute grub and supplies, and keep main fires from spreading or uniting. He was fairly successful in this until August 10, when a wind arose to fan all blazes to renewed vigor and danger. The air over the range darkened with smoke as flames leaped skyward.

On the fire lines, Pulaski's men plied axes, mattocks, shovels and wet gunnysacks in an acrid murk. Sweat poured from their soot-smeared bodies. Their eyes were red-rimmed and swollen, their lungs seared by flames.

The practice was to clear a fire line eight feet wide by cutting off the brush and trees, shoveling away the parched moss, leaves and humus until the mineral soil was exposed. This line was sometimes cut close to the advancing fire, at other times far enough ahead so the intervening space could be backfired to stop the oncoming blaze. Such lines had to be patrolled constantly so if wind-whipped embers dropped beyond they could be put out immediately, or if new fires were set, additional fire lines could be run around them at once.

Crews managed to corral the new fires set on the 10th. But that emergency left the fire lines more extended, the patrols thinner, the whole situation more ticklish. And to keep everyone's nerves on edge, the wind continued to blow, not very strong but with maddening capriciousness.

On August 8 President Taft signed the order authorizing the use of troops for fire fighting. Supervisor Weigle immediately requisitioned four companies of Army men— two for Avery and two for Wallace. Red tape delayed their arrival and not until August 15 did the men ordered for Wallace detrain: two companies of Negro troops of the Twenty-fifth Infantry from Fort George Wright near Spokane, who, in charge of two white officers, marched down to the ball park to muster roll.

Nothing was so romantic to sixteen-year-old George Tabor and his friend Bob Moffatt as real, live, uniformed soldiers, and they hung around the ball park big-eyed with interest. When the Negro infantrymen started up Placer Canyon they tagged along. Both George and Bob were Wallace boys who had hunted, fished and hiked in these hills, and when it turned out Weigle had no one to send along, the boys proudly guided the troops to Livingston's Ranch, two-and-a-half miles up the winding canyon, where they were to camp.

Supervisor Weigle didn't care a whit about the skin coloring of the troops. What concerned him was that as woodsmen they were green as grass. Many were Southerners who had never seen real mountains or tall timber before. The experienced Forest Service men he might have assigned to direct them were in the hills. Even more serious, he was short of fire-fighting tools with which to equip them.

Under such circumstances he could hardly expect them to be of much help. He set them at the easier task he could find, that of patrolling the rear Placer Canyon fire lines a mile or two farther up the canyon from Livingston's. He expected no trouble in that quarter.

4

The people living in the little towns of the Coeur d'Alenes, not weary and absorbed like the fire fighters, had plenty of time to think about the dangers which surrounded them, and it spoke for the hardihood of the miners' and shopkeepers' families that they had not fled days ago.

A fabulous lead and silver belt, richest in the world, had been discovered in 1886 embedded in the seams of the Coeur d'Alene mountains. The mining hamlets which sprang up—Wardner, Kellogg, Osburn, Burke and Mullan, as well as Wallace, the Shoshone County seat—could find no place except at the bottoms of deep canyons. There they crowded in, with tightly forested mountainsides rising sheer about them. Often the canyons were so narrow that not all buildings could be fitted in along the canyon floor. Houses were dug back into the embankments, as at Burke, or stood along terraced streets gouged from the upright forest walls, as at Wallace.

In the summer of 1910 all these townsites were natural fire-traps, since the only exits were through other narrow, forest-lined, tinder-dry canyons which might spring into flame at any moment. As the terrible heat of August continued and surrounding fires spread, nerves grew frayed. Apprehension deepened. After August 10, the sun was shut out by a pall of smoke and everyone moved in a torpid gloom. The mines were closed down—the Bunker Hill & Sullivan at Wardner, the Hecla at Burke, the Morning at Mullan—and miners turned to as fire fighters.

In all the towns, talk was of nothing but fire, and in Wallace when the wind was right, ashes, cinders and smoldering embers from the Placer Canyon fire fell into downtown streets. Special fire brigades were formed to extinguish this incendiary material. Yet there was no general exodus from the towns. People stuck stubbornly to homes, jobs and businesses.

On August 19, Ranger Pulaski came into Wallace for

supplies, and hurried home a mile up Burke Canyon where he lived with his wife and small daughter.

Pulaski, a descendant of the Polish Count, Casimir Pulaski, hero of American revolutionary fame, was a fine looking man, above average size with an erect carriage and some of what we call polish. He was well educated, had a good vocabulary, spoke excellent English. Yet he was a practical, down-to-earth woodsman. There was nothing his men could do he couldn't do better, no job at which he scorned to work beside them. He had been sixteen years with the Forest Service and was a popular woods boss.

His wife, Emma, looking at him with the eyes of love and concern, saw his soot-grimed clothes, his taut, lined face, his bloodshot eyes; saw him sink into his favorite chair as though he could never rise again.

"I've never seen so many miles of fire!" he told her. "Never seen the timber so dry! It's nightmarish—unbelievable. Wallace will surely burn. I don't see how anything can possible save it. It's you and little Elsie I keep worrying about. I had to come home to tell you what to do. If the town starts to burn, don't try to go down that way. Go in the opposite direction, up the canyon here. I've thought it all out, and the old tailing dam on up the gulch is the safest place. If the fire comes, take Elsie and stay at the dam till the danger's over."

She had never seen him so pessimistic and it frightened her. "But what about you?" she demanded. "What's going to happen to you out there in the mountains?"

"Oh, I can always take care of myself—that is," with a shrug, "unless the whole shebang blows up and there's no place to go."

She wanted to cry out, "Oh, please don't go back!" But she was a ranger's wife and her duty was as stern as his. She kept silent.

An hour later Weigle telephoned to report a new fire had broken out in the back confines of the west fork of Placer Creek. He had already sent additional men in. Would Pulaski hurry back to take charge of them and get a crew and supplies up the ridge to the new fire as fast as possible?

Ranger Pulaski turned to his wife. "I'll have to take the stuff I came after up by buckboard as far as the pack camp at the end of the road. Can you come along, bring the rig back to town? I'll tie my saddle horse on behind."

"Of course I'll come." Wanting desperately to weep she was nonetheless glad of the chance to remain at his side as long as possible.

5

Taking little Elsie with them, they picked up the supplies in town, drove down Bank Street to where it bumped into the west hill, then turned south on King Street.

King, after two blocks as a conventional city street, became a narrow, winding road along Placer Creek, where the few straggling houses were pushed back against confining canyon walls.

Presently, leaving all habitations behind, they entered the wilder canyon, where mountain shoulders heavy with timber shut out all but a smoky strip of sky. Now and then they crossed the creek on plank bridges.

As a Forest Service ranger's wife, Emma Pulaski had lived and traveled much in the outdoors and had learned to love it. She knew the mountain scenery of this part of Idaho in its many seasons, and usually she rode along savoring the flavor and beauty of all she saw. On other trips along this way she had scarcely taken her eyes off the cottonwood trees shimmering in the sun along the creek; had watched the creek running noisily over rocks of tan, sienna and brick red, had often got out to pick wild violets among the clover and dandelions on the canyon floor, to count the butterflies, large and small, wafting their colored way along the dank stream side, or to thread her way along the low canyon walls to see the wild blue clematis and wild coral honeysuckle climbing over thorn and other bushes to get their blooms into the pure, clear sun.

But today the water was all but gone from the creek, and along its course the greenery hung sear and wilted. Before they reached the pack camp the road had become little more than a double-rutted trail, and each jolt brought her spirits to a lower ebb. At the camp Ed turned the wagon around and got out to unload.

South through the cleft of the canyon lay the St. Joe ridge, where, below a long saddleback, she saw the fire-demon with which her husband had come to grapple. In this view it looked not merely a sinister, smoke-robed figure but a monster with awful red teeth tearing at the very heart of the mountain. She closed her eyes to shut out the terrible sight.

Ed Pulaski, having bade their daughter goodbye, came to take his wife in his arms. "I may never see you again," he said.

Then he was gone and she was driving back. Her senses came acutely alive. Ed might die in that flaming inferno. So might these beautiful forests she knew so well and loved so much. Even as she had stamped forever on her consciousness Ed's beloved, broad-shouldered figure, so must she memorize for all time each bend in the deep canyon road.

Never before had she noted so clearly the tall white pines glinting silvery-green in the sun, their needles gathered into clusters at twin-end like so many stars ;the tamaracks looking so frilly and frivolous; the young cedars holding out branches as lacy and lovely as fronds of maidenhair fern; the old cedars standing as rugged individualists, ragged with strips of sagging bark; the hemlocks bristling with stubby-needled limbs, decorated by tiny cones: and the firs with their thick, intricately patterned branches so closely draped.

At the lower forest edge the trees clothed themselves to their very feet. Beween their trunks she glimpsed mysterious dark recesses — hide-aways for dainty ferns and orchid ladyslippers, pathways for furtive lynx and wily fisher.

When a big black animal came out of the thicket and

ambled across the road, it seems so natural a part of the scene that she was only slightly startled.

"Mama, what is that?" whispered little Elsie.

"Only a big, black dog, dear."

It was a bear of course. As she watched it climb a bank and disappear her compassion welled for it too, a vital living being like Ed, like the great green trees, like the tiny, endearing yellow violets called "Johnny jump-ups." All were threatened by those dreadful, red devouring teeth.

As she reached King Street her husband's words echoed in her ears: Wallace will surely burn, and she saw again how tightly the town was mountain hemmed. Through the main east-west Mullan Canyon flowed the south fork of the Coeur d'Alene River. Where Placer Creek came out of the south to join it, a roughly triangular flat was formed. On this flat Wallace lay with a half dozen interlocking mountains standing over it like green, inverted V's.

Bank, the main and longest street, had room to run only from King to First and on to Ninth—exactly ten blocks. Streets parallel to it were but two to seven blocks long. Cross streets were three or four blocks long. To create a little more room for dwellings, two or three streets had been slashed across the base of the south hill.

The river cut the flat near the north hill, leaving room beyond its banks only for the tracks of the Oregon Railroad & Navigation Company and the Northern Pacific branch line.

The flat ended at Ninth and Bank where the canyon walls pinched in almost to the narrowness of the river. The road crossed the river by a wooden bridge and ran winding into a smaller flat at the mouth of Burke Canyon, out of which Canyon Creek joined the South Fork. This was an industrial outskirt given over to warehouses, railroad shops, an oil storage tank, and the ugly buildings and scrap piles of the Coeur d'Alene Iron Works. Within the canyon mouth houses nestled and low on the east hill sat the Catholic Providence Hospital.

As Emma Pulaski drove home she kept thinking: If the fire comes, where can people go? West down the main Mullan Canyon a narrow valley wound to Osburn, five miles away, and Kellogg, twelve miles away. Those who lived in the main part of town could perhaps flee in that direction. But she and her neighbors were cut off from downtown Wallace by the narrowness of Burke Canyon and the bottle-neck at Ninth and Bank. The town of Mullan lay seven miles east, while Burke lay squeezed within the confines of its own canyon seven miles north. The way to both towns was through declivities so narrow that roads and railroad lines ran through the timber. Yes, Ed was right and the tailing dam, whatever its hazards, would be safer than the canyon roads. But who cared to be safe if Ed and the other fire fighters were to die, and if all these beautiful forests and even the town were doomed? Her head pounded to think of it.

6

The next morning, that of August 20, dawned stiflingly —if night turning into a hot murk of saffron and slate gray, with a dull burnt-orange knot showing up sickishly where the sun should be—if that could be called dawn. People woke coughing, their throats raw, and saw again the boiling pillars of smoke over the mountains to the south. The hours dragged on, singularly oppressive, and around noon a wind similar to the one on the 10th started up.

In Kellogg, O. M. Vang went into his back yard, dug a big pit, lined it with boards and heavy paper, and buried the family's new shiny sewing machine.

Near Mullan a farmer fearfully eyed the barn where he had dynamite stored, and hitched team to wagon, loaded the dynamite on board and started up Deadman Gulch toward the National Mine tunnel.

At Murray, an old gold camp on Prichard Creek twenty miles north of Wallace, Mrs. Margeurite Corbeill and her children Vance and Nina stood on the porch of the cabin they were occupying and watched a fire burning on the mountain face east of town near the Terrible Liz Mine.

Mrs. Corbeill had already come seven miles down from the Paragon Mine where her husband Ike worked when the mine crew had been called out to fight a fire nearby. She had not fled far enough, she reflected, as she watched this new fire throw down ashes and cinders into the main and only street of Murray. When the wagon stage come in from Wallace that night, she was going to get on it and put more distance between her and all this danger.

In Wallace itself, on King Street, Tom Nicholson loaded everything he owned on a wagon, took it down to the other end of town to his little tobacco factory, the Wallace Cigar Company, which stood near the river east of Seventh Street. Other King Street residents packed up valuables and took them to homes of friends on streets considered safer. Pioneer Margaret Mallon, made of sterner stuff, remained at her home at No. 2 King.

Yes, King was the street down which the fire would surely come if it burst out of the canyon. But in other parts of town houses and places of business might be lost through fires set by falling brands. "It might be my house, my business," people reasoned, and all week they had been busy putting new or increased fire insurance on their buildings. On this ominous Saturday morning everyone who had not already attended to this matter of insurance decided they had better do so. Fire insurance offices became madhouses. Clerks could not cope with the business, and office managers, getting panicky themselves, closed up shop in the early afternoon.

To Mrs. Hannah Beswick who visited Wallace that day, this tenacious sticking—people might pile on insurance but they made no move to quit the town—seemed fantastically foolhardy.

Mrs. Beskwick was herself a fugitive from the forest fires. With her two daughters she had been spending the summer with her husband Norton, manager of the Gold Chrome mine near DeBorgia, Montana, forty-five miles from Wallace over Lookout Pass in the St. Regis River drainage.

Also visiting at the mine was M. L. Brain, a successful

Chicago mining promoter, who is spite of the masculinely abbreviated name was a woman and mother of Elmer Brain, a young assistant of Norton's.

Two weeks ago Norton had decided fires were creeping too close to the mine for comfort and had sent the women out. Mrs. Brain left for Missoula while Mrs. Beswick went to stay with friends in Mullan, where in spite of general smokiness and fires burning back on the St. Joe ridge, everyone felt safe enough.

On the 20th she left to make a trip to Spokane but stopped en route to visit friends, the Henry Ellars family in Wallace. They invited her to stay overnight and she was considering the matter when her daughter Zoe, who hated visiting with all the passion a teen-ager can muster, cried and begged to continue their journey. Giving in, Mrs. Beswick promised they would take the afternoon train.

At the depot, ashes and cinders crunched underfoot, and as they waited Mrs. Beswick noted how the whole little town, normally so attractive and picturesque in its cupped hollow with mountain-sides of tightly - braided green climbing about it, today cowered brown and ash-gray under an angry smoke cloud.

All at once she jumped back in alarm as an object hurtled out of the sky. Part of a tree branch, fully a foot long and still blazing, crashed at her feet.

Thoroughly frightened, she cried out to the Ellars, "How do you dare stay in this town!"

"Oh, it's been like this for ten days," they replied with maddening stoicism.

"Though it does seem some worse this afternoon," Mrs. Ellars added a bit apologetically.

"Why, it's crazy to stay here!" insisted Mrs. Beswick. "It's downright dangerous. You'd better take the train with us right now and get out of here. Stay in Spokane till things get better."

Her friends only laughed at her fears and handed her and her daughters aboard the westbound train. As she sank into a seat she gave thanks to tempermental Zoe for insisting they leave. Imagine staying all night in a town where fire struck out at you like lightning from the sky!

7

Yes, things were worse that afternoon, as Mrs. Ellars had admitted, and an hour later events took an alarming turn. The wind drove the fire across the trenches in Placer Canyon. The soldiers on duty there, having little knowledge of what to do and almost no tools to do it with, were easily routed. Groups of disorganized Negro infantrymen began straggling out of the canyon into town. Weigle, fearing to get the troops trapped at Livingstan's Ranch ordered the officers to break camp and move their men into town to the ball park.

As smoke poured down on Wallace the day grew so dark lamps had to be lighted at 3 p. m. In most quarters all calmness evaporated. Nuns from Our Lady of Lourdes Academy at King and Bank, known locally as the "Sister's school," left to take refuge at Providence Hospital in the far east end of town. Most other King Street residents who had not already done so fled hurriedly. They hauled suitcases and trunks, furniture and hastily packed household articles down to the OR&N depot across the river at Eighth. Joined by the more fearful citizens from other parts of town, they demanded a special train out of town.

Mayor of Wallace was young Walter Hanson—not a full-time mayor but a practicing attorney who acted as city father on the side. Usually his duties in this town of 3500 people were not very exacting, but today the questions were coming at him from all sides. Was the town going to burn? What ought people to do? Should they flee now? Was he going to order a special train?

The mayor's trouble was that he didn't know the answers. The fire was still out in forested Placer Canyon, and just how severe was the threat to the town he could not say. Hoping that Weigle with his forester's knowledge could help him, Hanson walked over to the Forest Service office.

Weigle had had a hectic morning. With so many fires

burning, with so many crews in the woods, with all his own
men out on jobs, he had been left with the tremendous
task of buying and dispatching food supplies in a dozen
directions, of trying to round up more camp gear, more
cooking utensils, more tools, more pack mules, more
men—more *everything*—and get them moving into the
woods. As many items had long since been exhausted, it
meant trying to work miracles.

Then the wind had risen and with it his sense of tension. With the Placer Canyon line breached and no crew
left there to check the flames, God alone knew what would
happen next.

He repeated that to Hanson. "God only knows what's
going to happen next, I don't. Still, the fire is out in
green timber. That should check its speed. So should
the winding, downward course of the canyon. It's more
apt to top a ridge up there than come down this way.
But no one can say for sure. I'll order my saddle horse
brought round and ride up and look the situation over.
A lot depends on the wind. If it dies down we'll be okay;
if it gets worse, all hell may break loose. In the meantime
—yes, it might be a good idea to have a relief train standing by—just in case."

At 4 o'clock in the afternoon Weigle started up the
canyon. At that very hour a strange and unreal hush fell
over the Bitter Root Range. People in the dark, suffocat-
ing streets of the town, as well as men on the fire lines
noticed it and later attested to the phenomenon.

Moving air currents stopped. Smoke hung motionless.
Sound waves ceased to travel and the world turned mute.
An extreme rarity of air, a tenuous, mysterious atmosphere developed, as if a vacuum bell had been fitted down
over the whole heated hell.

Weigle noted the change. "Thank God, the wind is
dropping," he thought.

But this was no ordinary cessation of wind. This was
the dead-center eye, the vortex of the hurricane. It was
that moment of extreme calm, that absence of all motion
with which nature warns of the coming cataclysm.

8

Two different Big Creeks have their source opposite each other high on the slopes of the St. Joe Mountains, one making its way north to the Coeur d'Alene River, the other south to the St. Joe.

On the middle fork of St. Joe Big Creek, not far below the main ridge, a stretch of fire line in a narrow, forested canyon was the special charge of Ranger John Bell and a gang of thirty-seven men—one of the crews under Pulaski's general supervision. All afternoon the men had worked in the muggy, smoky darkness, plying their shovels and gunnysacks, sweat pouring in rivers from their bodies, eyes staring red-rimmed from their minstrel-black faces.

Only a few of Bell's men were native to the Coeur d'Alenes. Joe de Marco, a young Forest Service worker, came from a large Italian family in Murray. Walter Ingersoll lived in Kellogg. Upton B. Smith, known as "Smitty" was only twenty-one but a well-known character around the lead-silver mines. George W. Cameron and William J. Elliott, his friends, were also miners.

The rest were floating laborers and adventurers. Jean Viettone and Dominic Bruno were Italians, Tony Butcher an Austrian, Chris Omiso a self-styled hobo. Steve Marquette hailed from Iowa, Chris Hanson from South Dakota, G. N. Ward from San Francisco. Others were from equally far-flung points, with equally varied backgrounds.

The floaters had simply been broke, needing a job— any job. A few had wanted to see the country. The local men had either volunteered or been forced to duty in the emergency. All had signed up with the Forest Service for 25 cents an hour and board and room. Room under the starry sky. "Bring your own bedroll," was the order.

All had signed up, that is, with the exception of two homesteaders. Roderick Ames, age 35, had a fine claim on a little tributary stream called Ames Creek, where he had built himself an imposing cabin. He had come up from Kellogg the day before to bury his household articles and other effects, but finding a crew so close had stayed to lend a hand in the hope of saving his own valuable stand of white pine timber.

Joseph Beauchamp, an older man, claimed a quarter section directly up the canyon, where his unpretentious cabin stood in a two-acre clearing. Desperate to keep the fire from advancing and burning him out, he too had volunteered to help Bell's crew.

All afternoon the wind blew, not overly strong but so persistently pushy the men had to pit all their grit and guts against the fire to keep it in check. As the men relieved each other on the fire lines, those off duty relaxed a little. Everyone was exhausted. No ear was attuned to the eerie silence that fell upon the woods. The wind dropped. No breath of air stirred. The smoke ceased to rise upward. For a little time nature achieved some unfathomable stabilization in that vastness of expanding heat waves.

Then a breeze stirred. The men tasted it oven-hot on their lips and the smoke screen shifted. The breeze stiffened, bringing at last a blessed freshening of air. The smoke pall rolled back to reveal the sun low in the sky, where it shone red as a mad bull's eye.

That was the prelude: then the thing struck. A bank of violent wind smashed into the heart of the coralled fire like a clenched fist. The blaze lifted as a live, fluent body, bent its flame tops across the cleared fire line and ran away into the green, unguarded forest. Overhead winds careened, snatching up live brands and embers and hurling them on ahead.

Men of the crew stood stupefied. Only Bell, the experienced Forest Service hand, understood what had happened. Tornado winds had struck. He shouted, "Run! Make it for Beauchamp's clearing! For God's sake—go!" And he dashed off to shout the same command to the men running up from the far fire lines.

Then the race was on—the race for that opening in the canyon where Beauchamp had cleared away the timber. On the heels of the fleeing men came the roaring walls of fire, and with them a brutish wind which knocked down weak-kneed trees and old snags, and then bowled on ahead carrying flaming branches, pine cones and streamers of moss.

The men burst into the clearing just ahead of the inferno. Bell led the way to a small pool in the creek which ran near the cabin. "Into the water!" he ordered. "Keep down and as wet as possible."

As many as could threw themselves headlong into the shallow depth. But there was not room for all, and Joe Beauchamp called, "I've got a tunnel that's just the place. Follow me!" The remaining men ran after him to a bank where he had dug a cellar-like hole for burying his valuables.

With thirty men cowering in the pool and seven huddled in the short tunnel, flames closed in on the clearing.

9

Ranger Pulaski led his new gang to the fire which had broken out behind Striped Peak, back from the west fork of Placer Creek. His men had one good laugh. A green cook, hired from Spokane, brought with him his white cook's apron and his tall, white chef's cap. What a look on his face when he learned that the washtubs, boilers and five-gallon tins dumped to the ground from pack mules were the cooking pots, and camp was only a gathering of these vessels, together with food supplies and packs of tinware dishes, under an old tarp. Camp and kitchen were open to every wind that blew.

Fortunately the other cook, Frank Foltz, a Latour Creek homesteader, had worked in lumber camps, and George Howard, the camp flunky, was a woodsman from Wallace. They showed the fancy chef how to bank an open fire with logs and then under the sky to bake hams, cook mulligan stew, and boil washtubs of rice and potatoes.

Late on Saturday afternoon, as Foltz was ready to call the first crew in off the fire lines for evening grub, a blast of high wind smote the surrounding forest. Dead trees toppled, green ones bent double, the tarp tore from its pinnings, and heat and smoke rolled in from the fire area.

Pulaski, who had been out on his saddle horse inspecting the farther limits of the blaze, wheeled into camp, shouting above the roar of the sudden storm: "The fire lines are broken! The Big Creek fire's coming over the hill. Quick!—we'll be surrounded. We've got to hit the trail."

Turning to Howard and another camp helper, he ordered, "Hurry! Dig some holes. Throw in all the tools and gear you can before we leave. I'll round up the men."

"What about the grub?" demanded Foltz.

"No time for that. Each man will have to grab what he can, eat it on the trail. We got to get out of here. We're right between the two fires, and if we get caught where they come together—we'll all be goners."

As he rode forward the wind became so strong it nearly lifted him from the saddle. Smoke thickened until the men he encountered loomed only as darker shadows in the general murk—some already running from the leaping flames, others standing as though paralyzed. "Get into camp," the ranger bawled. "Take a blanket from the camp stock—grab what grub you can carry. We're pulling out."

By the time he had assembled all forty of his men his voice was beginning to fail from so much shouting. He gave up his horse to S. W. Stockton, an old Texas ranger turned prospector, who was so crippled by rheumatism he would never make it if he had to walk. Another man put a bridle on a pack horse that was in camp.

It had turned pitch dark except for the pink glare of the surrounding fires. "Line up single file," the ranger commanded. "Keep your eyes on the man ahead. If anybody falls out of line, let out a yell. Foltz, you bring up the rear. We'll try to make Wallace." He led off, the reins of the saddle horse in his hands.

In a mile they came out on Franklin Ridge. Downward the smoke thinned out and below a steeply timbered slope they could see a mountain tarn. Some of the men, panicky by now, begged to go down to the lake. "We could save ourselves by getting into the water."

But Pulaski knew all about the lake; he had discovered it during an early forest survey, had named it for his daughter Elsie. He shook his head. "No use trying to go down there. The banks fall away right at the shore. We'd only drown."

Instead he led along a ridge northeast, then down a slope to try to pass below the fire they had been fighting, But as he came out on the lower slope, he saw the way ahead barred by new fires. Smoke poured in so heavily as to blot out the men in the column. To keep contact each fire fighter had to put his hand on the shoulder of the fellow just ahead.

The column went on until flames seemed to dance on every side. Men began to moan and pray with fear and the column came to a demoralized stop.

"No use getting scared yet," snapped the ranger, "I'm going to get you out of here."

In one direction dark trees appeared beyond the moving flames, and Pulaski, placing a wet gunnysack over his head, dashed through the fiery wall, then came running back again.

"We can make it through that way," he announced and led them around the edge of the flames. Again they were in smoky forest.

But they were completely cut off. He had seen that during his foray ahead. Their only hope now was a couple of prospect holes of the War Eagle mine a short way down the canyon. Fortunately he had seen that the way to the largest and safest of the two was open, and he led the men toward it between crackling walls of fire.

The tunnel he had chosen was 100 feet long, with enough room to hold them all. The timbers at its mouth were smoking, but he ordered, "In there quick, men! It's our one chance."

A greenhorn fire fighter cowered back, bawling in hysterical voice, "We'll roast to death in there."

"You'll roast out here. Get in!" Pulaski pulled his revolver.

Soon he had herded them all in except three of his best men, whom he set to scooping up water from a pool at the tunnel mouth. When they had thrown enough on the timbers to cool them, they led the horses in. Then, to keep out as much smoke as possible, Pulaski supervised the hanging of blankets on old nails and splinters at the tunnel entrance.

"Lie flat on the ground," he ordered the men. "Keep your noses near the trickle of water. Or in the damp earth. The air is better down there."

Yet even along the tunnel floor men choked and gasped for breath and one big fellow screamed. "I've got to get out."

The ranger pushed the man back, then stood upright at the tunnel entrance with his revolver drawn. "It's death to the man who tries to pass me," he said.

For he knew it was torturous death outside. He could hear the fiery winds, risen to new heights of fury. As the tumult passed over, burning trees fell across the tunnel mouth.

10

Supervisor Weigle was able to ride nearly four miles up Placer Canyon. He encountered fire before that but it was on a slope overhead and he went on until he met the main body of the blaze enveloping the canyon wall to wall and devouring trails and roads as it came.

In the canyon the wind was not severe and the fire was traveling neither fast nor furiously. It advanced, however, in a hot display of naked power, with searing noises and waves of cindery smoke. Its direction was down the canyon toward Wallace.

On his way back toward town, the supervisor still debated the fire's potential for destruction to Wallace. So much depended on wind, on humidity, on the essentially erratic nature of forest fire itself. At the moment the danger to the town seemed not too immediate but who could say what would happen? Would it be wisest to advise an evacuation?

Two miles out of Wallace the supervisor met a man staggering up the road and recognized him as young "Speedy" Swift who lived above at the mouth of Hord's Gulch, not far from where Weigle had turned back down the canyon.

"Were you at the ranch?" Swift demanded of Weigle. "My wife and baby are up there—liable to be burned. I'm sick, been in town to the doctor. I don't know if I can make it or not, but somebody's got to go up there and get them out alive." His face looked ghastly and he tottered against a tree.

Weigle knew well the danger of getting trapped in the inferno above but he answered quickly, "You get back to town and into bed. I'll ride up and bring them out."

As he neared the mouth of Hord's Gulch he found an arm of the main fire had run into the gulch. Had the ranch already been swept by fire then? Was it too late to save Mrs. Swift and the baby?

The wind had toppled so many trees across the trail ahead that he was forced to tie his horse to a bush and to pick a hot-footed way through the burning tree trunks. As he came within sight of the clearing he was almost afraid to look. But there it was through some miracle: the cabin standing against a background of blackened trees. Around it men were throwing water on it from buckets.

These men, a dozen in number, were fire fighters from one of Pulaski's crews. They had been working higher up the canyon and when they were forced down by the advancing fire they ran into the clearing for safety. They had taken Mrs. Swift down to the shallow waters of the creek, settled her down with the baby on her breast, and covered her over with wet blankets. The trees had burst into flame around the clearing, the barn had caught and burned, but the men with buckets had saved the house. The big danger seemed to have passed now, but they would guard the house for awhile longer and when they were sure it was safe from sparks, they would bring Mrs. Swift and the child with them to Wallace.

Weigle, needing to return to his own duties, picked his way back along the debris-choked trail, thankful he could report a narrow escape to young Swift rather than a tragedy.

As he reached the unburnt trail his preoccupation was broken by a sudden roaring of wind. He looked up to see a tempest of violence hit the main canyon fire. He recognized the danger at once and started to run toward the bush where he had tethered his horse. Before he could cover the distance a sheet of flame reached out and enveloped the road ahead.

Fire was behind him now and fire ahead. His only chance was a prospectors tunnel which appeared as a dark hole along the canyon wall. He wheeled toward it.

Smoke cascaded in to blind him but he groped his way ahead and found the tunnel entrance. As he ran in, the flames were at his very heels and behind him the debris at the tunnel mouth flashed up, sending a billow of smoke and flames in after him. Fortunately, a small flow of water trickled along the floor. He splashed his face and clothes, then soaked his hat and held the wet felt to his mouth and nose. Even so he began to choke.

Desperate now, he remembered that outside he had crossed a bare dump pile of rock and earth. Still holding his hat to his mouth he ran out and threw himself down on the bare, gravelly expanse. Scooping away the dry top dirt he buried his nose in a damp hollow. The gravel seemed to act as a filter and the air came to him purified. He could breathe again. Prone and motionless he lay, flames whipping back and forth above him like cat-o-nine tails.

11

When Weigle failed to return as expected, Mayor Hanson himself set out on foot up the canyon to learn what he could of the danger in that direction. Several others

also made the trip, drawn as people always are by anything of a disastrous nature.

Harry McLeod, a linotype operator, was on duty that
day at the *Idaho Press,* a little rival sheet of the *Times,*
and he kept worrying about the high south hill. Of the
many pyramid-shaped mountains which stood about, this
was the one which formed a backdrop for the business
district, rising almost perpendicular above Bank Street.
The streets gashed at its base seemed hardly to mar it,
and it towered upward steep and proud, so thick grown
with young forest clear to its peak as to appear at first
glance to be wrapped in one flawless piece of green velvet. Only close inspection revealed the faintly pointed
markings of individual tree tops.

An incredible mountain it was—so perfect in its beauty
that McLeod could look upon it a thousand times a day,
each time with pleasure. By habit when he came to the
desk for a new piece of copy he always gazed upward at it.
About 2 p. m. he saw, to his dismay, a column of smoke
rising behind it. This was a new and different column
from the one hanging over the Placer Creek fire and obviously rose from a new blaze. Where was this new fire?
Just around behind the mountain face? Or on some ridge
far back? He could not tell, and felt consternation that
this velvet perfection he so admired might be endangered.

When he got off work at 4 p. m. he walked up Placer
Canyon to figure out if he could where this new fire was.
After a couple of miles he could see ahead to a slope
where red flames were tearing through green tree tops
but could not make out the relation of this blaze to the
pillar of smoke that had worried him.

Harry McLeod lived with his mother and brother in a
house on Bank between First and Second. His mother
was out of town, but on returning from the canyon he
found his brother Rod home ahead of him. Rod, who
worked at the post office, had brought with him a hand-
cart used for hauling mail, and he insisted on packing
up the things dearest to their mother and taking them
out of town to safety. Harry wasn't at all sure the town was

in danger but he went along with Rod's idea and helped pack two trunks. Together they set out along the road west pulling the trunks on the postal wagon. Under his arm Rod clutched a paper bag containing a loaf of bread and a dozen oranges. Provisions for the road? Harry asked him.

At 5 p. m. Roy Kingsbury came from a meeting of the Federal Mining Company. He was a mining man who owned part interest in the Wallace Hospital, which sat flush against the hill at First and Cedar. As he was much worried about the danger to the hospital, he got on his motorcycle and rode up the canyon to observe the progress of the fire.

He sped on until he saw the blaze ahead on the slope. But the wind was not blowing hard at this hour and the fire seemed to be traveling but slowly. Reassured, he rode back down to the hospital and sat down to dinner with the resident physician, Dr. St. Jean.

During the dinner the wind rose to sudden fury and went shrieking past carrying swirls of smoke and debris. He and the doctor rose quickly from the meal and together set out up the canyon on foot to see what this sudden change portended. The gale which had sprung up was such a mean one they had to lean against it as they walked. They soon came in sight of the fire and found it on a frightening rampage. It tore along the slope with such a powerful uplift that great trees were being pulled up by the roots and knocked flat with explosive bangs.

They turned and almost ran back to evacuate the hospital. Dr. St. Jean was getting out his fancy new automobile (one of the two horseless carriages in town), and Kingsbury was calling Sutherland's Livery Stable for additional conveyances when Mayor Hanson walked in, having returned down the canyon not far behind them.

"Yes, I think you're wise to get the people out of here," he admitted. "It looks pretty grim. By the way, Bill Osburn phoned me earlier, told me he could make room in the Osburn Hospital for as many patients as we wanted to bring down there. I'm going over and suggest Leonard get his patients out too." This was a reference to his brother, Dr. Leonard Hanson, who ran the Hope Hospital on the second floor of a building at Sixth and Cedar.

"You think the town's really going to burn?" asked Kingsbury.

The mayor lifted an uncertain hand. "I don't know what is going to happen. But I'll feel better when these two hospitals are emptied, I can tell you that. Right now I'm on the way back to my office to issue an order for every able-bodied man in town to report for volunteer fire duty. Not only that but I'm going to threaten them with jail if they don't obey. It looks like we may see plenty of hell before this night's over."

12

The Worstell family, about a year previously, had moved aside the old building in which the late William Worstell had started a furniture business in 1888. On the northeast corner of Seventh and Bank they had put up a fine, new two-story brick building. Its main floor gave ample room for a large display of new furniture, the upper floor served as storage space, while second-hand furniture was relegated to the old frame building now adjoining it east on Bank. Bruce G. Worstell ran the store, with some help from his brothers, Attorney H. E. Worstell and Probate Judge Lawrence Worstell.

H. E.'s law offices were in the Otterson Building on Bank Street. That Saturday afternoon he worked on a case until 5 p. m., then walked the few blocks home to dinner. As yet unmarried, he lived in the family home at 205 River, where he found his mother Mary wringing her hands. "Oh, Harle, the fire is on the way down King Street! The whole town is going to burn!"

Attorney Worstell had his own firm conviction that the town was in no danger at all, and he said, "Oh, Mother, calm down. Who says the fire is coming down King? I know of no one who says it. Who is this authority who is so sure the town will be reduced to a cinder?"

His chiding attitude of cross-examination reassured her somewhat. Yet she persisted, "What if the fire does come? What am I to do?"

Not able to take her quite seriously, he said, "Well, there's a lot of wide open spaces down at the ball park. Nothing down there to burn. If you get too worried, just go sit on home base and you'll be safe.

The family had a huge investment in the store and his one real concern was that a stray spark might set it on fire. After dinner he decided to go and help Bruce keep an eye on it. Perceiving that his mother was truly upset, he turned to her before he left and said, "Honestly, Mother, I don't think there's the remotest chance of the town burning. But they have an emergency train standing by over at the depot. If you get too frightened, go get on that train and you'll be all right."

On coming out of the house he found that the relatively mild wind which had been blowing when he walked home had now turned into a real gale. A gale so fierce he was forced to take shelter along the sides of buildings and hang on to lamp posts at corners. This shook his certitude somewhat and he turned in alarm to the southwest, where the wind came tearing out of Placer Canyon. The same black smoke cloud churned there, looking no nearer the town than before.

The same fierce wind buffeted the car in whch Mayor Hanson and his doctor brother delivered to the Osburn Hospital the last load of patients from the Hope Hospital. As they drove back, a violent gust reached in, whipped the cap from the mayor's head and bore it away into the smoky atmosphere. As he saw it go he thought, "Oh, well, Mother never liked that cap anyway. Thought it was unbefitting the dignity of my office." And he made a vow: "If we get through this night and there's any town left to be an official of, I'll buy me a new plush hat worthy of a great Lord Mayor."

This gale-force wind boded Wallace no good, he felt sure. But as yet no flames were visible around the town and he could hardly order an evacuation when nothing was on fire and in the end nothing might burn. All he could do now was wait and see.

Mayor Hanson asked Leonard to drop him off home, where he lived with their mother at First and Bank. Mrs. Hanson, like Mrs. McLeod down the street, happened to be away visiting and Walter fixed himself a lone, late meal. Around 8:30 he went out to wet down the yard and house against wind-blown sparks.

The Hanson house was a substantial frame one on an ample corner lot. Just across the street from it the mountain bounding Placer Canyon on the east rose straight up and curved round to merge with the high south hill.

The mayor got out the garden hose. He sprinkled down the yard. He poured water on the clapboard siding. He squirted water up to the shingle roof. With his head tilted back he turned toward the hill and saw there beyond the roof peaks a sheet of flames, far up, shooting out of Placer Canyon, wrapping around the curved side of the mountain, and then, like a streamer in the wind, blowing out across the south hill. Moving with a crackling roar, with a resinous snapping and popping, it surged through the green tree tops like an angry red breaker and tore on east above the town.

Stopping only to turn off the water, the Mayor of Wallace ran bare-headed and in shirt sleeves up Bank in the direction the fire had taken.

East of Worstells on Bank stood a little planing mill, and next to that the Wallace *Times* in a two-story frame building. Around the backdoor of the *Times* was gathered an untidy mass of discarded newsprint and cans of old solvent used in cleaning type. Some of this waste material had overflowed into space between the newspaper plant and its next-door neighbor to the east, the false-fronted, one-room insurance office of Joe Whelan.

Overhead the wave of traveling red fire bore on, rushing with a roar west to east, cutting a flaming swath across Harry McLeod's velvet green mountain, spewing out fireworks like Roman pinwheels. A big burning brand, describing a neat arc in its course, plumped down near the backdoor of the *Times* into the ready pile of refuse. In an instant newsprint and solvent were flaring.

Like most other businesses in Wallace, the *Times* stayed open until 9 o'clock on Saturday night. Inside someone shouted, "My God, look at the hill!" R. G. Chambers, a linotype operator, hurried out the front door to see what was happening. As he stepped to the sidewalk he saw flames shooting along the side of the building. He tore back in yelling, "The place is on fire! Everybody out!"

Across the street Mrs. E. W. Stewart of the Home Hand Laundry saw the flames leap up. She rushed to her North Idaho Company phone. "Operator! Operator! Call the fire department. The *Times* is on fire!"

At the Coeur d'Alene Hardware Company store, diagonally across Seventh and Bank from Worstells, Clerk Edwin Kribs was on duty that evening. Around five he had gone home to dinner at the apartment where he lived in the 200 block on Bank. Neither he nor his wife had felt much concerned about the fire threat.

As closing hour approached Kribs was waiting on a man and woman who told him they had just moved to Wallace and were staying with friends until they could get some household articles together. They were buying dishes, pots and pans. One of them, happening to look up from their purchases, shouted, "Omigod, fire!"

All three ran to the window and, sure enough, saw the second-hand furniture store next to Worstell's brick building on fire. "But we just came from there," the man said incredulously. "We just bought our furniture there."

"We already paid for it," the woman said in the same incredulous voice. "It will all be burned." The two ran out toward the burning store, as if somehow to retrieve their purchases.

Kribs, feeling incredulous himself, followed them out and without even bothering to lock the door, started down the street toward home. Overhead the south hill flared weirdly and behind him buildings burst newly into flame.

13

The speeding mayor arrived to see the blaze already set and spreading. He ducked into the Rocky Mountain Phone Company, a half block down Bank, to make sure the fire Department had been called, then dashed up to his office in the Otterson Building, taking two steps at a time, to retrieve some cash he had left in his desk drawer.

He heard the fire bell begin to toll and hurrying back arrived at the fire scene along with Fire Chief Fred Kelly and the hose cart. Already the fire had spread from the *Times* to the planing mill and Worstells' old building on the west, and from Whelan's east to a rooming house called the Coeur d'Alene Hotel.

"Looks bad, Fred," said Mayor Hanson to Chief Kelly, raising his voice to be heard above the crackle and snap of the fire.

"Afraid so. With this wind we'll never stop 'er from spreading east."

"Had we better evacuate?"

"Probably best. With luck, though, we might not lose more than the east end."

The mayor hurried back to the phone company. The switchboard was swamped now. People trying to locate members of the family, friends warning friends, excited voices reporting the fire, hysterical voices demanding what to do.

The seven girl operators were sticking to their posts and working frantically, even though the light of burning buildings and burning mountains flickered over the switchboard. Some were upset, crying into the mouthpiece on their breasts.

The telephone office manager ordered lines cleared so the mayor could make emergency calls: to the fire station to order the bell rung as a signal for evacuation; to the infantry officers to request soldiers to help load the trains; to the chief of police to suggest he open the jail and take the prisoners to the city park for safety; to Kellogg to alert the neighboring town to the problem of Wallace refugees, who would soon be pouring in.

Hanson turned to the manager. "We're ordering all women evacuated. Can you let the switchboard girls go?"

"Yes, yes," agreed the manager excitedly. "I've got to leave myself—see my mother and sisters get out safely."

On down Bank Street, Edwin Kribs dashed into his apartment, shouting to his wife, "The east end's on fire— the whole town'll probably go. Grab what you think's important and we'll head for the train."

"We'd better take Alice with us," said his wife. She referred to their neighbor, Alice Woodward, who was alone in another apartment with her tiny daughter, also named Alice.

Kribs ran to get Mrs. Woodward, giving her time only to find her purse, gather up a few necessities for the baby and wrap the infant in a blanket.

The fire bell tolled in long strokes. In a few minutes they were out of the building.

The streets were by now a scene of pandemonium. People who had horses and rigs were galloping about gathering up families and friends and heading for the west-end canyon road to Osburn and Kellogg. People on foot were running in all directions: Some rushed home to rescue wives and children, valuables and pets; some hurried to the houses of neighbors and friends to be of help; some dashed to business establishments to snatch up money or valuable papers.

Panicked people sped along empty-handed, knocking others down as they tore toward the depots. The cautious type carried satchels and suitcases previously packed for a possible exodus. Those who had remained unworried till the last moment clutched bundles hastily done up in sheets or old blankets.

Mothers pulled wailing children by the hand. Here and there a bent-backed man tugged a heavy trunk along by hand, its bottom grating screechingly over the pavement. An old woman carried a bird cage with the bottom out but with parrot clinging squawkingly to its perch.

An old man tumbled out of his house, one leg in his trousers, bobbing along erratically as he tried to get the other leg in.

A few grim-faced householders were sticking it. They were busy hauling furniture into yards, digging holes to bury possessions, running to put out the burning brands which were falling all around. To those stubborn ones, bent on preserving what they owned, the crowd as it surged toward the depots cried out, "The town's lost! Come on with us and save yourself!"

Mrs. Kribs, carrying the baby, brushed hot embers from its blanket. They met a neighbor who called, "Don't try to go across by the depots. It's burning up that way. Cross lower down."

They headed directly for the river, which during the past hot dry weeks, had become a shallow stream with many rocks protruding. Those who had crossed ahead of them had already thrown down planks to form a precarious bridging. They teetered over and arrived along the railroad track.

14

Harry James, yardmaster for the Northern Pacific, had put in as harried an afternoon as the mayor himself. One scared brakeman had skipped, leaving the yard crew shorthanded, and the water tank-car had been in demand every hour. That piece of equipment had certainly paid for itself. With its hose attachment immersed in the river, the powerful pump on board could throw a stream of water 300 feet. One spot fire after another had broken out along the brushy hillside above the tracks, and another bad fire had started near the NP depot, but using the tank-car equipment they had managed to put out all the blazes before they got out of control.

In the afternoon came the order for special trains to be made up. James supervised the switching, using all the passenger coaches he had (even one from the Burke stub line), boxcars, even flatcars, then kicked these trains over to the OR&N line. For the NP branch line came west out of St. Regis, Montana, ran through a number of little Montana towns, crossed Lookout Pass, switchbacked down Mullan Canyon and ended at Wallace; whereas it was thought safest to send all trains out in the opposite direction to Kellogg and Spokane, reached via the OR&N.

All afternoon and evening townspeople pestered the station agents at both the NP and OR&N depots demanding to know when the trains would leave. But there were no running orders. Those orders were obtained only after the fire swirled out of the canyon and dropped on the town. And at the height of the confusion a work-train car got a wheel off the NP track blocking the way east of the NP depot.

When the fire bell rang the evacuation signal, everyone rushed for the relief trains, which stood in the yard west of the depot. As the crowds went streaming in that direction, Yardmaster James hurried over to give the OR&N crew a hand.

He found a sea of people pushing, shoving, clawing for entrance to the limited coach space. The conductor, valiantly attempting to load women and children first, seemed lost in the seething mass. A pregnant woman had started up the coach steps when a man came dashing up in a panic, pushed her roughly aside, and tried to throw himself into the vestibule. The yardmaster, seeing this outrage, waded in, collared the man and pulled him down to the trackside. "Go hunt yourself a flatcar!" he shouted, taking a swing at the fellow.

Next a drunk tried to stumble up the steps into the car. James pulled him back, too, and he started cursing. The yardmaster spun him around roughly, headed him back across the river. "Get back over there! If the town burns you might as well burn with it!"

A burdened-down mother handed her baby to a friend while she climbed on board with her bundles. Just as she entered the car the brakeman slammed the door shut, announcing the coach was full. "My baby! my baby!" wailed the mother until the brakeman opened the door and the child was handed up.

Above: Before the fire, the honky-tonk town of Grand Forks, Idaho. Below: Immediately after the fire, bars and taverns were doing a brisk business in tents.

Oregon Historical Society

Above: A packtrain takes the trail at Avery, Idaho, during the 1910 fire.
Below: Avery several years later.

Black smoke and searing flames threatened forest and cabins in the St. Joe Valley.

A pillar of smoke boils skyward from the fire on Big Creek, a tributary of the St. Joe River.

Seven men were roasted to death in Beauchamp's tunnel when burning logs rolled down over the tunnel mouth.

Beauchamp's homestead ranch, on the middle fork of St. Joe Big Creek. Many took refuge from the fire in the water of a little stream that ran through the clearing.

The old woman with the bottomless bird cage found room in one of the coaches but other passengers so resented the cage taking up valuable space they threatened to throw it out the window and the old lady after it. Another woman had to be restrained from jumping out the same window. She had forgotten to bring her purse, her money and her valuables.

Walter Hanson, seeing people flee across the river to the trains, noted among them able-bodied, unencumbered men who in accordance with his orders should be serving as volunteer fire fighters. Ironically, some were prominent citizens who should be trying to save the town rather than their own skins. When he remarked on this to the chief, Kelly answered, "Oh, let the bastards go—we're better off without them."

But the mayor was angered and meant personally to see that no such deserters left town on the trains. When he arrived at the depot, he found one of the companies of men of the Twenty-Fifth Infantry there to assist him.

"Captain," he snapped to the infantry officer, "I want no one on these trains except women, children, old people or sick people—or men who are taking their families out to safety."

At that moment the mayor's eye fell on a well-known town gambler already fatly ensconced in a coach seat, leaning back waiting for the train to start. "Take that man off!" Hanson exploded.

In a few minutes the officer returned to report. "One of my men asked that fat fellow to move out of the coach and he refused. We have no orders to use force on civilians."

"I can tell you," the mayor cried, now thoroughly riled, "these people are going to obey the U. S. Army even if they are civilians! If they don't move, prick them with your bayonets. Captain, I'm giving you orders to do just that!"

The gambler came off the train.

But it was a losing battle. Mrs. James, the yardmaster's wife, staying in their house across the river from the tracks, watched the relief trains go by that night and saw the sides and tops of cars black-dotted with clinging men.

The Kribs and Mrs. Woodward found a place in a box-car where lumps of coal and coal dust crunched underfoot. A few wooden boxes had been thrown into the car and these were given to women who had babies to hold. Others were forced to stand, or if they weren't squeamish about coal dust, could sit on the floor. Many stood, for it was only a twelve mile ride to Kellogg.

In a far corner of the car sat Mrs. Rush White, clutching to her bosom a blanket-wrapped child ill with scarlet fever. She had phoned her doctor for instructions and he had said, "You'll just have to take him, that's all. Oil him up good, be sure he's warm, and keep him away from other children. He'll be all right."

As the train started west Mrs. Woodward and other mothers gave Mrs. White a wide berth.

<h2 style="text-align:center">15</h2>

Conductor George Washington Jones of the Idaho-Northern Railroad, a little branch line running to Murray, heard via telegraph the news that Wallace was burning. He took a train of a few coaches and boxcars down to Enaville, connection point with the OR&N parent line, and asked George Wheatley, the Enaville agent, to call the Spokane dispatcher and offer the train for service in evacuating Wallace.

"Tell Jones to get his damned train back on the Idaho-Northern and keep it there," bellowed the dispatcher to Wheatley. "I've got seven locomotives between Wallace and Kellogg and don't know where the hell any of them are!"

In Kellogg, the OR&N station agent, N. H. Brooke, was roused shortly after nine by a loud knocking at his door and a voice shouting, "Hey, Brooke, you're needed at the station. It's the fire."

As was his wont Brooke had locked up the station after the last scheduled train had gone through. Now as he struggled into his coat and hurried to the door he couldn't imagine what was wrong. The forest fires nearest to Kellogg were one behind Kellogg Peak and another in Deadwood Gulch but both were under control and the town was not considered in any danger. The railroad station itself must have caught fire, he decided.

But as he neared the tracks he saw no smoke. "What's up?" he demanded of a lounger.

"Wallace is all hell on fire. They're shipping everyone down here."

Unlocking the station, Brooke called his telegrapher, ordered him back for emergency duty. The two were soon swamped by railroad detail and Brooke was glad to see Stanley Easton arrive to take charge of the refugees when they came in.

Easton, president of the wondrous-rich Bunker Hill & Sullivan Mine, was the most influential citizen in town and functioned in unofficial capacity as mayor, and it was he whom Mayor Hanson had called.

The mine president had quickly organized a relief committee with headquarters in the McConnell Building. Under his leadership, committee members had canvassed private homes for those who could take in women and children; they had got merchants to unlock stores and provide blankets; they had opened the Odd Fellows Hall as a place to bed down men; they had arranged with a coffee shop proprietor to dispense coffee and doughnuts at the depot to the stricken people.

All was in readiness when the first relief train arrived. Shaken and bewildered Wallace citizens poured from it, women weeping, babies wailing, all saying, "Wallace is lost." It had become a cry of mass despair: "Wallace is lost." Women sobbed and said, "You could look behind— it was like the fires of hell—Wallace lost, our homes burning . . . "

Helen McBride, who took in two refugee mothers and their daughters discovered one woman was clutching under her arm a fresh-baked loaf of bread wrapped in a blanket.

Stanley Easton felt so sorry for one weary old man that he took him up to the mine office to sleep on a couch. On the way the old fellow kept cursing his own folly. "There I was, comfortable as I could be, living down in East Texas. One day a man came along selling mining stock and sucker that I was I put a thousand dollars into shares. This summer I decided to come up and see what I'd bought. But I found the whole country on fire and never got near enough for a look. Right now I wouldn't care if that mine were worth ten million dollars, To hell with my thousand bucks! To hell with the whole state of Idaho! I'm going back to Texas and I'm going to stay there!"

Trains kept arriving, some unloading all passengers, others taking those who wanted to go on to Spokane. Many people were too keyed up to sleep and kept milling around the station all night. The old lady got separated from her bottomless bird cage with parrot and it sat on a railroad bench all night. Men kept coming in to hand Brooke telegrams to be sent to relatives and friends. "Wallace is totally burned," these messages invariably read. When Brooke pointed out that according to latest reports a part of the town stood, they repeated in dazed and dogged fashion, "Wallace is lost."

16

Providence Hospital, on the outskirts of Wallace's east end, was a square, four-story brick structure. It sat low against the timbered mountain which divides Mullan Canyon from Burke Canyon. Crowded behind and to one side were an isolation building, a wash-house, a garden and a barn. A small hayfield stretched along the NP tracks which ran in front of it and on into Mullan Canyon.

This location had been considered so eminently safe it was not thought necessary to evacuate Providence along with the other hospitals. For the fire had been imagined as moving forward in a predictable path. Instead it behaved irrationally. It flipped clear across town, set the east end ablaze and pointed its flames due east up Mullan

Canyon. It spread up Bank Street, consuming shacks, rooming houses and stores. It leaped across the Eighth Street bridge to set the two OR&N depots afire—a new one, recently built, an old one still standing, used as warehouse space. It spread south of Bank to the large Coeur d'Alene Hardware warehouse at Ninth and Hotel.

With fire blazing on both sides of the main thoroughfare of Bank, the Burke Canyon addition was virtually cut off from the main part of Wallace.

At Providence Hospital Father Francis Bonara frantically called the NP depot begging for a relief train to evacuate the twenty-five patients, fifteen sisters and ten nurses and attendants. The resident physician, Dr. F. Leo Quigley, not trusting the NP's harried half promise, phoned livery stables one after another, demanding conveyances. All their equipment was out, he learned, but Sutherlands, realizing the plight of people ill and immobile, promised to round up some rigs and send help.

Sister Anthony, sister superior of Providence, was visiting St. Patrick's hospital in Missoula. Father Bonara placed a call to her. "Wallace is on fire," he shouted into the phone. "The wind is this way and flames are headed toward the hospital. We're trying to get a relief train—livery stable rigs—anything we can. I thought you should know we are having to abandon the hospital."

All Sister Anthony could do was assent to this emergency measure. Hanging up the phone in Missoula, she was very much upset. She crossed herself and prayed silently for the safety of those at the hospital. Then she added a prayer that the hospital facilities themselves might escape destruction. "Spare it, Dear Lord, the place where our work of mercy is done, and in thanksgiving for granting this favor, Dear Lord, we will erect in a prominent place a statue of the Sacred Heart of Jesus."

In Wallace the chances did not look good. Before any conveyances could arrive from Sutherlands, an ambulatory patient who had been out viewing the situation ran in to say the Bank Street Bridge had caught fire.

Now they were cut off by road. Their only hope was the railroad.

A segment of NP track ran into the Burke Canyon mouth forming a Y. There, in front of the Federal Mine mill stood an engine and caboose. Throwing professional dignity to the howling spark-filled wind, Dr. Quigley ran down and grabbed the conductor by the arm. "We've got to get the patients away from the hospital! Can you bring your train up?"

Conductor George W. Brown, known to fellow trainmen as "Kid" Brown, lived on Canyon Avenue across the flat from Providence Hospital and next door to his brakeman, Mike Nicholson. Both men had been away from home all week with a work train in Saltese. That evening, hearing that Wallace was in danger and unable to get an answer from the NP dispatcher, they decided to make a caboose hop over Lookout Pass to check on Brown's wife and small child and Mike's teenage son, Jimmy, who had been left alone while Mrs. Nicholson and Mike's daughters were away visiting in Nevada.

As the men rode into Wallace they saw Jimmy come running down to the Canyon Street crossing; for he knew his dad's engine whistle and this was his favorite way of welcoming him home. Slowing to pick him up, they continued on down toward the NP depot to check in and take on water and coal. But fire had already invaded Wallace: the south hill flaring, the east end buildings ablaze. Ahead all was confusion and the track barred by a car with a wheel derailed.

The flames were traveling rapidly toward Canyon Avenue, Brown saw as the caboose train backed up the main track and onto the Y. He sent Jimmy dashing off to tell Mrs. Brown to hurry down to his engine—to warn neighbors they had better come, too. He would run them out to safety on his train.

Brown had not yet happened to think about the hospital but when the doctor came pounding up with his frantic appeal, he immediately understood its peril. "Of course, Doctor, I'll do anything I can. But I don't have room on here for so many people. Maybe I'd better run down to the yard and hook onto a boxcar or two." The ball-up, fortunately, was farther down the line.

"Yes, but for God's sake, hurry!"

But Brown, as he neared the yard, discovered that the OR&N depots were now on fire and nearby, also ablaze, were the boxcars he had meant to annex. There was nothing to do but run ahead again.

At the Canyon Street crossing he stopped to gather up Mrs. Brown and some of their neighbors: Mrs. Graffenberger and her several children; Mrs. M. Rule and her black-eyed twin granddaughters, Doris and Dorothy Baldwin, eleven years old; Mrs. J. C.Anderson and Fred Anderson, wife and son of an NP engineer; Mr. and Mrs. O. W. Bass, Lizzie Schilling and Mr. and Mrs. E. C. Young.

He then ran ahead to the hospital, where sisters and nurses were helping patients out to the track. Some, ill and confused, tried to pull back and return to the hospital building. Several wept despairingly. One man hobbled out on crutches. Nurses came forth carrying two small babies. The pale mothers were brought out on stretchers, as was one post-operative case.

The caboose became overcrowded and full of confusion. Mrs Graffenberger had trouble rounding up her children. Mrs. Rule cried out in distress, "Mercy sakes, I've left my purse—forgot my money!" And little Sister Joseph Antioch, smote suddenly by remembrance of three county patients housed in the basement, scuttled out to make sure they weren't being left behind.

Nurses, sisters and attendants who were able bodied climbed aboard the coal tender. Dr. Quigley had decided to remain at the hospital but Father Bonara came forth carrying the Holy Sacrament, which it was his duty to protect, and scrambling atop the water tank, he settled down clutching the Sacred Host to his chest.

By the time all were loaded there were nearly a hundred people on board. The caboose was so full that Brakeman Mike Nicholson had to stand on the bottom step of the caboose with his hands on the grab-irons to hold the passengers in. Just ahead of him an old lady kept saying, "But I have no money to pay my fare." Mike boomed, "Lady, the last thing we're worried about on this trip is fare."

By now the buildings of the Coeur d'Alene Iron Works, at the edge of Burke flat, were burning. Nearby stood a big oil storage tank, which if it should suddenly explode, would spew fiery hell in all directions.

The way west was thus impassibly barred and Conductor Brown had no choice: he would have to take his freight of human beings east along the branchline toward Missoula, even though wind-whipped fire was moving into Mullan Canyon.

Having no running orders, the little train set out with whistle blowing frantically.

In the caboose distress and confusion mounted. Mrs. Graffenberger had counted off four of her small children but was missing Willie, age seven. Everyone searched for Willie, even on the coal tender and aboard the engine, but he was not to be found. "He was right beside me," cried the distracted mother. "How could he just disappear?"

The Baldwin twins, Mrs. Rule's dark-haired granddaughters, were discovered weeping in a corner. "Grandma got off to get her purse. She didn't come back."

The nuns also became upset to discover that Sister Joseph Antioch had failed to return to the train before it started. One sister cried, "Tell the conductor to stop, and I'll walk back and find her." But Sister Elizabeth, who was in charge, shook her head. "No, that would not be wise. We will pray to God to take care of Sister Joseph."

The train sped east between the burning hills.

17

Sister Joseph Antioch was only twenty-two years old and very tiny—in fact, less than five feet tall. A tender young French-Canadian novitiate lately arrived from the mother house in Montreal, she was a stranger in a land where even the language was foreign. As yet her English was rudimentary.

By the time she ran back in from the train the hospital lights had gone out but candles had been left burning in the vestibule. She snatched one up and hurried down the stairs and into the patients' room. "Oh, a most good thing I have come back," she thought, "for there they are, all forgotten, still in their beds, poor old things."

To the men she called, "Quick. Get up! We must all leave! Fire."

To her amazement they did not move but merely stared at her with utter lack of comprehension.

Suddenly she realized that in her excitement her English had deserted her and she was babbling to them in French.

Running to the window she lifted the curtain and pointed outside. Flames could be seen leaping and dancing above the Iron Works buildings on the flat below. Those flames were far more eloquent than any words, French or English. The men sprang from their beds.

Outside she heard the train whistle sharply.

"Oh, hurry, hurry!" she moaned as she helped them into their bathrobes.

Dr. Quigley, candle in hand, put his head into the room apparently making rounds to be sure that everyone was out of the building. "Oh, you're taking charge of these patients, Sister," he said. "Good!" He was gone again.

Sister Joseph herded the patients up the stairs ahead of her and out the front hospital entrance. There her eyes grew large and wild. Where the engine and caboose had stood the track was empty. The train had gone!

Her knees buckled and she sank down on the steps. All had been rescued but her! The other sisters, the nurses, Father Bonara—all had gone on the train. Only she had been left behind. She alone in this new and frightening land, flames all around, responsible for these three patients whose language she did not even speak. Oh, she was of no use and they would all be burned alive.

She dissolved into weak tears.

Then her faith came crowding in. No, no, she was not alone. God was still here. He would take care of her, show her what to do. Squaring her small shoulders she led the patients back into the building.

In the hall she saw Dr. Quigley with a nurse, Miss Royal, at his side. She was astonished for she thought everyone had left on the train.

"What are you doing still here?" shouted the doctor.

She was still unable to summon any English but conveyed by gestures that the train had left them behind.

"Well, we'll have to get you out of here somehow." The doctor pushed her and the patients out the back door. Behind the hospital, Eugene Rohr, the gardener, was bringing the horses from the barn. "Rohr's going to drive the team and wagon away from here to save them. I'll see if he knows some safe place to take you."

Presently the bewildered sister was helped up on the wagon seat beside Rohr. Two of the patients got in behind. The third patient, Dan Darrow, younger and spryer than the others, elected to remain with Dr. Quigley.

Rohr drove off up Burke Canyon.

The little sister began to cry again. "Where are you taking us?" she asked.

The gardener said kindly, "Where there is no fire. To a lady who speaks French."

18

In the early evening hours, as the outlook worsened in the lower reaches of Burke Canyon, Emma Pulaski paced the floor. Her turmoil was not so much over the threat to her own safety and that of Elsie; mostly her tortured thoughts were for her husband, and the other fire fighters who might be trapped, and for the whole mountain region in its travail.

Having lived with Forest Service talk so long, knowing the fantastic dryness of this peculiar summer, she understood far better than those around her what a hurricane like this meant—one which shook the house to its foundation and seemed about to tear the roof off.

This was the possibility the forest rangers had not even dared to think of. For no fire could be kept in check against wind like this. All the guarded blazes would go out of control, would unite and tear remorselessly through those seas of green.

Hurricane-driven fires would run like greased lightning, would strike with the force of battering rams, would jump impossible miles, sear anyone and anything in their path. They would play what tricks they pleased, burn where least expected, skip over what they wished. Those wild-running fires would respect no boundaries and no barriers, and if they gave any man quarter, it would be through sheer caprice.

Could Ed possibly come through such a night alive? And what of all the other husbands and fathers, sons and brothers in the fire fighting crews? She heard Ed's voice, "Oh, I can save myself—unless the whole shebang blows up and there's no place to go." This, she knew, was the whole shebang blowing up. Would there be any place of refuge for him and his men?

When little Elsie knelt to say her nightly prayers, the mother added, "And ask God to bring Daddy and all the other men home safe." For perhaps the Almighty would listen more compassionately to the words of a little child than to the prayers which were rising from her own heart.

The tension was giving her another of her headaches. After Elsie was tucked in, she went to lie on her own bed. Presently a knock roused her. A neighbor came in excitedly. "Pack your things and get ready to leave with us. We're all going to the tailing dam for safety."

Out the window she could see people already trundling loads of furniture and other possessions up the road toward the dam. But as yet no flames could be discerned which threatened the smoky canyon. She shook her head. "No, I'm not going to run away unless the fire actually comes."

It came. A half hour later she saw the flames leaping

along a ridge behind Wallace. Fire zigzagged up and down the slopes like streaks of lightning and flashed across the mouth of Burke Canyon.

Hell opened with all its terrors. Too numb to feel much of anything, she wrapped the sleeping Elsie in a blanket and carrying the child in her arms, headed for the tailing dam.

*   *   *

At the same hour in Murray, Mrs. Corbeill and others met the incoming stage, suitcases in hand, ready to flee from the Prichard Creek canyon. The driver shook his head. "You may as well forget it," he said. "Wallace is burning and there's fire up and down all the canyons. There's no place to go."

19

After the girl operators left Wallace, District Plant Chief W. E. Samuelson and a helper, Jack Leonard, took over the switch-board at Rocky Mountain Bell. Calling in to Missoula to report to District Supervisor McKenzie, Samuelson heard McKenzie respond with a hearty "Good! I'm glad you're keeping service going!"

"Well, we'll stick as long as we can," Samuelson said dubiously.

"What do you mean?" demanded McKenzie. "How near is the fire?"

"Wait a minute. I'll have Jack take a look."

A pause. "He says it's half a block."

"Traveling which way?"

"This way."

The line went dead.

Leonard was right. At first the fire had moved due east, but later the wind had subsided a bit giving it more scope for action in other directions. Now the flames were back-tracking toward Seventh and spreading toward the south hill as well.

The base of the hill jogged back along here, giving room for two very short streets, Hotel and Residence, paralleling Bank. The fire, crossing to the south side of Bank, sparked the Pacific Hotel, which was a frame rooming house, then ate through the block to Hotel and on to Residence.

Residence, true to its name, consisted of rows of small houses. Directly above it, carved in the hill, were two more streets with scattered houses, Maple and Pearl, which were reached either by tiers of steps or by a steep, switchback road. The fire climbed the hill, touched off houses on Maple and Pearl one by one. Some owners had long since fled but others stood by doing what they could to save their property. James J. Boyd, a retired railroad man, refused to leave until his house was actually flaming. At the last moment he rushed back in to save the family parrot.

On Hotel Street towered one of the town's sustaining businesses, the Sunset Brewery, in a four-story brick building. In front of it on a railroad siding stood two boxcars of malt, two of sugar and two of grits. These were ignited, and as they burned set fire to the loading platform.

Herman Wickard, a baker, ran in to rescue a dog named Maggie from the brewery engine room. As flames licked inside to gut the building, Maggie was all that was saved. Fully two thousand barrels of beer burned. To the guzzlers on the fire department and among the volunteers it was the saddest sight of the night. The precious golden beverage ran out of the brewery in a great river and flooded the nearby streets. Fire fighters waded to their knees in beer foam.

At Seventh and Bank, H. E. Worstell was sticking to his first opinion. The town as a whole was in no danger of burning, he maintained, and he felt nothing but scorn for those he saw scuttling to the trains. Yet his own worst personal fear had been realized. The Worstell establishment was on fire. So far the fire was confined to the old store and a stout fire-wall stood between it and the new. If only the fire crews would pour some water at this spot they could easily save the brick building. But Fire Chief

Kelly was deploying his men and hoses elsewhere. Wild with helplessness, H. E., Bruce and Lawrence Worstell gathered in the street and watched to see if the fire-wall could withstand the heat.

On three of the four corners at Seventh and Bank the buildings were of brick or masonry—Worstells on the northeast, the Shoshone County Courthouse on the southeast and the narrow *Idaho Press* building next door to the larger Coeur d'Alene Hardware Store on the southwest. Also, at Seventh and Cedar the seven-story Hotel Samuels was a brick building. This made Seventh the logical place to try to stop the fire. The weak spot in the defense lay between Worstell's and the river, north on Seventh. The Wallace Cigar Company, the two-story St. Elmo rooming house and its shacky annex buildings— these were wooden structures. Where Seventh intersected Cedar Street and dead-ended on the river bank, the fire station, also a flimsy wooden building, spanned the street end and adjoined a row of wooden buildings down the north side of Cedar.

As the fire chief conceived it, the crucial things was to stop the fire's progress through this section of wooden buildings and keep the fire from spreading down Cedar, and it was here he decided to make his stand. For if Cedar went, then the business district would go and with it the whole town.

At this hour, when things were the hottest, the McLeod brothers returned to town. On reaching Markwell's Milk Ranch, two miles out, Harry had stated flatly that was as far as he was playing horse to any postal cart. The brothers secured Markwell's permission to store the trunks in an outbuilding, and they hurried back to Wallace to find their house intact but Harry's beloved hillside slashed by fire and still flaming upward. The rival *Times* had burned, and fire played across the street from Harry's own place of employment. The fire chief was pouring water on the fire station—a strategy that later made him the target of some good-natured ribbing.

Edwin Kribs, having settled his charges in Kellogg,

hopped a locomotive back to Wallace. On the same engine was Jack Soulders, who had left his family with Kellogg friends; Bob Strachan and Bud Morley who had found places for Bud's wife and three children and widowed sister-in-law and child.

Also on the engine was one woman, Gertrude Lent, chief operator in Kellogg for Rocky Mountain Bell. She had phoned Samuelson to say, "Could I be of help up there?"

"You sure could," he boomed. "You could take over in here. We got plenty of work on the outside. If things get too hot we'll see you get out."

So while other women were fleeing, Miss Lent rode into Wallace and took over the switchboard. The lines to the west were buzzing, but those toward the east were down.

In fact, *all* communications were cut off east of Ninth and Bank; road, railroad, telephone, telegraph. No one knew what had happened in the Burke addition, which had been isolated since 9:30. What had happened to the patients at Providence Hospital? Had they perished? What about the others living in that area? Concern was so great that Mayor Hanson organized a party to try to climb around the fire by way of the north hill above the tracks and to reach the hospital if humanly possible.

As for Wallace proper, everything east of Seventh had burned by 11 p. m. except the Court House and Worstell's brick building, and not even these were safe. The heat from other burning buildings ignited the wooden window frames of the Court House. Only the quick work of County Commissioners John Murphy and B. R. Adams in chopping the burning frames away with an ax kept the county building from being gutted. In the rooms of the Hotel Samuels soldiers stood ready with buckets of water to douse window frames there. At Worstells, though the fire-wall still stood, flames had licked over and heat was buckling the roof of the new store.

At midnight Mayor Hanson declared martial law.

Midnight, too, brought another problem. For earlier as

pressure in the fire hoses fell, the water coming through became choked with ashes and cinders. The water supply was brought by flume from a little dam up Placer Creek, and it was feared that dead birds and animals might have fallen into the reservoir or flume. Mayor Hanson declared the water supply contaminated and advised the men to drink beer.

But Wallace had Sunday closing, which meant that at midnight the saloons would have to shut up shop and lock their beer away. To forestall this the mayor issued an order temporarily rescinding the Sunday closing law.

When thirsty fire fighters reported the taverns were closing anyhow, Walter Hanson walked over to the nearest one, the Wallace Bar. "Don't you understand you are to be allowed to stay open?" he demanded of Simons the proprietor. "The water's no longer fit to drink and we're going to need all the beer there is in town."

Simons hesitated, then burst out, "But Sheriff Moffatt came by—*he* says we've got to close."

The mayor pulled himself up to his full height. "But I've declared martial law and I say you can stay open, I don't intend to be responsible for people dying of typhoid. I order you to stay open and if Jack Moffatt wants to make something of it, just send him to me."

The saloons of Wallace stayed open, and to the eternal credit of beer and whiskey not one man contracted typhoid.

20

Mullan, seven miles east, was but half the size of Wallace, with a population of 1700, and was not held in so tight an embrace of mountains. It sat against the hillsides where Finn Gulch opened into the Mullan Canyon. Along the Coeur d'Alene River South Fork, which flowed past, a small uneven valley opened out, stretching nearly a mile to the east.

The town had a couple of major streets running east and west with the valley, a few cross streets, a mass of unpretentious one-story frame buildings out of which rose a small number of two- and three-story brick buildings. There were eleven saloons. The town had no mayor but functioned through a citizens' committee.

Mullan's chief pride was its volunteer fire department, a venerable institution formed in 1895. A fire bell, bought in 1905, hung on a ten-foot scaffolding in the vacant lot by McCrae's barn. It summoned men to fight town fires, called townspeople to church and rang the curfew at night.

A hose cart was an even newer acquisition. To fires near the station it could be pulled by hand but to those farther away it was hauled by whichever man got there first with his team—to earn the coveted fee of $2.00.

Out of the low, muggy smoke screen pressing down on Mullan that Saturday afternoon came hurtling burning branches, and smoldering pieces of bark. The fire bell rang constantly and the hose cart was on the go. Home owners helped by getting out their garden hoses to wet down houses and yards and put out fallen embers.

As the wind increased toward evening, news came that Wallace was doomed, and with the gale whipping out-of-control fire east up the canyon, prospects for Mullan were not good, either. The citizens' committee ordered all able-bodied males to the defense of the town.

Like many others in Mullan the Harvey S. Taft family lived in a house perched on a hill above the business district. Before going down to join the fire fighters, Taft hastily dug a pit in his garden and told his wife to start packing their valuables.

As she gathered up extra clothing, pictures, china, silver and keepsakes, Mrs. Taft paused now and then to make a worried trip to her front porch. From that vantage point she ordinarily had an excellent view of the canyons and ridges toward Wallace. But today the mountains were veiled in heavy smoke, through which she searched for signs of flames. Seeing no actual fire she went back to her work somewhat reassured.

As 9 o'clock approached and she made one more anxious scanning trip she saw it: red naked fire tongues lick-

ing through the haze over a ridge behind Wallace. She
stood rooted in fear and fascination, until she heard her
husband run in calling, "Get the children ready while I
throw the boxes in the pit and bury them. There's a
relief train on the way up from Wallace and you and the
children had better go out on it."

They dashed away from the house a short time later so
sure they were leaving it to the flames they did not even
bother to lock the door.

Downtown they found all in confusion. Residents of
Finn Gulch, fearful of being trapped in its narrow confines, were streaming into the main business section,
staggering under armloads of possessions or pulling trunks
along by ropes. Other people rushed to and fro, some with
seeming purpose, others in frenzied indecision.

At the station they learned that Wallace was now afire
and one fleeing train had arrived, overburdened with
nuns, fathers and hospital patients. The engineer had
added a couple of boxcars to give more room; and the
conductor, after reshuffling his load, had taken aboard as
many Mullan women and children as he could find space
for; then the little train had started on east again. Members of the citizens' committee patrolled the station platform with guns and brickbats to make sure no men left
town.

Another train was expected and more people came
flocking in. As they waited they milled about and talked
excitedly. But what arrived was not the train but the fire.
It appeared out of the dark canyon and ran across the
south hills like an agile, loud red monkey, climbing one
tall green tree only to jump to the next, and the next,
until it topped the ridge. Streams of flames shot out over
the town and struck somewhere in Finn Gulch, then
leaped back across the river into the green forests and ran
away east along the railroad track.

Now there was forest fire on every side: west toward
Wallace, south toward the St. Joe ridge, north up Finn
Gulch, and east along the branch line. This gave rise to
the quandary: Was it safer to stay or to go? Might it not

be as well to take a chance on the town as to take a chance on a train?

Eastward to Lookout Pass the country was wild and steep, and the NP branch line, making its way to the summit on the Montana line, looped about in switchbacks and took fourteen miles to travel a distance that was only about 7 miles in a straight line. At one point the tracks crossed the famous S bridge—a great structure 140 feet high and 840 feet long, bending from one hillside to the other in a 14-degree reverse S curve to take advantage of the terrain on both sides of the canyon. This and fourteen other trestles were all of wooden construction and the right-of-way was but a narrow defile between solid lines of timber. If fire should close in, there would be no place to flee. A rumor ran through the crowd that one trainload of people from Wallace had already been trapped and burned.

A good many people decided to throw their lot in with the town and left the depot. The Tafts, among others, remained an hour longer until the station agent announced that fire had crossed the railroad yards in Wallace and no trains could get through.

Harvey Taft led his family back up town and found a room for them at a hotel, then went out to join the fire crews. Having put the children to bed, Mrs. Taft sat numbly by the window that looked out on Earle Street and watched the burning hills.

21

On the Idaho-Montana line, Lookout Pass, 4727 feet in elevation, divides the Coeur d'Alene River drainage from the St. Regis River drainage. The east slope, though still all ridges and canyons, is not quite so rugged, and the NP track as it descends makes its biggest switchback in the vicinity of Borax siding. It then passes through Taft, Saltese, Haugan and DeBorgia, joining the main line at St. Regis. In 1910 all these towns lay within the borders of the Lolo National Forest.

With the coming of the fire emergency, Supervisor

Elers Koch of the Lolo placed Assistant Ranger Frank
D. Haun in charge of fire control in the west end, with
headquarters at Saltese. Among other things, Haun put
Ranger Roy A. Phillips to patrolling the NP track from
Saltese to Lookout Pass.

At first Phillips legged the twelve miles to the Pass and
legged them back again, one round trip a day. Later he
was supplied with a railroad velocipede, which greatly increased his efficiency. He could then make three round
trips a day and still have time for an occasional patrol
trip up the Milwaukee line for a different view of the
country.

Hardly a day passed but Phillips spotted some telltale
smoke column. Many were railroad-caused fires and he
had authority to call out section gangs, extra gangs and
railroad tank-cars from all over the division, which gave
him a highly mobile and effective fighting force. While
he was on patrol he handled thirty-five fires and kept all
under ten acres, an excellent personal record.

In connection with the August 10 flare-up, a fire
broke out on Bullion Creek west of Borax siding. As this
was across the Idaho line in the Coeur d'Alene National
Forest, Phillips kept reporting it to Supervisor Weigle,
but Weigle was swamped with so many new fires he was
unable to take action at once.

When the fire burned on toward the Montana line,
Phillips got twenty-five men from Missoula and dispatched them in from the Montana side under John S.
Baird, District One lumberman. Shortly afterward Weigle
sent a crew of sixty under the foremanship of S. M. Taylor, a woodsman and prospector from Wallace. Taylor
began to cut fire lines along the west side of the blaze
while Baird worked along the south side.

When the fire continued to make headway toward the
Lolo, Ranger J. E. Breen of the Taft Ranger Station was
placed in overall command and given 150 more fire fighters. Roy Phillips was taken off patrol to help Breen boss
this large crew, which was sent in from Borax to the north
and east sides of the blaze along the Montana border.

About August 15 the Bullion fire crews were augmented by a company of Negro infantrymen under Lieutenant Titus, who set up camp not far away from Breen and Phillips on the same burn.

By August 19 Phillips felt the northeast sector to be relatively safe and set out to ride clear around the fire on a tour of inspection. He found the fire lines completed except for a couple of miles on the west. A wind was blowing, pushing the fire down on Baird's south lines but these seemed to be holding. The fire was in pretty good shape, Phillips felt.

August 20 was mostly a routine day for the Bullion fire crews. Phillips and his men were having trouble holding a piece of fire line on a rocky, precipitous slope and in the end had to cut a new and safer line lower down. In the afternoon they saw a big black cloud forming in the west. "Maybe it'll rain," they said hopefully.

Darkness fell before they got the new line ready to leave for the night. As there was little danger during the hours of high humidity Phillips did not leave night patrols out. With all his men he set out for camp in a darkness so smoky and impenetrable that without lanterns or lights of any kind they had trouble finding their way. When one man stumbled off the path it took much shouting through brush and trees to set him straight.

About 9:30 when they were within 100 yards of camp Phillips was astounded to see a great brand fall out of the dark sky and crash not far away. "Now where in the hell did that come from?" he asked in wonder. The fire they had left had no such force.

He was too weary to figure it out. He sent a couple of men to locate the brand and put it out, then ate his supper and fell into bed.

Around midnight he felt a rude hand on his shoulder and opened his eyes to find the camp cook standing over his saying excitedly, "Hey, wake up and listen to that!"

He listened and heard over on the NP branch line a train whistling and whistling as it descended the switchback.

"What do you make of that?" demanded the cook. For trains never whistled along here where there were no crossings and no towns.

"It must be a warning of some kind," Phillips hazarded as he climbed out of bed. Then on reaching his tent door he saw in the sky a great red glow—a glow that had not been there when he went to bed.

"That's what it is all right—a warning! The engineer is trying to wake everybody along the track. The whole St. Joe ridge is on fire!"

The camp itself, situated as it was on an old burn, would be safe enough, Phillips decided. But over on the Borax siding was piled a whole stack of camp provisions, unloaded from a boxcar that day. They certainly couldn't afford to lose these supplies if fire should sweep Borax.

On Ranger Breen's shoulders was the responsibility for the whole ranger district and he had gone into Taft for the night. This left Phillips in charge. He awakened several of his most trusted men and with them set out for Borax, a couple of miles away. They quickly buried the supplies and were ready to start back when a railroad speeder came putting in with Ranger Breen aboard.

"I've just had a warning call from Haun in Saltese," he announced. "All the fires in the Coeur d'Alene are out of control. The winds are hurricane force and coming this way. Wallace is already burning and Mullan surrounded. My orders from Haun are to keep the crews where they are if they're safe, or if they're not to move them out. But he thinks we can hold out here on the burn."

Breen joined Phillips and his men and all started back for camp. By now the flames were coming over the crest of the ridge and trees were hissing, popping, exploding and falling. On the Borax bridge they met a group of their own men tearing out of the woods in a panic. A good half of the crew was there, with Lieutenant Titus and his soldiers not far behind.

"We're heading for the Borax tunnel!" cried a foreman, leader of the group. "It's the only place we've got a Chinaman's chance to save our lives."

"Well, you can stop right here," said Breen in a commanding voice. "I can tell you there's a big draft through that tunnel in the best weather. Any fire that comes will be pulled through there just like through a chimney. If you want to get roasted quick that's a good place to do it."

The men began to look uncertain but kept glancing in terror at the fire-fury behind them on the ridge. "But where can we go?" they cried.

"Camp is the safest place," said Phillips. "The old burn's not liable to burn again. Besides, we've got plenty of men to run a quick line around it and backfire from there."

The men were willing to listen to the rangers and agreed to return to make a stand on the burn—all except the foreman and one follower. But when these two saw they were being left alone, they too turned and accompanied the others back to camp.

On the west side of the Bullion fire, S. M. Taylor and his crew went innocently to bed that night sleeping in the open. Around 1:30 a. m. a big burning ember sailed down, struck the blankets of a sleeping man and seared his leg. The yell he let out woke Taylor and the crew. It woke them only just in time, for they discovered a wave of fire rolling up Bullion Creek toward them with the speed and roar of an express train.

One of the men, Larry Ryson, had worked at the Bullion Mine nearby, and Taylor, himself a prospector, knew where the mine entrance lay. "Run like hell, boys!" he called. "I think we can just make it to the tunnel." They all dashed wildly up the hill and reached the tunnel mouth just ahead of the fire.

Most of the men found room at the rear of the tunnel but a few crowded into smaller drifts along the way. Edward Everett Hale found himself in one such drift and discovering that one fire fighter had snatched up his blankets as he ran, Hale organized the men into shifts of fifteen minutes apiece to hold the blankets to the drift entrance to filter out smoke. Even so, fumes leaked in so thickly acrid they all gasped, coughed and felt near suffocation. Men prayed and moaned. Others gathered around the light of a candle stub to write their dying messages.

It was to his old mother in Birmingham, England, that Hale's thoughts turned.

"In Bullion Mine, August 21, 1910, 2:05 a. m. Mother dearest: This is my last. I am in charge of fifteen men in a drift. We are trying to hold out the smoke but chances are slim for us all. Forgive me if I have ever mistreated you, for I do love you. Goodbye. Ed."

Later he lay down on the drift floor hoping the air was less poisonous there, or if not, determined to take his last smoke-filled breath quietly and slip away without fuss.

22

West out of Missoula, Montana, the Chicago, Milwaukee, St. Paul and Pacific Railroad parallels the Northern Pacific main line to St. Regis, then shares company with the N P branch line along the St. Regis River as far as Taft. There the two sets of tracks part company, the branch line continuing northeast to Mullan and Wallace, the Milwaukee Road turning sharply south toward the St. Joe valley.

To gain the upper reaches of the St. Joe drainage, the railroad must first attain the Bitter Root Divide. Upward from Taft the tracks rise steeply, cutting back and forth across the mountain face, clinging to toeholds cut in cliffs, plunging through tunnels, crossing trestles over yawning gorges. At 4200 feet the railroad gains the summit at St. Paul's Pass, runs through a two-mile tunnell (known locally as Taft Tunnel) and emerges into Idaho.

Down the Idaho side of the Bitter Roots the line twists and turns along the St. Joe North Fork and its tributaries, making one lengthy looping switchback, passing through myriad tunnels and across sixteen bridges. By the time it meets the main stream of the St. Joe River at Avery, twenty-five miles from the summit, it has dropped 2000 feet in elevation.

On westward it travels the whole length of the beautiful St. Joe valley before it takes off across the wheatlands for Spokane.

The timber of the St. Joe drainage, famous for stands of Idaho white pine, is so extensive it is today included within boundaries of its own, those of the St. Joe National Forest, with a million and a half acres. In 1910, however, this vast area was but a stepsister district within the Coeur d'Alene National Forest.

So undeveloped was the whole region of St. Joe swiftwater that for the sixty miles from the Bitter Root Divide to the boom town of St. Joe City the most magnificent virgin forests were penetrated only by the thin line of the Milwaukee Road—the Milwaukee so newly built it had opened to rail traffic only the year before, in 1909, and had not yet completed all fill and bridge construction work. In that sixty miles Avery with a population of two or three hundred was the largest town, the other railroad stops having but a handful of people.

Between Avery and St. Joe City homesteaders had come in to take up white pine timber claims on Marble Creek, Trout Creek, Prince Creek, Big Creek, Slate Creek and other streams accessible by hand-poled boat, or, more recently, by railroad. Even in these creekside canyons there were no settlement centers, no roads, very few trails. Back from the railroad hundreds of square miles lay unsurveyed, uncharted, trackless — a maze of mountainsides so precipitous a ship's ladder would be needed to climb them. The big or main fork of the St. Joe flowed for fifty miles through unbroken wilderness before it approached the railroad line at Avery.

Avery had been hacked from the forest when the site was selected as railroad division point on the western edge of the Bitter Roots and a roundhouse and a few other minor railroad installations built there. At its feet lay St. Joe swiftwater, at its back climbed a steeply timbered mountain. Along its main and only street were located the railroad commissary, beanery and bunkhouses, while back on a knoll stood Pearson's false-fronted, white-painted store, "Dry Goods—Groceries—Hardware." Most of the railroad workers lived west of main street near the roundhouse in what was called Shacktown, at the mouth of Hoghead Gulch.

No saloons were allowed within the national forest, and the one honkeytonk was the Forty-Nine Dance Hall on the east edge of town, where liquor was sold on the sly.

Also on the east edge of town stood the Avery Ranger Station, headquarters for District Ranger Ralph N. Debitt. He together with Ranger Kottkey of the Falcon station on the St. Joe North Fork was responsible for fire control through all this tremendous forest wilderness. And fire was all over hell's half acre—up toward the St. Joe Mountain divide, at several spots on the North Fork, south in the St. Joe headwaters, and God knows how many other places as yet unreported. So many fires had been set by locomotives along the Milwaukee right-of-way that the railroad company had been forced to hire men to walk the track as fire spotters.

The situation was wildly impossible. Debitt had crews on Big Creek and also only six miles west of Avery on Setzer Creek. Kottkey had men near Falcon and on Bird Creek, while Supervisor Weigle had sent Ranger Joe Halm into the St. Joe headwaters.

The Setzer Creek fire was threatening Avery iself, and Debitt was grateful to see the arrival of two companies of Negro infantrymen from Fort George Wright, who under command of Lieutenant E. E. Lewis set up camp near the Forty-Nine Dance Hall.

On August 20 Avery became rife with news and rumor borne in by railroad crews and railroad telegraph. A wind had sprung up and fire was coming out of the Benewah Lake country, topping a ridge and threatening the town of St. Maries, eighteen miles downstream from St. Joe City. At St. Joe City fires were racing along the hills. Flames were pointed upstream toward Avery.

Between 4 and 5 o'clock the winds hit Avery and the

Setzer Creek fire began to perform like an Apache dancer. Two fire fighting crews of seventy-five men each were working in that vicinity. One crew was guarding the far side of the fire, with its camp set up on Storm Creek, the next stream west. This crew had been supervised by Debitt himself, who, on going into Avery on other business, left it in charge of Foreman James Shehee. The second crew, with Foreman William II. Rock in charge, was holding the line on the east ridge north along the creek.

When the wind struck, Debitt realized the danger of a fire trap and dispatched Deputy Sheriff Charles Sullivan at a gallop to warn the two foremen to get their crews into town as fast as they could.

By the time Sullivan reached the Storm Creek camp blazes had already jumped the fire lines in several places. Most of the men were much relieved when Shehee ordered them to take off for the safety of railroad and town.

Among the crew, however, was one disgruntled group composed mostly of Butte copper miners and tough Butte skidroad characters. A number were raw recruits who had arrived by train from Missoula in the middle of the previous night. All they knew about timber and fire fighting was that after a night of little sleep and a day of grueling heat and smoke they didn't care for any part of it. Ready to settle down in camp to nurse their grievances and blisters they received Shehee's orders with sullen displeasure.

Pat Grogan, big Butte miner and leader of the group, swore roundly and said, "Them scaredy-cat rangers are always getting their wind up about something. I can't see no danger here and I don't feel like no six-mile hike this time o'day." He together with twenty-seven others who shared his sentiments refused to budge.

As the main part of the crew set out for Avery around 6:30 the rear contingent glanced behind and to their horror saw the blaze tearing through green timber and heading directly toward the Storm Creek camp.

In Avery Debitt was busy burying records at the ranger station and preparing to evacuate the town. He requested a relief train from the Milwaukee and while it was being made up sent Lieutenant Lewis's infantrymen knocking on people's doors, telling them to throw their belongings together and be ready at the depot in forty minutes. Trestles would undoubtedly burn, the station agent warned, and it might be days before any train could get back in. In that event the food situation would be critical and Debitt instructed the soldiers to round *everyone* up to go—yes, even the Setzer Creek fire fighters as they straggled into town.

At the depot the townspeople were hysterical and soldiers had to be stationed at the doors of coaches to keep order and load women and children first. All men, with a few exceptions, were herded on board, too, and the train pulled out west, destination Tekoa in the wheatlands.

Smoke rolled in as thick as though night had fallen and the roar of the approaching fire seemed to shake the hills. Debitt advised the lieutenant to try to get the troops out of its path, and the army officer commandeered a Milwaukee work train, loaded the infantrymen aboard and ordered it away west.

A handful of Milwaukee employees still remained and as the train passed the roundhouse it whistled for the men to hurry on board to save themselves. But the Milwaukee crew, led by Roundhouse Foreman Ralph W. Anderson, Hostler Charlie Swanson and Blacksmith Helper Tom Huff, elected to stay and try to save the railroad installations.

Telegrapher Delmar and another man crossed the river to put the torch to the south slope, while Anderson and helpers set blazes along Hoghead Gulch. Away roared these backfires to meet the oncoming charge.

23

Earlier that afternoon, as the day turned to premature night, Engineer Johnnie McKedon, with Lew Bradway as his fireman, left Avery on a helper engine to pull Train No. 264 to the top of the Divide.

All along, fires burned not far from the track, flames crackling but invisible through the smoke shroud, out of which howling winds were flinging ashes, cinders and bark. Never had the grind to the top of the mountain seemed so long as through that stifling, choking, furiously churning murk.

At Taft Tunnel, when they reached it at last, the helper was cut off and McKedon and Bradway started back for Avery. At Falcon, halfway point on the return trip, "Ma" Van Antwerp, the telegrapher, was famous for her cherry pies and the men stopped at her shack for a bite to eat. The talk was of nothing but the fire which was boiling all around the isolated little railway station.

"It looks bad to me," McKedon warned. "I'd advise all of you to pile on my engine and get out of here while the getting is good."

"But the telegraph is needed more than ever in an emergency like this," Ma protested. "And along the cleared right-of-way here we ought to be safe enough. What worries me are those folks down at Grand Forks."

Grand Forks was a notorious little settlement a mile away at the base of two intersecting canyons—a resort for gamblers, wild women and other nefarious camp followers who had flocked in during construction of the Taft Tunnel.

"From what I hear," Bradway commented, "that hell-hole down there is so hot that no mere flames could sear it."

Ma was too worried to be amused. She called in her two relief telegraphers, Bea Flynn and Zelda Pearl, and after a conference they announced, no, they guessed they would stick it out. It wasn't fair to the Milwaukee to desert their posts in time of need.

McKedon and Bradway climbed back aboard their engine and started on down the smoke-draped tracks. Five miles away at Kyle, Old Man Martin flagged them down. His daughter Maud, the Kyle telegrapher, ran out calling up to McKedon excitedly, "Ma Van Antwerp has sent out an SOS. Grand Forks has already burned. The people have run up out of the timber to Falcon. Now the fire's all around Falcon and she thinks the depot is going next. She asks for you to come back and get them out."

McKedon stopped only to hook onto a boxcar on the Kyle siding, then began to back up the grade toward Falcon.

*   *   *

The news that the slopes of the Bitter Root Divide had sprung into a mass of galloping flames was telegraphed to C. H. Marshall, superintendent of the Milwaukee railroad division between Deer Lodge and Avery. He immediately dispatched the work trains in that area to the rescue of those along the track. "Don't pass anyone whoever it is," said he, "and put every living soul on board whether they want to go or not."

The division's chief carpenter, C. R. Lanning, was in Taft that day making a personal check on fill and construction work, and he stepped aboard the work train which made a mercy run up the east slope to Taft Tunnel. On the way they picked up section workers, construction workers, trackside dwellers, and all the people at the Bates & Rogers construction camp not far from the east portal. With nearly 400 people on board they made a dash for the big bore at the summit.

In the long tunnel everyone was safe enough. But what about people living and working on the west side of the slope? Conductor Harry V. Vandercook and Engineer Blondell volunteered to take the engine and a couple of cars down to rescue as many as they could. "Okay," said Lanning, "we'll make a try for it."

Descending the west slope with the shortened train was like entering a furnace. Flames leaped across the track, trees burst into torches, toppled and crashed, their flare tops putting the torch to the next trees.

Yet the risk was worth it. They found railroad men and homesteaders gathered along the track so paralyzed by fear some had to be lifted on board. A group of Hungarian track workers cried and prayed, clutching their bedrolls, and seeing help arrive, tumbled on board in such panic they jostled others rudely aside.

They picked people up at Roland and Adair and with forty-seven refugees aboard started back up the hill. But they saw the would never make it all the way back to the Taft Tunnel and ran into a shorter tunnel for protection.

Carpenter Lanning was still worried about the people living at Falcon and Kyle, and he, Engineer Blondell and Conductor Vandercook unhooked the engine and rode it back down the mountainside. But by now bridges were burning and they found the way ahead blocked. They tried to back up the slope only to discover that behind them another bridge had burst into flames. Blondell threw the throttle wide open, and the three men lay down on the deck to protect themselves from the heat. The engine was wreathed in flames as it sped over, the men expecting each moment to be their last on earth. But the bridge held and they plunged to safety in a short-bore tunnel beyond.

Meanwhile, Engineer McKedon, backing up the slope toward Falcon was not at all sure he would make it. Wind had toppled trees across the track which he had to push aside with his pilot, and twice he stopped to throw water on burning bridge timbers.

All Falcon seemed on fire—but, no, the depot still stood, its platform teeming with section workers and their families, the motley band from Grand Forks and the women telegraphers. They jumped quickly on board and McKedon gunned ahead out of Falcon.

Fire ringed Kyle now, too. Maud Martin, her father and several younger stair-step Martins waited with bundles of belongings, ready to pile on board.

McKedon's next worry was the trestle between Kyle and Stetson, but at last his headlight, boring feebly through the smoke, picked it up still standing and not yet on fire. He whistled triumphantly into Stetson and stopped to rescue the section crew. The engine and boxcar were by now so crowded that some men had to climb atop the locomotive tank and some cling to the running boards.

The overloaded little train whistled into Avery at 2 a.m.

24

At 6 a. m. that Sunday morning Hannah Beswick awakened in her Spokane hotel room to hear a raspy voice shouting loudly in the streets below, "EXTRA! EXTRA! WALLACE BURNS!" She jumped from her bed in such alarm she awakened Zoe too.

"EXTRA! EXTRA!" repeated the raspy voice. "ALL IDAHO GOING UP IN SMOKE. MONTANA TOWN BURNS TOO!"

Zoe started to cry. "Oh, Mama, what'll become of Mr. and Mrs. Ellars. And Daddy, too."

"Now, Zoe, don't get all upset," her mother said sharply. "Newspapers get out extras to sell papers. They always make the headlines as frightening as they can. That doesn't mean all Wallace is burning. It probably means a few houses caught on fire. I'll go down and get a paper and find out."

As she walked from the elevator she was amazed to find the lobby in a state of utter confusion. Wild-eyed people in various states of distress and disarray occupied all chairs and sofas while others sat on suitcases or oddly wrapped bundles of belongings.

"It's the truth all right," the clerk assured her. "Wallace has burned. People have been streaming in from there all night. Everybody crying and families separated, and nobody knowing what's happened to those left behind." He managed a faint smile. "Why, I had one lad, about seven years old, name of Willie, who came marching in all by himself. 'Wallace is too hot for me,' said he and asked for a room."

"Did he get one?" asked Mrs. Beswick, her human curiosity temporarily surmounting her anxiety.

"A lady who is a neighbor recognized the boy and took charge of him. His name is Graffenburg or something like that. Nobody knows what became of his family."

Kitchen brigade of Joe Halm's camp on Timber Creek, at the headwaters of the St. Joe River.

FIRE FIGHTERS
AT BREAKFAST
AVERY IDAHO

Breakfast-time for fire fighters in camp near Avery, Idaho.

Scenic home of the old St. Joe Ranger Station before it was razed by the 1910 holocaust.

Tents temporarily replaced the Station after the fire.

Charred entrance to the War Eagle tunnel where Ranger Ed Pulaski and forty men took refuge when trapped by the great Bitter Root Range fire, August 20, 1910. Five men died of smoke suffocation in the tunnel.

The Pulaski family and friends at Sunset Peak Ranger Station. Left to right, rear row: Ranger Ed Pulaski, Emma Pulaski, Elsie Pulaski, and Elsie's friend, Gladys Noxon. In front are Mr. and Mrs. Straw.

Emma Pulaski stands at the burned-out mouth of the mine tunnel on Placer Creek where her husband, Ranger Ed Pulaski, nearly lost his life fighting the rampaging forest fire.

The newsboy with his racous cry of "EXTRA" came into the hotel lobby and Mrs. Beswick grabbed a paper from him. Bold black headlines leaped out at her:

WALLACE IS SCORCHED BY FOREST FIRE LOSS $500,000

High Winds Send Burning Embers on Idaho Cities and Blaze Sweeps Many Blocks

HUNDREDS FLEE FOR LIFE

Immense Area in Coeur d'Alenes a Seething Mass of Flames—Fire Spreading and Vast Amounts of Property Doomed to Destruction

"I told the Ellars they should come with us!" she exclaimed as she read. "What has happened to them? And what, oh God, has happened at the Gold Chrome mine?"

* * *

Not only in Spokane was the plight of Wallace the big headline story that morning. In Seattle and Portland the *Post-Intelligencer* and the *Oregonian* got out extras. By wireless the news flashed to every part of the country, and in New York City over their Sunday morning coffee cups readers of the *Times* learned that "Forest Fires Set Wallace Ablaze—Populace of Idaho Town, To Which Flames Advance All Day, Flee in Terror—Trains a Refuge for 600."

Even in England the burning of the forests of the American northwest proved a story of spectacular interest.

From Washington, D. C., President Taft sent word to Idaho's Governor James H. Brady that additional troops would be made available for fire fighting and that Army Chief-of-Staff General Wood would give aid in every possible way.

In Boise, the state capital of Idaho, Governor Brady on Saturday had sent emergency orders for Idaho's state militia to return from war maneuvers at American Lake in Washington State; and on Sunday morning the Governor made public announcement that he stood "ready and willing to do anything within my power as chief executive or personally to alleviate the sufferings and protect life and property in the stricken district." He sent a personal representative to Wallace, with a promise that he would later try to visit the area himself.

Relief campaigns got underway, with Spokane's Mayor N. S. Pratt appealing for bedding, clothing and money to aid those made destitute by the fire. Elks clubs as far away as New Orleans subscribed funds to send to Wallace victims.

25

While the outside world wakened to news of the calamity in the Bitter Roots that Sunday morning, in the silver mining town of Wallace, hub of the disaster, no one had been to bed.

All night long Fire Chief Kelly's crew had poured water on the buildings along Seventh Street. All night long the volunteer brigades had put out other fires as brands rained down from the hills. All night long Negro infantrymen had patrolled the streets to forestall any looting of empty houses. All night long James Gyde and others had superintended backfires touched off along the west hill back of Wallace Hospital.

As daylight came on these different groups began to realize their efforts had paid off. The fire chief's strategy had been sound. The St. Elmo Hotel and its annex buildings had burned but the fire station had been saved, and this had stopped the flames from spreading on down Cedar Street. The Seventh Street line had held and only one-third of the city had burned.

East of Seventh all that stood were the brick walls of the new OR&N depot, the gutted brewery building, the windowless Court House, the tall brick chimney of the St. Elmo, a brick foundation, and the new Worstell building. A portion of the Worstell roof had burned causing much smoke and water damage inside the store.

In the east end almost everything that was combustible had already been consumed. The fire was burning itself out and danger to the rest of the town seemed past.

From the Burke Canyon addition came good news. The relief party sent out in the night had broken through to discover the Providence Hospital evacuated and happily still standing. To some it seemed miraculous. Dr. Quigley and Nurse Louise Royal had remained on the roof for hours, each with a hose in hand, while on the ground level the patient Dan Darrow had handled a third hose. When the hospital water supply gave out, the enterprising trio was able to manipulate the Federal Mine mill fire equipment, draw water from the mill flume and continue the fight till the danger was over. They saved not only the hospital and its outbuildings but also the nearby Anderson Lumber Yard. Doctor, patient and plucky nurse were heroes and heroine of the hour.

The hospital had been safely evacuated, but what of those patients, nuns and townspeople who had climbed aboard "Kid" Brown's engine and caboose? Were they still alive? With all wires down along the branch line it was impossible to learn of the train's progress and safety, and wires to Missoula via Spokane elicited the alarming news that the train had not been heard from on that end. The fire as it ripped on up Mullan Canyon, consuming the S bridge and other bridges, could easily have trapped and burned the little caboose train. Were all aboard the train dead?

Mrs. Rule, on discovering herself left behind by the train, had decided to try to save her little house, and she turned to with garden hose and wet sacks. When the multitude of sparks seemed to be getting beyond her, a man she did not know appeared and helped her, and when the danger had passed disappeared without telling her his name. In the morning her daughter, Mrs. Baldwin, returned from her camp cook job to learn her small twin daughters were on the missing train. Grandmother

Rule and Mrs. Baldwin could only pace the floor and hope the girls were not dead.

Meantime searchers among the east end ruins discovered the body of James Boyd near his burned house, apparently overcome by smoke in attempting to rescue the family parrot. And in the smoldering remains of the Coeur d'Alene rooming house another body was found, as yet unidentified.

26

Out of the gutted Placer Canyon that Sunday morning stumbled first one man and then another.

The first appeared about dawn. Hair wild, hat gone, skin blistered by heat and blackened by soot, he was scarcely recognizable as Supervisor Weigle. He told how at his place of refuge near the mine entrance he had lain for hours beneath whipping sheets of flame, saved only by the breathable air filtered to him through dirt and gravel. When at last he dared rise and go seek his horse he found it burned to death. On foot he groped his way back to Wallace through smoky blackness lit only by fires eating at stacks of waste that yesterday had been the proud green forests of Placer Canyon.

The second man, who appeared later in the morning, was in even worse condition: clothes all but burned off, eyes glazed, voice a rasping wheeze. As he reached King Street he gasped out to the first patrolling soldiers he met, "Pulaski's crew—men dead—others bad off—need doctor."

The man was Frank Foltz, Pulaski's camp cook. He was taken to Mayor Hanson, who, after hearing his appeal for aid, hastened to organize a relief party. Weigle had been sent to Hope Hospital for attention and was in no condition to go out. Hanson rallied some of the town firemen and asked for a doctor to accompany them.

Both hospitals had been open for emergencies all night, Dr. Hanson and Dr. Max T. Smith standing by at the Hope, Dr. St. Jean and Dr. Mowrey at the Wallace, treating burn and smoke-poison cases as they came in. All the doctors were worn and weary, but Dr. Smith consented to join the relief party.

As they set out up Placer Canyon Dr. Smith carried his medical case, but the mayor took along his brother's prescription for treatment: a bottle of olive oil and a bottle of whiskey—whiskey donated by the Wallace Bar.

"The thing to do when you find the men," Dr. Leonard Hanson advised, "is to give them a stiff drink of olive oil followed by a stiff drink of whiskey, and get them back to town."

* * *

Around the tailing dam in Burke Canyon the flames began to die away about five in the morning. Like sleepwalkers Mrs. Pulaski and her neighbors rose and made their way down the canyon road. To their astonishment they found their homes still standing, though fire still smoldered all about.

Emma Pulaski was alone and in inner despair over her husband's chances of having lived through the night. Her neighbors, realizing her plight, took turns coming to sit with her. Late that morning she noticed how sad their faces had grown, how softly they tiptoed around the house. "They've heard bad news," she said to herself, but she could not bear to ask for fear they would tell her Ed was dead.

Requesting her neighbor friend to keep an eye on Elsie, Emma went to lie on her bed and try to make her mind blank of all thought. "Oh, Emma, look!" the neighbor cried.

She leaped from her bed to the window and saw, down the road, one burned tattered figure leading another burned, tattered figure toward the house.

"O my God, it's Ed," she gasped and went rushing from the room. As in a nightmare she reached the road and ran stumbling until she was near enough to see it was George Howard leading Ed home and that Ed was burned and ill and blind.

There in the middle of the road she reached her husband and clasped him in her arms crying, "Oh, but you're alive—you're alive!"

Later, sitting for days beside his bed in the hospital she heard from him the story of how he had rounded up his men and led them to the War Eagle tunnel and had guarded the entrance to keep the crew from racing out to death. Half crazed, the men had fought for places along the air-bearing trickle of water on the tunnel floor until one by one they had lost consciousness. Presently he too, had slumped down unconscious.

He had wakened, how many hours later he did not know, to find the air clearing and some of the men stirring. "Come on outside, boys," a voice said, "the boss is dead."

"Like hell he is." he answered, but when he tried to get up he found that flames and smoke had so seared his eyes that the world was dark to him, and his men had to lead him outside. All were desperate with thirst but they found the stream so choked by alkali ash as to make the water undrinkable. Rocks were still too hot to sit on.

Pulaski ordered the roll called, and six men failed to respond. Five of those missing were found dead of smoke suffocation in the tunnel, with one man unaccounted for. The horses were wheezing so badly that Pulaski ordered them shot.

All the men were burned and sick and parched, but everyone could at least hobble, even the old Texas ranger, Stockton. When dawn came they started for Wallace. Pulaski, fearing that the ones who were worst off would be unable to make it all the way, sent Frank Foltz, who was small and quick, on ahead to ask for help.

No trail nor track remained, and down Placer Canyon they crawled over smoldering stacks of logs on hands and knees. With shoes burned off, clothing in rags, skin blistered and smeared with ashes and mud, they looked more like scarecrows than men when they met Mayor Hanson, Dr. Smith and the rescue party. Nor could Pulaski's crew stomach anything offered them: not olive oil, nor whiskey, nor even the coffee brought to them by a party of women farther down the trail. As yet all they could swallow were tiny sips of water.

The crew was taken to Hope Hospital for first aid. Pulaski refused to remain there, insisting that he must go home to Burke Canyon to find out what had happened to his wife and child. After he learned they were unharmed he returned to the hospital to rest and recuperate. The doctors said his sight might come back; or, if not, he would have to learn to live without it.

27

On that same Sunday morning Dr. T. R. Mason was breakfasting leisurely in his home in Kellogg. Around 10 a. m. the phone rang and an excited voice said, "Some men have been burned and we need you up at the Constitution Mine at once."

The doctor felt a bit disgruntled to have his leisure interrupted but he knew a doctor's life is not his own. So he merely shrugged, phoned the livery stable and finished breakfast while his saddle horse was being brought around. Then without changing out of his patent leather shoes or his best Sunday suit of fawn-colored gabardine he set off for the Constitution, hoping to patch up the burned men quickly and return to his day of rest.

Instead, at the Constitution, which was on the east fork of Pine Creek, he found Shift Boss Pengally in a highly agitated state. "My God! do you know the whole damned St. Joe ridge burned last night! Swept everything before it. A guy named Krause just came in from Big Creek and says a whole crew got caught up there, some dead, others burned. They were under Ranger Bell—clear to hell and gone over the other side of the ridge. We've called you to go in with us, as the men are in a bad way."

It took Dr. Mason a moment to digest these facts. The men weren't here then, but somewhere out in the mountains, God knew where. His spirits sank into his patent leather shoes but as he had no real choice of action he merely said, "Okay, who's going in with me, then?"

"Well, we've called Dr. Knudson and he's on his way up from Kellogg, too. We've rounded up a posse of twenty-four miners, and Walter Johnson, shift boss at the Last Chance, is going to lead them in. The posse's to start out on foot, each miner carrying a blanket to wrap the sick and injured in. As soon as I can talk to the mine officials and get a pack string together, I'll send some grub in after you."

By noon the members of the posse, together with the two doctors, were tramping up toward Elsie Peak. At first there were rough trails and the going was fairly easy. Then they reached the burned area and the trip became an ordeal such as Dr. Mason could never forget. What only yesterday had been tall, thick, pungent green forests now lay as blackened piles of crisscrossed logs, still smoking—piles 20 feet high in places, over which they climbed, crawled and sprawled as best they could. Once Dr. Knudson lost his footing and fell between the logs, and by the time they got him out they had to beat the fire from his clothing. The ground, too, still smoldered and the men constantly stepped into burned potholes and hot foottraps. Shoes charred and feet became sore and blistered.

By late afternoon they were traveling high in the Coeur d'Alene Big Creek drainage. As night came on smoke hung so murkily no ray of starlight penetrated and their way between the charred tree trunks and by and over the piled refuse heaps was a truly Stygian journey. Their only guide was the tiny glow of what was called a Palouser: a lard can with a candle struck through the hole in the bottom, the tin acting as a reflector for the small gleam of light.

Arriving at a seemingly impassable barrier of heaped logs they halted till daylight. Then in the weird smoky light of dawn they climbed a long hogback and passed over the hump into the St. Joe Big Creek drainage.

Some of the men were so tired they had lagged and the posse was now strung out. Not far behind the indefatigable Walter Johnson, Mason struggled along still carrying his doctor's grip, which had become heavier and heavier with each passing mile. His beautiful fawn-colored suit hung in sooty ribbons and the remnants of his handsome shoes barely clung to his feet. He discovered he was staggering and collapsed on a nearby log.

Johnson doubled back to see what the trouble was.

"I don't know if I'm going to make it any farther," the doctor confessed dubiously.

"What you need is food," said Johnson. "I know where there's a logging camp and unless it's been clear burned out maybe I can rustle up something. You just sit and rest." Dr. Mason remembered then he had not eaten since his breakfast at home yesterday morning.

In half an hour Johnson returned with sandwiches and a pail of hot coffee. In Dr. Mason's whole life food and coffee had never been such a Godsend. He was enormously revived and able to go on. With Johnson, too, had come a logging boss who had agreed to guide them the rest of the way. It proved not far to a place of blackened ruin the logging boss called Beauchamp's clearing. There, huddled in the lee of a big stump were Ranger John Bell and what remained of his crew.

28

Not waiting for Dr. Knudson and the rear contingent of the posse to arrive, Dr. Mason began treating burns and congested lungs. "There's twenty-eight of us come through," said the ranger. "Ten dead. Seven or eight badly burned or pretty sick."

The men passed before him: Ranger Bell with bad burns on face and neck, wheezing and coughing from chest congestion; Tom Farlet with burns and bronchitis; Peter Schmidt, little finger burned away, burns on face, lungs badly congested; Fred Owen, burned face and seared lungs; John Lassig, burns on face and an injured eye; Walter Ingersoll, burns and congestion and a broken leg; John Graham, burns and bronchitis; Joe de Marco, burns and near pneumonia; and the rest of the crew with lesser burns, bruises and wheezing.

Applying salve and gauze, administering medicines, the

doctor listened to the tales of their terrible experience. They had lain in the shallow creek, submerged as far as possible, splashing water over the exposed parts of their bodies and clothes. Even those who could find a fairly deep spot had to keep their faces above the surface and when the great trees around the clearing caught they could feel the heat searing and blistering faces and necks. At the height of the fury the suction-like draft toppled one huge tree across the creek. As it fell it pinned down "Smitty" Smith and his friends Elliott and Cameron. The first two died almost immediately, but Cameron lived two hours in utmost agony.

And as the timber on the hillside above Joe Beauchamp's tunnel burned, flaming logs rolled down across the tunnel mouth. Inside were the homesteaders Beauchamp and Ames, the two Italian workers Bruno and Vittione, the Austrian Tony Butcher, the tramp Chris Omiso, and C. Buck. From the creek the men heard the dying screams of the seven as they roasted to death inside the blocked tunnel.

Beside the creek the men started to panic but Walter Ingersoll threatened them with his gun, ordering them to stay down in the water. Then the gun became so hot he had to toss it away and get into the water himself.

After two hours the worst was over. Heat and flames subsided so they dared climb out on the bank. No longer was there any cabin or any clearing—only a charred waste of canyon. Weakened and in shock, the men stood shivering, bitterly cold in their wet clothes. Bell dispatched H. D. Krause, who had come through the ordeal better than the others, off to summon help. The rest of the crew, using the big stump as a windbreak, dug themselves beds in the warm ashes.

By now the remainder of the posse had come in. While Dr. Knudson assisted Dr. Mason, the posse members undertook the gruesome task of removing bodies from under the tree trunk and from the tunnel. Identifying the bodies in the tunnel was difficult, as the heat had been so intense that tobacco cans, razors and coins in the pockets

of the dead men had melted and the metal had fused together.

Posse members dug a long shallow pit as a common
grave for the ten victims. Foreman Johnson asked Dr.
Mason if he could say a few appropriate words at the mass
burial. The doctor shook his head. "I can patch up their
bodies but I'm afraid I can't do anything for their souls."

It was Dr. Knudson who rose to the occasion. The
sermon he preached there in the wrecked and desolate
canyon over the bodies of the men who had met such a
terrible end was the most moving Dr. Mason and members of the posse had ever heard.

Even yet the ground retained heat absorbed from the
fire's blast. When all patients were treated Dr. Mason
dug himself a bed in the warm ashes, burrowed down
and snatched a few hours of much-needed sleep. When he
woke the pack train had come in with the grub.

29

It was Tuesday before Dr. Mason got back to Kellogg.
That was the day the posse and pack train came out from
Big Creek by way of Placer Canyon to Wallace. The trip
out was less arduous since they were better equipped
and also made contact with a party sent up to meet them.

This second party had left Wallace on Monday for the
War Eagle tunnel. The men had located what was left of
the missing member of Pulaski's crew—a body found not
far away on the hillside where the man had apparently
lost his way or tripped and fallen and so failed to gain the
tunnel. They wrapped the grilled remains in a blanket,
also identified and wrapped the five bodies in the tunnel
and sent them to Wallace by pack train.

The rescue party then cut trail up the canyon toward
the St. Joe divide. Twelve miles from Wallace they met
the Johnson posse coming out and helped in getting Bell
and his crew to town. Some of the men were in such bad
condition they had to be tied on the mules. Only when the
sick and injured had all been put into hospital beds in

Wallace was weary, begrimed Dr. Mason free to head for home—never to retrieve his lost, leisurely Sunday.

The Wallace hospitals became so filled with fire injury cases that an emergency call went to Spokane for extra nurses. And through these crowded wards pretty Mary de Marco searched, weeping as she went. "But Joe is my only brother—he can't be dead." Happily, when the Bell crew was brought in from Big Creek she found brother Joe de Marco among them, burned and ill, but still alive.

Other fire fighters out of Wallace had close calls—like George Burden, whose head was split open by a flying branch—but no other lives were lost.

Many mules and pack horses were burned and supply-train operations brought to a halt. Hundreds of men, routed from their camps, poured into Wallace, headquarters of the Coeur d'Alene National Forest, expecting to draw their pay and head back where they came from. But all was temporary disorganization. Timekeeper's records had been burned, buried, or simply not made up and turned in during the emergency. What was more, most of Weigle's headquarter's force who should have dealt with the problem were on rescue missions.

Mayor Hanson arranged for a special relief headquarters to be set up to deal with the influx of homeless, temporarily moneyless men. A cookshack-type eating place was established in a vacant store and the men bedded down at night in the courthouse—even in the jury room.

One fellow when asked what he did for a living said, "I'm a fire fighter by vocation, a booze fighter by avocation." Their vocation gone, many were heartily pursuing their avocation in the local bars. One drunk visited the Forest Service office and demanded his money in such abusive language that Weigle threw him down the stairs. Additional deputy sheriffs had to be hired to keep order.

Presently rangers and foremen came in from the hills, timekeepers' records were dug up or written up, red tape run through and the men paid off. The town's floating population thinned.

30

Mullan, that Sunday morning when Wallace was discovering itself out of danger, was not so lucky. In Mullan
the fire which had jumped into Finn Gulch was burning
back over the ridge and coming down on the town from
the north.

To backfire was the only hope McGinnis put the
match to the hill behind the church while others set similar fires along the grade on Chloride Hill all the way to
the Midnight Mine property and the Morning Mine mill,
and as far as the Lucky Friday mine. Soon the whole
north slope was ablaze.

Every man was needed in the battle for the town. Yet
some had to be spared to form a rescue squad. At dawn
Sunday morning Jim Danielson, the young foreman in
charge of the Stevens Peak crew, came dragging himself
into town badly burned and obviously injured. His men
had been trapped about 9 p. m. Saturday night with fire
raging toward them from all sides. They had taken refuge
on a mountain meadow after first burning off the bear
grass and other vegetation. Here they should have been
safe, but the onrush of flames created heat so intense the
humus soil caught and spotty fire rolled over the meadow
a second time. They protected themeselves as best they
could beneath their blankets but all had been badly
burned about the face and hands, and one man, Walter
Beaman, had inhaled a fatal dose of smoke.

The rescue detail, dispatched with pack train to the St.
Joe ridge, returned in early forenoon. Frantic as Mullan
people were fighting for their homes and businesses and
all they possessed, they never forgot the sight of that pa-
thetic crew as it came into town. The pack animals carried
two men who could not walk, and also the body of the
dead man. The other fifteen walked single file holding
their burned arms in the air.

The men were taken to the office of Dr. James R. Bean,
above Dr. Key's Drug Store. After giving the men first
aid, Dr. Bean bedded them down on cots brought over

from the William Coumerihl Furniture Store. A couple of railroad bridges damaged by fire between Wallace and Mullan were hastily repaired, and at 2 p.m. a train arrived from Wallace to transport the injured Danielson crew to the hospital.

In the Rocky Mountain Bell office in Mullan, Ruby Watkins, the manager, and her two switchboard girls, Olevia Parker and Helen Clubb, remained on duty all night and all day, with hardly time to eat the food brought to them by Helen's mother, Maggie Clubb. They were warned they might have to leave the building at any moment and hurry to nearby Mill Creek for safety. But it was important to keep the switchboard open, not only to report new fire but to keep people from panic. One woman kept calling in, and when one of the girls answered she would say, "Just wanted to be sure you were still there."

Some Mullan people had fled. The train which took the Danielson crew also evacuated townspeople. A second relief train left at 7 p.m. and a third arrived and filled up. But as night came on humidity increased sharply and reduced fire danger to zero. Anti-climatically, people climbed off the train and went back home.

The Harvey Taft family, returning to their house that night, found it just as they had left it. One neighbor, however, discovered unexpected damage. On exhuming her belongings, she found her beautiful stemware broken, her precious china chipped and cracked. In her excitement she had tossed the dishes and glasses into the pit recklessly by the apronload.

No house or place of business in the town of Mullan was burned. All that was lost were the buildings of the Midnight Mine and a miners' tent town nearby, together with some prospectors' cabins built in the timber fringes on the north and south slopes.

Mullan, raking up the cinders and ashes, counted itself fortunate after all.

Murray and Burke had come through, too, without

serious loss, partly through luck, partly through the night-long and day-long battles of their defending forces.

31

On the other side of Lookout Pass in the St. Regis River valley the little towns of Taft, Saltese, Haugan Junction and DeBorgia also fought hard for their lives that Sunday. Each was but a small clump of false-fronted shacky buildings along the railroad track, none of them with more than two or three hundred people.

A couple of years before, during the building of the Taft Tunnel, Taft had been a riproaring construction town with a population of several thousand. Now, even though most of its glory and its construction workers had departed, it was still rough, tough, and tall-timbered. With fire headed toward it from Lookout Pass Saturday night, it seemed doomed, and all women and children were evacuated on the Wallace refugee train which came in about midnight.

In the light of early morning, flames climbed into the surrounding tree tops. By then Ranger Breen had returned to town, having left his Borax crew making a stand on the burn. Determined to save Taft and with it the ranger station and a large supply of Forest Service lumber piled nearby, he hastily organized a fire brigade, calling into service all who could grasp a shovel, wield a gunnysack or throw a pail of water. This was not so many as it should have been. All night long the saloon habitues had been busy trying to drink up the town liquor supply before it should burn. By the time the fire actually arrived, a number were too tipsy to help.

The town of Taft burned—everything except the Taft Hotel, another small building, and a part of the Forest Service lumber. One drunken man, too disorganized to flee a flaming house, was badly burned before he could be rescued. Ranger Breen put the injured man on his speeder, took a couple of the man's lumberjack friends along as attendants, and hurried him to Saltese to the doctor.

Saltese in 1910 was a small boom town with both the

Buffalo and Monitor mines running full blast. Mike Linn, who ran a hotel in Missoula, also owned a hotel in Saltese and on the critical Saturday of August 20 was in town on business. With him were his two teenage children, Harry and Anna, and their cousin, Jennie Linn of Wallace, daughter of Mike's brother Ole and his wife Anna. Jennie's was an exchange visit, for meantime Mike's wife, Tillie, was staying with the Ole Linns in Wallace.

The three teen-agers were having such a royal time together, were so busy with pranks, talk and silliness they paid little attention to the gathering tension among the adults around them. That night they were asleep in the hotel when Mike Linn pounded on their doors, shouting "Get up and get dressed—it looks as if the town is going to burn." When they tumbled sleepy-eyed into the lobby, he told them he had decided to send them to Missoula for safety. He gave them each some money and told them to hurry down to the depot and report to his friend, the station agent, who would put them aboard a train. When they got to Missoula, Harry and Anna were to take Jennie with them to the Linn home and stay quietly until their parents arrived. Mike was going to remain in Saltese to try to save the hotel.

Being out alone after midnight with money in their pockets, and down along the railroad tracks where they were usually forbidden to go, was a superb adventure to the children. They reported to the station agent but found the train wasn't in yet. So they went next door to the Small Brothers' Restaurant, ordered sandwiches and pie, giggled and cut up. It was a great lark. When the train pulled into the station, the agent had to come after them. He hustled them aboard a box car. Harry and Anna, who thought they knew everyone in Saltese, were fascinated by a group of women gathered in one corner, who wore long bright-colored gowns or flowered kimonas. Where had they come from? and if they were ready for bed, why did they have such heavy paint on their faces? It was quite a mystery.

Haugan Junction and DeBorgia were not yet thought

to be in danger. The relief train went on through without taking any more passengers.

But around 4 a. m. Ranger Frank Haun of Saltese got a message through to Town Constable Joe Mayo in DeBorgia. The fire was traveling fast and the situation serious. He better think about evacuating the town. Also would Mayo send warnings out to the fire crews on Big Creek, the tributary to the St. Regis River which flowed in from the south in that area?

The DeBorgia constable, after first sending an SOS to the NP for a relief train, borrowed a bicycle and peddled out to Billy McGee's ranch. He asked McGee if he would ride to Big Creek to spread the warning. Mc-Gee consented provided Mayo would help him catch his saddle horse. The pasture was so shrouded by smoke it took the two men an hour to locate and rope the horse. As dawn broke, McGee rode off toward Big Creek, and Mayo returned to DeBorgia.

Later that Sunday morning, Ranger Hays, who had come from the Gallatin National Forest to boss one of the Big Creek crews, received McGee's warning. He led his men to Saltese, where he arrived at noon to find the town still threatened but unburned, with Rangers Haun and Breen and Deputy Sheriff Ed Hill leading the fight to save it. Hays and his crew pitched in to help.

A work train whistled in from Missoula with a big supply of buckets and a section crew meant for the relief of Wallace. With bridges burned in Lookout Pass, the train could not get through, and Deputy Sheriff Hill ordered the section crew to the defense of Saltese. Led by some toughs who had boarded the train as refugees, they refused. Hill arrested one gun-flourishing leader. The work train crew, defying Hill and the rangers, took the train back down the track to return to Missoula.

The Saltese doctor dressed the burns of the injured man whom Breen had brought down from Taft. Wrapped in absorbent cotton, the patient was then placed in a boxcar as the safest place in case the town should burn. One of his lumberjack friends, who had been helping to dispose of the Saltese liquor supply, decided to look in to see how he was doing. As the boxcar was dark he struck a match. In his unsteady condition he lurched and ignited the dressings of the injured man, who with a shriek bolted the car and ran blazing and screaming down the tracks. Some fire fighters managed to throw him to the ground and beat out the fire but he died soon afterwards.

Anti-climactically the work train with its belligerent section crew came puffing back into town. Fire had jumped on ahead, burned out bridges and blocked their way. Now they had no choice: to save their own necks they would have to help save Saltese. They piled off the train.

A fire line was strung out and backfires set. In the evening hours on Sunday the timber fringing the town burned, with flames whipping out to try to ensnare town buildings. With plenty of men, plenty of ladders and plenty of buckets, water was poured on every roof and the fire forced around the town. Only a few outlying buildings were lost.

That same evening, as fire closed in around Haugan Junction people took refuge in a nearby pit, sharing space with deer, bear and other frantic wild creatures. A few hardy men remained in the hotel bar attempting to beat the fire to the whiskey . The hotelkeeper himself poured the drinks and led the gallant race.

In DeBorgia, the NP relief train ordered by Mayo arrived from Missoula. With it came Supervisor Elers Koch of the Lolo, who dropped off at DeBorgia while the train went on to Haugan Junction to rescue people there.

Koch at first attempted to rally the men of DeBorgia to set backfires, but when he saw it was too late for that, ordered everyone aboard the train when it returned. All obeyed except Al Whitman and a couple of families living on the outskirts of town. Whitman saved his own house, the Ed Albert house, and the new schoolhouse— three buildings standing in a row. The Thomas Hogan family saved their place, the first ranch west of town, by carrying belongings to a nearby creek and putting out fires which started around the house. The Mike Dewy place, east of town, escaped, too.

All the rest of DeBorgia burned—sixty-eight buildings in all. Haugan, too, was consumed to the ground.

As the train sped east, the Haugan hotelkeeper, now roaring drunk, waved one last whiskey bottle in a defiant gesture of farewell to the flames. But the fire was not to be outwitted so easily; it played tag with the refugees all along the track and followed them menacingly close to St. Regis.

32

Ranger Breen, helping out at Saltese that day, had become increasingly worried about his Borax crew. Receiving no word from that quarter by late afternoon, he took Ranger Haun's suggestion and got on his speeder to ride up and check on the men.

Above Taft the fire was still burning all along the right-of-way, shooting now and then across the tracks. Fearing ties might have been charred and rails would give way, he geared the speeder down as slow as possible. Just before reaching Borax he saw three shadowy figures loom out of the thick smoke. One was Roy Phillips. Breen brought the speeder to a quick stop, jumped down and grabbed Phillips' hand. "Am I glad to see you, Roy!

Phillips was scorched, ragged and obviously dog tired. I'd begun to think you fellows hadn't made it."

"No, we're all okay at the camp. But we had a close call, I can tell you that. When our backfire met the main fire— you never saw such a swoosh of flames! Came right down on the camp, smoke, fumes, cinders and burning pine needles. Everything swirling around so thick you couldn't see and everybody choking. But we'd wet everything down and when the air cleared nobody was badly burned and nothing on fire. But some were sick with smoke and others blinded. One fellow wanted to kill himself because he thought he'd never see again, but he's all right now."

"What about Titus and his men?"

"They worked right alongside us and they came

through fine, too. But I've got some other news that's not so good. That was what I was coming down to report. The timekeeper from Taylor's crew got through to us this afternoon to tell us eight men died up at the Bullion Mine. The whole crew ran for the mine when the fire came up the creek. Most of them went way back in the tunnel or into drifts along the way, and even back there the smoke got so thick some of the men wrote their last will and testament but they lived through. The eight who died were probably dropped by smoke before they could get far enough inside. Or else they stopped too close inside where an overhead air shaft sucked in smoke. Anyhow, when the others started coming out they found these eight dead by the entrance. The whole crew was smoke poisoned and the men have gone to Wallace for treatment. Taylor needs somebody to come up and help identify the bodies and bury the dead."

"Could you go, Roy?"

"That's what I thought I'd do. But decided I had best come down and report in first. Now you can carry the bad news back to Haun and he can wire Missoula."

The following morning Phillips took Lieutenant Titus and John Baird with him and hiked up to the Bullion Mine. He and his helpers identified the dead as Larry Ryson of Wallace, who had once worked in the mine; Val Nicholson and Leslie Zellers, both of Gem, a little mining hamlet up Burke Canyon; Aaron Benton of Wisconsin; Thomas Welch of Spokane; Louis Holmes of England; S. D. Adams and Ernest Elgin, parts unknown. Phillips' men blanket-wrapped the bodies and placed them side by side in a shallow trench.

33

In Spokane the morning of August 22 the front page of the *Spokesman-Review* spilled over with great black headlines:

WALLACE FIRE LOSS $1,000,000

50 Dead, 180 Missing in St. Joe Area

WESTERN MONTANA FORESTS, WITH SMALL TOWNS VANISHING

AWFUL FIRES RAGE FROM BRITISH COLUMBIA TO OREGON LINE

THOUSANDS OF REFUGEES IN MISSOULA

Taft, Montana, Has Been Burned, Saltese Surrounded By Fire. DeBorgia and St. Regis are Seriously Threatened. Haugan, Montana, is Destroyed.

Solid Line of Fire From Thompson Falls, Montana, for 50 Miles to Idaho Line With Belknap, White Pine, Noxon and Heron Burning.

Mrs. Beswick took in these announcements of disaster with a sinking heart. The Ellars had fared all right. She had been able to get through to them by phone and had learned they had gone by team and wagon down near Markwell's Milk Ranch and had slept in the open all night. Back in Wallace they had discovered no damage to their house, but were still keeping a team hitched to a wagon because of danger from the backfires burning along the west hill not far above their house.

But she had been unable to reach DeBorgia, and her anxiety over her husband at the Gold Chrome Mine was acute. With a sea of flames engulfing all western Montana, with fire pouring from Lookout Pass all the way to St. Regis—how could the men at the mine possibly have escaped?

Even as she tried to shake off a gloomy sense of foreboding she turned a page and came upon a one-column headline:

MEN AT MONTANA MINE FEARED LOST

"DeBorgia, Montana, Aug. 21 (Special) —No word has

been received here from the Gold Chrome Mine. Fire is known to have swept the area. Manager Norton Beswick and a few men had remained at the mine to try to save the mine and mill buildings, and it is feared they may have lost their lives . . . "

Even as her knees sagged and despair ran through her she managed to cling to a wild hope. "Norton knows how to take care of himself! He could have found a way to escape. They don't *know* he's dead, and I won't believe it, I *just won't believe it*—not until I know for sure."

In Wallace Mrs. Mike Linn and the Ole Linns, Jennie's parents, were full of anxiety about Mike and the three children. With Taft lost, with Saltese surrounded and perhaps burned by now, anything could have happened. Or has Mike and the children managed to get away to Missoula? The Linns in Wallace tried wiring Montana by way of Spokane.

In Missoula, when the train had finally arrived, Harry and Anna had taken Jennie home with them as instructed. None of the three had got any sleep on the train but they were too keyed up to go to bed. With the big house to themselves they had a wild time chasing up and down stairs, laughing, shouting, banging on the piano and singing at the top of their voices.

They became so noisy a neighbor came over to see who was tearing the house down. With relish they told her how they had jumped out of bed in the middle of the night and ridden a boxcar away from Saltese.

"You crazy kids!" cried the neighbor. "Don't you know Wallace burned last night—maybe Saltese too by this time. Your parents are probably dead this minute and you carrying on like this. Shame on you!"

After that they were quiet and abashed—until a telegram came, a plea from their folks in Wallace to hear what had happened to them. A wire from Wallace must mean Jennie's parents and Harry's and Anna's mother were still alive. They cheered up and decided Mike Linn must be all right in Saltese, too. They began trying to phone Wallace but it was late that night before they got through, and then the hookup was by way of Chicago. "Yes, yes, we're all right," they shouted into the phone.

They never did confess to the adults what a good time they were having until the neighbor put the damper on.

In Wallace the good news spread that the refugee train had arrived safely in Missoula. Mrs. Rule and Mrs. Baldwin learned that the twins were all right and in good hands. Mr. Graffenberger located his family in Missoula and was able to tell his wife that little Willie, through some circumstance not yet understood, had turned up in Spokane.

The passengers had adventurous tales to tell. "Kid" Brown's overladen train had set out, its whistle blowing continuously, and a few miles east of Mullan, at Larson near the Snowstorm Mine, had stopped for water. As the fuel supply was nearly exhausted, Conductor Brown meant to stop next at Dorsey, where a coal supply was maintained for winter pass emergencies. But the fire was so close on their tail that he dared not pause, and the big S bridge flamed beneath them as they crossed. Jimmy Nicholson helped scrape up the last remnants of coal to heave into the firebox, and providentally it proved enough to carry them over the hump. On the downhill side of the pass they needed steam only for the air brakes.

Here and there they stopped to rouse homsteaders from their beds and bring them away with nothing on but a coat thrown over their night clothes. They stopped, too, to add boxcars and evacuate towns along the way. Reaching St. Regis at last, they waited for Conductor Ahart to bring up a passenger train from Missoula to take them the rest of the way. Mrs Ahart came along with the makings of sandwiches and coffee, which she passed out with Jimmy Nicholson's help. Ravenous Jimmy found there was not enough to go around and ended up hungry himself.

Amid all the confusion a woman gave birth to a baby. On arrival in Missoula she and the baby were hurried away to a hospital, as were the other invalids on board. The nuns, nurses and Father Bonara were welcomed at St.

Patrick's Hospital. Other refugees were taken in hand by a Missoula relief committee, women and children being sent into private homes, men given lodging and meal tickets. In a few days they began returning to Wallace by way of Spokane.

Already others had returned from Osburn, Kellogg and Spokane. Those who like the Kribs, Mrs. Mary Worstell and the Ellars lived in the main part of Wallace west of Seventh found their homes and apartments intact. On King Street there had been no damage at all and it was ironic that only those who had taken belongings to the other end of town had lost anything—some in the burning of the OR&N depot and Tom Nicholson in his cigar factory.

A sadder return awaited those who lived in the east end or at the entrance to Burke Canyon. Fifty homes had burned there—fifty families left with nothing but the clothes they wore and a few possessions they had carried away. The homes of Kid Brown and Mike Nicholson were reduced to charred timbers fallen about the foundation stones, and both families lived the following winter in railroad work cars.

As for Sister Joseph Antioch, the little lost nun, after spending a safe night with the French-speaking LeMieux family, she was put on a train for Spokane, met by nuns from Sacred Heart Hospital, and later united with her own Sisters of Charity when they returned from Missoula via Spokane.

Sister Anthony, with Sister Elizabeth at her side, was first to visit Wallace to inspect the hospital. She found it in perfect order—not even a shock of hay in the field burned or in disarray. Pausing to give thanks, she remembered her promise to erect a statue of honor to the Sacred Heart of Jesus, and she vowed, "It shall be done."

But though the hospital had come through with no straw disturbed, the fire loss in Wallace stood at a million dollars. Insurance company adjusters arrived and paid off claims in batches. Telephone and telegraph companies dispatched repair cars and repair crews. The NP sent special work trains and section crews. Wallace, beginning to repair and rebuild, was no longer news. The spotlight shifted to the St. Joe Valley.

34

The town of St. Maries, at the confluence of the St. Joe and St. Maries rivers, knew many hours of suspense the afternoon and evening of August 20, as fire out of the Benewah topped the nearest ridge. Barges were lined up end to end to form a bridge across the St. Joe River so that if the wooden waterfront buildings should be ignited, people could escape to the slough and meadow beyond, where there was nothing to burn and water to keep them cool. Frantic householders piled furniture and other belongings on the river bank, where the side-wheeler *Idaho* stood by.

The fire jumped over St. Maries. From peak to peak it went leaping to Mount Baldy and beyond, scattering flames all along the valley. At St. Joe City (or Ferrell, as the waterfront town at head of navigation was called), the propeller-driven *Colfax* waited with steam up, ready to take people down river. Backfires saved the town.

On Big Creek, where the Milwaukee Lumber Company had been building a railroad spur, the company lost its six construction camps, with camp crews barely escaping with their lives. The great reservoir of white pine timber the spur had been meant to tap was totally destroyed.

Homesteaders along Marble Creek, Trout Creek and other creeks which flowed through heavy white pine timber were wiped out—not only their cabins but the timber stands they had hoped to sell for big money.

Lovely mountain brooks became ugly, debris-filled, ash-choked streams. The ash made an alkaline solution so poisonous it killed fish until they floated belly-up by the thousands.

In Avery when the rolling crown fires and the backfires set by the Milwaukee employees met, the heat became so intense it drove Roundhouse Foreman Anderson and his helpers into the roundhouse pit for relief. When they dared reemerge hours later, they found the backfires had slammed the main fire back from the railroad installations and the town. All buildings still stood.

The work train carrying Lieutenant Lewis and his two companies of infantrymen backed into town. The way ahead had been blocked by burning bridges, but when they had tried to return they found the track behind barred by fallen trees. For hours they had shunted back and forth along a short piece of track, dodging reaching arms of flame. At last the fire had subsided and a crew of soldiers had cleared the rearward track. The return of the infantrymen to Avery was warmly welcomed, for among their number was an army surgeon with medical supplies for treating burn and smoke-congestion cases.

When dawn broke Ranger Debitt assembled a party to go to Setzer Creek to learn the fate of the men who had defied orders and remained in the Storm Creek camp. What the searchers found chilled the most callous among them.

Fire had torn up the gulch and through the camp, and from gruesome evidence left behind, only hard-headed old Pat Grogan, leader of the revolt, with a mongrel dog beside him, had stood his ground as the flames bore down. His body, a heap of charred flesh and bones, was the only one found at the camp site. His watch had stopped at 7:27.

All the others had tried to outspeed the flames and their bodies were scattered along the canyon for half a mile. In their last frenzy some had tried to climb the canyon wall and their heads were turned back in grotesque positions as though watching death overtake them. The body found farthest up the canyon yielded a watch stopped at 7:34. The man had gained seven minutes of life in his mad sprint before the fire.

Later that day, Lee Hollingshead, the young ranger boss of a crew of sixty on the west fork of St. Joe Big Creek, came in to report a story no less terrible.

On Saturday afternoon when the big blow hit he and his men had been working near the edge of a large burn.

He at once ordered every one to its center where he felt they would be safe enough. All obeyed except nineteen who panicked instead and tried to outrun the fire down the hill. In their path lay Hank Dittman's homestead clearing and cabin, and into the empty, one-room cabin they had dived for protection.Timber crowned around the clearing and the cabin roof caught. When flaming timbers began to fall through on them they were forced into the fiery walls of flames outside. One man seemed to have escaped. Eighteen bodies were found near the burned cabin, all seared beyond recognition.

On Saturday afternoon when Deputy Sheriff Sullivan had ridden out to give warning, he had discovered himself cut off from the William H. Rock crew, working north along Setzer Creek, and a great deal of anxiety about the crew had developed. So Debitt was much relieved to have Rock report in. He told how he and his men had been forced to take refuge on a flat, meadow-like area burned the previous day. He ordered everyone to lie flat and keep his blankets over him. As surrounding timber exploded with fire, columns of flame shot hundreds of feet in the air —a spectacle so terrifying that one man, Oscar Weigert, rose in a panic, rushed away from his fellows and shot himself with his own pistol. The other men remained where they were and came through all right.

Twenty-eight dead on Storm Creek; eighteen at Dittman's cabin; one with Rock. Forty-seven in all. HEAPS OF DEAD AT AVERY, read a *Chronicle* headline. And out of that heap only a few bodies could ever be identified. All the Forest Service had to go on was the men's names in the timekeepers' records and in most cases there was no way to match up names with bodies so badly burned.

Along the Milwaukee line, as refugees came out of the Taft Tunnel and shorter tunnels they found ties burned and rails buckled in heat so intense it had even consumed pick handles and other wooden tool handles thrown down by workers along the right-of-way far from other combustible material; and at the ends of bridges as water had boiled out of barrels, staves had charred as fast as the water level fell.

Chief Carpenter Lanning, emerging to survey the damage, discovered fourteen Milwaukee bridges, from 120 to 775 feet in length, destroyed between Avery and the Divide. Grand Forks had burned, as had the St. Joe Ranger Station near Falcon, and most buildings in Falcon and most in Kyle. At Adair, a car of oil and one of dynamite had exploded on the tracks, igniting a nearby construction camp and honkeytonk town.

And though backfires had saved some towns, the sad fact was that the backfires themselves had proved tremendously destructive forces. Combining with and augmenting the original savagely traveling fires, they had helped create a conflagration which had burned nearly every stick of timber in the whole St. Joe range. All the way from St. Joe City to Avery, on up the North Fork and clear to the Divide, the magnificent virgin white pine forests of Saturday—among the most valuable saw timber in the whole Pacific Northwest—were by Sunday reduced to a graveyard of blackened boles and blitzed rubble.

Through the endless miles of this ruin, search parties still sought missing men and missing crews. One by one they reported in, and on August 26, Debitt wired Weigle that Hank Kottkey and his men, feared trapped and burned, had been found safe on Bird Creek.

But south in the St. Joe headwaters, Joe Halm had not been heard from.

35

At Washington State College, Pullman, Joseph B. Halm had won Pacific Northwest fame as a football player. Graduating in the spring of 1909 he had accepted a job with the Forest Service to do boundary work in the Coeur d'Alene National Forest. Later he had to laugh at himself as the fraternity-type dude in silk shirt, straw hat and pinched-in shoes who reported to Ranger Pulaski, who was to show him the ropes. A few thousand mosquito bites and many heel blisters later, Joe had learned what a tree blaze was.

During the 1909 fire season Halm was put on his own patroling the NP branch line between Mullan and Lookout Pass, making frequent side trips to Stevens Peak to scan the country. In reporting the first fire he spotted from that high point he described it as "just over the ridge", instead it turned out to be in the Cabinet National Forest, twenty-five miles away.

But by 1910 Ranger Halm was an experienced hand in the thick of the desperate fight against the spreading fires. Late in July Weigle dispatched him on a difficult mission to the far south end of the Coeur d'Alene National Forest, where a blaze was burning in the mountains dividing the headwaters of the St. Joe and Clearwater Rivers.

The area was so remote Halm took his crew by train to Iron Mountain, Montana (within the Lolo near Superior), then followed the old Cedar Creek mining trail sixty-five miles into the wilderness over the Bitter Root Divide, to Chamberlain Meadows at the headwaters of the north fork of the Clearwater River.

After a fortnight of helping Ranger Friday cut lines along the south side of the blaze, Halm moved with his crew over the low divide into the St. Joe headwaters. Camp was at first set up on Bean Creek, later moved to My Creek and finally to Timber Creek.

Here they were in forest which should have been feathery green, moist and tangy; instead the leaves hung withered as if by blight, and ferns and grass blades stood sear and brown, powdered with gray ash. In this depressing landscape the men moved like shadows through the stifling overhang of smoke.

The fire-fighting crew was supported by a supply line system of five base camps ten miles apart along the Cedar Creek trail and the St. Joe River. The packing was hired done by the son of an Iron Mountain saloonkeeper named Garreau who owned his own pack string. Young Garreau became increasingly lax and lazy about moving supplies, preferring to stay in one or another of the base camps along the way eating up the choice items out of the grub shipments. On August 18 the young packer refused to move needed supplies from Bean Creek to Timber Creek and when Halm insisted, insolently hitched his revolver on his belt, took his whole pack string and pulled out.

This left Halm and his crew of eighteen virtually grubless and helpless. The ranger did have a couple of other packers and a dozen head of pack animals but this was not an outfit large enough to bring in supplies for an additional sixty-five men expected to join the crew. He would have to try to guard the fire with the small number of men he had on hand.

The following day Halm and his two packers rode out to the nearest supply base, and Halm returning alone noticed how oppressively dark the afternoon had grown and felt a distinct sense of unease.

No sooner had he reached camp than most of his crew came pounding in off the fire lines. "She's coming!" the lead man gasped. "Let's grab our stuff, ranger, and get out of here. The whole country's afire!"

Joe Halm turned to find that out of nowhere and as if by sorcery the ridges to the northwest had sprung to rolling flames, out of which an inferno wind was spreading burning twigs and branches over the countryside ahead. "It looks bad," his foreman said as the rest of the crew came running up.

Halm took quick mental stock. The Timber Creek camp stood on a small cleared flat along the stream beneath tall pines and spruce trees. The creek, about fifteen feet wide and ten inches deep, was divided around a sandbar at this point, forming an opening in the timber about forty feet across. Small as this space was, it and the creek waters would afford some protection; whereas if they tried to outrun the fire and were overtaken along some narrow forest trail they would have no chance at all.

To calm his men Halm was deliberately cool and casual when he spoke. "Well, I'd say there was nothing to get excited about yet. It looks as if the fire might go over us. If it does come this way, we'll be okay if we get into the creek and stay in the water. Besides, it's time for supper and I for one am hungry. Let's have the cook rustle up some grub and after that we'll see how things look."

This suggestion seemed reasonable and the men relaxed, drifted apart and began to make trips to the creek to wash up for supper. But the fire was coming at incredible speed and before the cook could get the meal ready an awful roar drifted in on the wind. At its sound men regathered into groups, standing together for comfort, and staring fearfully, almost hypnotically at the boiling fire crest which swept toward them across the green tree tops. Three men who were friends ran suddenly to their bedrolls and started throwing their belongings together. "We're not going to wait here and be roasted," they gasped.

The ranger slipped into his tent and strapped on his revolver. When he came out men were pointing excitedly to a ridge opposite from camp. "My God, she's jumped a mile across the canyon," they said in awe.

Halm planted himself in front of the three men who were preparing to depart. He touched the holster of his gun as he said, "Not a man leaves this camp. We're going to stay by this creek and live to tell the story."

Turning to the rest of the crew he went on, "Here's what we'll do. We'll take everything we need to the bar in the creek. Each man grab a blanket, a couple tools and some grub for himself. Chuck the rest in the tent, drop the poles and bury it. Then everybody get to the sandbar. I'll see you through."

All hastened to obey except the three recalcitrant friends. For a moment they stood eyeing Halm, but seeing him hardfaced with hand still on pistol they decided to join the others. Soon everyone was running to the sandbar with armloads of canned goods, pans, pails, fire tools and blankets, or helping bury the extra supplies and equipment in the tent.

As the last man gained the bar the fire reached the

timber and closed in on the opposite side of the creek. Trees screamed in agony, flamed and crashed, their torch tops sending forth lassoes of flame to catch other trees and pull them down too.

Halm and his crew cowered in the creek waters, with burning brands raining down on them like hail.

36

After the great run of fires on August 20 and 21, humidity rose suddenly about 1 a. m. on August 22. Fires made little advance during that day or the next, and on the night of the 23rd a light rain fell, with snow on the peaks. The fire rampage in the Bitter Roots was at an end. Pockets of smoke and flame remained but were relatively stationary and predictable.

In the conflagration from 185 to 200 had lost their lives, according to tall newspaper headings, and from 400 to 600 were still missing.

Should Halm and his crew be counted dead? It was known that vast stretches of country at the headwaters of the St. Joe Big Fork had been ravished and speculations about him were dire. Some reports gave him a crew of around 85, others around twenty, with no one volunteering a reason for the large discrepancy.

NO TRACE OF PARTY UNDER HALM—SMALL HOPE FOR HALM, said the Spokane headlines on August 23.

On August 24, the Spokane *Chronicle* relinquished hope of any kind:

STAR ATHLETE BELIEVED A FIRE VICTIM

Joe Halm, Formerly Football and Base-Ball Man, With his Party, Lost in the Fire Saturday Night at Big Fork

Not Heard from Last Four Days

Famous "S" bridge on the N. P. branchline, between Mullan and Lookout Pass, after it was rebuilt over ruins from the 1910 conflagration.

Timber destruction resulting from the great fire. Joe Halm is on the right.

Bustling railroad construction town of Taft, Montana—before the fire.

Lookout Tower on Bitter Root Divide lurched crazily after flames swept through its wooden supports.

On August 25 Ranger Roscoe Haines, Ranger Charles Fisher and a search party headed out over the Cedar Creek trail for Halm's Timber Creek camp. Reports were anxiously awaited out of Iron Mountain.

Meantime, the newspapers were assembling a more general picture of the colossal fire damage, recounting other tragedies along the way.

On those two terrible days, August 20 and 21, fires had surged like great red rivers through that double tier of National Forests on both slopes of the Bitter Root Mountains—surged also along the Continental Divide through the Blackfoot, the Flathead and Missoula national forests. Not rivers in channel but rivers in flood, inundating the land in great irregular, destructive blotches.

The Coeur d'Alene Forest, central in devastation, had spewed fireworks north, east and south.

Fires in the Coeur d'Alene and St. Joe drainages had united to form a front thirty miles across at its widest point—a front which stormed the Bitter Root Divide and raced sixty miles east through the St. Regis Valley in the Lolo National Forest, all the way to the Clark's Fork River before its energies tapered to a diminishing point.

North and east out of the Coeur d'Alene Mountains two other fire streams swept into the Cabinet National Forest. After uniting to overwhelm a thirty-five mile section of the Clark's Fork Valley, they separated again to clamp lobsterlike claws ten and thirty miles long on the virgin forests northeast of the river.

In the Clark's Fork Valley, where ran the main line of the Northern Pacific, many ranches were lost, as were parts of the little towns of Belknap, Noxon, White Pine, Heron, and the railway station at Tuscor. Thompson Falls itself was seriously threatened. On Trout Creek Ed Donlon's sawmill was destroyed with most of his equipment, including twenty-five head of horses, the pigs in the pen, and thirteen million feet of white pine lumber.

On Swamp Creek out of Tuscor, Roy Engle's fire fighting crew found themselves surrounded and took refuge on a rock slide, where all escaped harm except four men who, panic stricken, dashed into the flames.

From the Cabinet National Forest a crimson backlash struck the Pend Oreille National Forest and fanned a local fire in DeFaut Gulch previously brought under control by the crews of William T. Brashear. Brashear, Foreman W. A. LaMonte and ten men were overtaken in the onrush and huddled under wet blankets—except two men who rushed wildly forth to their deaths. The rest were found unconscious from smoke by a search party under Deputy Forest Supervisor E. G. Stahl.

Along the North Idaho-Washington line, the worst fires were outside the boundaries of the Kaniksu National Forest to the west. Most destructive was one which came over the mountains from the direction of Deer Park and crossed the Pend Oreille River below Newport, where the country was well settled. Homesteaders were forced to flee for their lives. Three who refused to leave their farms, Mrs. Ernest Deinhardt, George R. Campbell, and William Ziegler, were burned to death.

In the Kootenai National Forest one blaze swept a large area at the head of Fisher Creek, while another, started on the Yaak River, traveled east into the Pipe Creek and Big Creek drainages, doing serious damage to mining developments near Sylvanite.

At the southern end of the Coeur d'Alene National Forest, fires of the St. Joe headwaters united with those of the North Fork of the Clearwater to lay in devastation a block thirty miles wide by sixty long—the whole north end of the Clearwater National Forest and the western edge of the Lolo.

Still farther south, a body of fire twenty-five miles wide in places made a headlong rush of seventy miles out of the Locksa and Selway River drainages into the Lolo.

In the upper Selway on Moose Creek, Deputy Supervisor Ed Thenon awakened in the middle of the night to discover erratic winds tossing burning branches around his camp. He led his crew of thirty to a sandy section along the creek, where, when a crown fire rolled through the surrounding timber, all were nearly roasted. The heat drove the cook into a seizure of violent insanity, while another young man began to dance and sing lullabies.

On the North Fork of Moose Creek, Ray Fitting, who was out scouting alone, took refuge in the creek under a ledge, flames whipping above the overhanging rocks and the heat intense. When dead fish began to float past him he got really scared, thinking, "If we're going to have boiled fish we're liable to have boiled me." But he proved a hardier type of fish and survived.

In the Nezperce National Forest, the town of Elk City nearly succumbed on Saturday night when surrounding timber burned, and only the quick work of Ranger G. I. Potter in organizing a bucket brigade saved it. Happily, forest losses were not so heavy here as farther north.

As for Ed Thenon's camp cook, he recovered his senses; but the Lullaby Boy, as he came to be called, continued to croon his comforting, sleepy-time melodies and had to be sent to an asylum.

37

At last there was news out of Iron Mountain, sent by Ranger Haines. Haines had ridden in ahead of the slower search party, had met part of the Halm crew coming out from Timber Creek, and had heard directly from them their story.

At the height of the fury, great trees had been twisted off and tossed about like broomstraws. A giant pine had fallen across the sandbar with such a crash that one man was knocked down by the rush of air, while others were showered with sparks and spray. Just below them a large driftwood jam caught and became such a roaring inferno that they knew if the wind should change and bring a blast in their direction they were lost. Already their drenched clothing steamed and smoked.

The crown fire stripped the trees it did not topple, then swept on, taking with it its powerful winds. The worst was over and Halm, counting blistered noses, found all his men were still with him, none seriously burned. But all were exhausted and in shock, and after drying their blankets over still-burning debris, they dug hollows under trees and slept. Dawn revealed the wreckage of their wilderness world.

Halm's worry now was his two packers. Taking a couple of men he hiked down to the first supply camp—or what had been the supply camp, for it lay in smoldering ruins. On they went to the second camp and found it burned too. A short distance beyond they came upon charred pack saddles with girths cut, and strung out farther along the burned trail the carcasses of pack animals. It was obvious the packers had decided to free the animals to fend for themselves while they made a run for it. But the fire had overtaken the pack string and doubtless the two packers had met the same fate somewhere farther along the trail.

Sadly Halm and his men started back for the Timber Creek camp but on the way a freak wind rose forcing them to take refuge in a cave-like hollow in a bank, where they watched already blackened trees knocked down like nine-pins.

After another night on Timber Creek Halm sent his crew out, but he and his foreman Walheim stayed to guard the camp until a pack train could come in to salvage Forest Service supplies and equipment. It was a week after the fire before the packtrain arrived, and it carried out the body of a prospector Halm and Walheim had discovered. A pegleg named Con Roberts, the prospector had lived in a shack not far off the main trail. He had started out for Iron Mountain with Mr. and Mrs. Pattison and five other miners, but in his crippled condition had not been able to keep up and had been overwhelmed by the fire. The rest of the party, after a terrible ordeal, finally reached safety. The ironic thing was that Con Roberts' little shack did not burn and if he had remained there he would have escaped.

As for Halm's two missing packers they eventually

made their way to safety, and later in Iron Mountain told their incredible tale . . .

The fire had already been roaring toward them when they had released the pack animals. They had kept a gentle little saddle mare, and while one man guided her head, the other held onto her tail, and thus took turns being pulled along by the beast, which was panting and much frightened by the spark-set fires crowning along the trail. At last they reached the Bitter Root Divide where the timber was sparser and behind them the progress of the fire was slowed. Getting far enough in advance to feel safe, they dropped exhausted into a bunk in a cabin they came to along the way.

Loud piercing whinnies of the little mare woke them to a pink glare in their faces. The fire had run them down. Timber around the cabin was blazing, and the barn where they had left the mare was already afire when they rescued her and dashed down the gulch. Trees had been mowed down right and left across the trail, but the faithful, intelligent mare worked her way over and under all barriers, and two miles farther on brought them out to an old placer digging and safety.

In a little over six hours they had crossed a mountain range and covered a distance of forty miles—a super-human feat explained only by the torturous death that was on their trail.

38

On the newspaper front many stories of lost and missing crews were proving false. Ranger J. M. Vandyke, with a crew of fifty-six, was not dead at Independence Creek, in the Coeur d'Alene North Fork country, as the *Chronicle* had reported. A dozen Milwaukee laborers reported dead out of Avery were accounted for. Six hundred men, claimed by newspaper headlines to be lost in the Montana woods, all checked in.

Nor were any lives lost at the Gold Chrome mine, as had been feared. In Missoula M. L. Brain was unable to get word from the mine, and being a woman of strong purpose she resolved to go check on her son. To reach DeBorgia and the mine took her three days—by railroad handcar, by wagon and on foot. Nearing the Gold Chrome she met her son Elmer Brain and Manager Norton Beswick on their way out. For seventy-two hours they had huddled in the waters of the nearby creek under smoke so thick they did not know whether it was night or day, while the fire burned itself out a mile away.

Two days later when he reached Missoula, Norton Beswick was finally able to get through by phone to his wife and daughters in Spokane, to let them know, to their overwhelming joy, that he was still alive.

Little by little the whereabouts of fire crews, mine crews, prospectors and homesteaders became known, until, with all the missing accounted for, the tally of dead could be made. And that tally proved that all early estimates of lives lost were exceedingly and misleadingly high. (Though to this day, old-timers in north Idaho and western Montana claim that many people perished whose bodies were never found in those millions of acres of burned timber.)

Seventy-eight fire fighters had died: seventy-two in the Coeur d'Alene National Forest, two in the Pend Oreille, four in the Cabinet. Seven others had died: two townspeople in Wallace, one man in Saltese, one prospector in the St. Joe country, and three homesteaders near Newport.

The toll stood at 85.

As for damage to forests, mills, mines and homestead, that could not be reckoned until the smoke had cleared away. *The pall of smoke was so tremendous as to constitute the most stupendous phenomenon of its kind caused by any fire at any time, any place in the country.* It produced a record for dark days in the United States and Canada which in the fifty years since has never been broken.

A gargantuan smoke cloud spread eastward with the prevailing air currents. It enveloped all the rest of Montana, all of North Dakota, great chunks of Minnesota,

Wisconsin and Michigan. It respected no international boundary but sifted one and two hundred miles north into the lower reaches of the Canadian provinces of Alberta, Saskatchewan, Manitoba and Ontario. Drifting south, the cloud covered half of the states of Wyoming and South Dakota. On east it blacked out the Great Lakes region, and flowed on through the St. Lawrence waterway nearly to Quebec.

This was the area in which smoke poured in so thickly as to turn day into night. In Butte and Helena, Montana; in Bismarck, North Dakota; in Casper, Wyoming; in Pierre, South Dakota; in the twin cities of Minneapolis and St. Paul; in Sheboygan, Wisconsin; in Sault Ste. Marie, Michigan; in Watertown, New York; and in Calgary, Saskatoon, Winnipeg, Toronto, Ottawa and Montreal, Canada, sun and daylight were shut out so completely as to cause artificial light to be used by day. On trains conductors carried lanterns to find their passengers and people in rural areas, with no access to news, were at an utter loss to explain the eclipse.

Actually the smoke cloud was observed over a far wider area. From Denver and Kansas City it could be seen in the sky. It drifted out over the New England States, on down the St. Lawrence waterway, out over the Atlantic. And westward a third of the way around the world, the British vessel *Dumferline,* 500 miles out from San Francisco, reported its crew unable to take observations for ten days due to the smoke haze hanging over the ocean.

Such was the phenomenon known as the Five Dark Days, August 20-25, 1910.

Only later, when this continent-spanning pall could be dissipated by time into space; only later, when the sun's rays could find their way to earth again—only then could foresters assess how much of the Pacific Northwest's timber wealth had gone up in smoke to make up the obliterating cloud.

By then William B. Greeley stood before a new map of District One—a map with burned areas showing in red. A

map which looked as though someone had flung the contents of a bottle of red ink in one angry, splashing gesture.
Big blotches covered huge chunks of twelve of the twenty-
two forests in the district, while other forests were be-
smirched by smaller blotches.

Those red areas represented 2,500,000 burned acres—
more than 4000 square miles—with 5,500,000,000 board
feet of timber destroyed.

Within national forest boundaries in other districts
an extra 1,000,000 acres had burned, destroying an additional 1,000,000,000 board feet of timber.

Figures for losses on private land were never completely assembled but ran at least another 500,000 acres
burned, with 2,500,000,000 additional board feet of timber destroyed.

*This is nine billion board feet of merchantable timber
reduced to ashes—and to smoke cloud.*

Such a figure is too huge to be readily comprehended.
Haul that amount of lumber by freight train, and figur-
ing 35,000 board feet per car, it will fill 257,143 railroad
cars. Make these cars up into our longest freight trains of
150 cars each and you have 1714 trains in motion—or one
continuous train 2400 miles long, stretching all the way
from Seattle to Chicago, and from Chicago to St. Louis,
Missouri. In 1910, such a supply would have lasted the
entire United States for the next fifteen years.

Who and what was responsible for such a staggering
national catastrophe?

Gifford Pinchot, former chief of the Forest Service and
noted conservationist, denounced the members of Congress, including Idaho's Senator W. B. Heyburn and
Montana's Senator Thomas H. Carter, who had blocked
adequate appropriations for fire fighting equipment. Heyburn replied that the accusation was "silly," while Carter
responded by calling Pinchot a "tyrant." Yet the fire itself
was a flaming testimonial of the need for greater fire protection—for all the trails, the lookouts, the telephones, the
maps, the pack outfits and the trained personnel which
might have cut the loss down to size. Out of the recrimi-

nations came a much needed reorganization and expansion of the Forest Service.

Yet inadequate defense could never wholly explain the freakish character of the Great Idaho Fire, as it came to be called. As of the morning of August 20, almost all local fires were under precarious control. Then—what happened? As Roy Phillips put it in a report to Missoula, "I have been through many tough fires .... and still I ponder on what factors were responsible for that great run of fire on those two days and nights." In the St. Joe Valley the fire was actually clocked at seventy miles an hour— faster even than prairie fire. This in the Pacific Northwest where hurricanes are virtually unknown.

Not until the burning of whole cities during World War II did the mechanics of what was termed a "firestorm" come to be understood. In *The Man in the Thick Lead Suit* (1954), Daniel Lang writes:

> "A fire-storm starts when the air above the confluence of columns of heat from a number of fires gets so hot that a violent updraft is created, as powerful as the strongest wind. The updraft of a firestorm heated to 1500 degrees Fahrenheit moves at a hundred and twenty miles an hour. In Hamburg firemen were sucked into the updraft. The cornices of buildings didn't fall, they floated upward. Wet blankets that people had wrapped around them were torn off. Families in basement shelters suffocated, because the air literally burned up. Some people have called these fire-storms 'hurricanes of fire' but even that is an understatement."

In such a manner—at a certain moment on the afternoon of August 20, 1910, the air over the Bitter Roots reached a surcharged pitch—brooded for a time with hot, murderous thoughts —then exploded into tornadoes of violence—lashed out with berserk winds.

"Dante's Inferno!" exclaimed one observer. "Yessir, we had a good big glimpse of Dante's Inferno!"

39

One by one, 116 injured fire fighters, all but 15 hurt in the Coeur d'Alene National Forest, were released from hospitals, mainly in Wallace. The majority were restored to good health but some suffered permanent damage to eyes, limbs or lungs.

In 1912 Congress paid off their claims. Collectively the 116 men had spent 1350 days in hospital beds and endured 850 days of later incapacitation. They received a combined total of $5,450.

Ed Pulaski recovered his sight but his eyes were never as strong again nor his general health as robust. He remained in the Forest Service and in connection with his work as a ranger invented a fire-fighting tool, half hoe, half ax, which is called a pulaski. That accomplishment, together with tales told of his courage, has made him the folk hero of the disaster.

In the end, the dead were taken from their shallow, mass graves and given more traditional burial (leaving behind in the mountain canyons such names as Cemetery Ridge and Deadman Gulch, which show on maps today). Those who had been native to the Coeur d'Alene mining region were buried in the Wallace cemetery, while the remaining fifty-four bodies were received into a special plot, acquired by the Forest Service in the St. Maries cemetery in 1912.

The dead were then mostly forgotten, the bereaved wore out their grief, and survivors scattered. Wallace and the smaller towns were all rebuilt. The courageous women operators of Rocky Mountain Bell Telephone were presented with gold medals in appreciation of their services during the emergency. And near the entrance to Providence Hospital, the promised statue of the Sacred Heart of Jesus was erected—a proud monument to faith which has stood for fifty years.

All in all the human community seemed to recover from the disaster faster than the land. Decade after decade, the canyons, ridges, slopes and gulches stood stark with ghostly snags and rotten with decayed logs. For a dozen years after the fire, ashes along the St. Joe ridge remained ankle-deep where the humus soil had been blasted as though by a blow torch.

In those years, an airplane leaving Clarksfork, Idaho, and flying for 160 miles southeast along the Bitter Root Divide to Moose Creek on the Selway River would have traveled seventy per cent of flight time over the 1910 burn, with the burn extending on an average of twenty-five miles on either side of the Divide. Even then the plane would have traveled over only three-fourths of the burned area, and to cover the other fourth, would have had to make a semicircular flight into Montana, from Missoula up the Big Blackfoot River, and northwest over the Flathead, Kootenai and Kaniksu national forests. The country below appeared to have been ravished by bomb warfare.

Yet there in the ruined acres nature was patiently at work. Between the snags and on top of rotting logs, the seeds of trees and bushes were sprouting. They struggled upward, hindered by erosion and reburns, helped at times by reforestation programs. The process was long and slow. Thirty years passed before the results were much in evidence, and forty years before the hills took on true beauty again. Even now, after a fifty year period, not all is as it was. Some slopes have become eroded, and many acres bear brush and less desirable evergreens where good saw timber grew before. And even where white pine and other valuable timber have come back, trees have not yet grown to their former size.

The mountains, however, enfold alder and lodgepole pine as tenderly as they do white pine, tamarack and fir; and nature, wiped out on three million acres, has been successful in restoring verdantly leafy and pungently pine-needled life to the Bitter Root Range. Again it is a country of bigness, no less vertically inclined than before—mountains in blue-green tiers running off to the horizon in every direction.

* * *

As for the human species, even out of disaster come moments of happy coincidence. Staff Sergeant Richard D. Peairs of Kellogg, Idaho, stationed in England during World War II, fell to talking to a tea-room waitress. When the young lady asked where his home was, he answered, "Oh a place you've never heard of—Idaho."

"But of course I know Idaho," exclaimed June Parker. "The Great Idaho Fire!" It developed that her father, A. J. Parker of Ipswich had been so impressed with news reports of the 1910 fire he had preserved a whole scrapbook of clippings and it remained for him a favorite moment of dramatic, tragic history.

To those buried in the Wallace cemetery—to those grouped in a circle around a special stone in the St. Maries cemetery—surely to them it was fitting that in Suffolk across the sea all that was known of Idaho was that they, the fire dead, had perished there. What developed was fitting, too, in a different way. The Great Idaho Fire having served as introduction, the army sergeant from America later married the girl from Ipswich and brought his English bride to visit those long-talked-of Idaho hills— which by then were refreshingly green again.

So, inexorably, does life go on—both for men and for trees.

THE END

APPENDIX I

The Wellington Avalanche

Notes and Bibliography

THOSE WHO REMEMBER

During the passage of a half century, one might suppose any event to have become clouded by time and legend, and those who lived through it, if any still survive, to be hopelessly scattered into the void. As my research was done mainly in 1956 and 1957, forty-six and -seven years after the disaster, I confess myself surprised and gratified to be able to trace the whereabouts of so many people who possessed direct knowledge of the tragedy.

I interviewed the following persons:

Raymond Starrett, now Safety Supervisor for Puget Sound Power and Light Company, Olympia, Wash. He is a tall, handsome man, still bearing on his forehead a large scar received in the Wellington wreck. He related to me his own boyhood memories of the ordeal at Wellington, and from him I also learned that his mother, Mrs. Ida Starrett, is still alive. She has been long remarried and I shall not divulge her married name or the name of the town where she resides for fear people will mention the avalanche to her; understandably she still cannot bear to think of it. As a result of her injuries she has been confined to a wheelchair for many years but retains a sweet and cheerful outlook. Raymond's grandmother, Mrs. William May, recovered from her injuries and remained a very lively person until her death at the age of eighty.

Carol Thompson, granddaughter of the Bailets, is now Mrs. Scott Holmes of Seattle. From her I learned that Mr. Bailets died in 1912, and Mrs. Bailets in 1938.

Josephine Williams Phillips, who was the second wife of Ross Phillips, also lives in Seattle. Brakeman Phillips died in 1952.

Annabelle Lee, retired after a long and honorable car-

eer as a nurse, lived in Seattle with my friend, the late
Miss Anna Moore, when I interviewed her.

Charles Andrews, G. N. electric motorman who saw
the trains swept into the ravine, is now retired and lives
at Richland Highlands near Seattle. A hale and hearty
man, he possesses a phenomenal memory which was of
incalculable value to me.

Andrew Pascoe, who later became a G. N. engineer, is
now retired and lives in Seattle.

Joe Beuzer is at present the proprietor of the Terminal
Hotel, Wenatchee.

Margaret Clark, who worked for the Bailets shortly
after 1910, also lives in Wenatchee.

Edward L. Sweeney, retired G. N. engineer living in
Spokane, dictated to me a statement concerning his experiences as engineer on Train No. 27, swept into the ravine at Wellington after he had left it to join O'Neil at
Scenic.

Mettie Longcoy Murphy, sister of Earl R. Longcoy,
killed in the avalanche, lives in Edmonds, Wash., where
I talked with her by phone.

Vincent O. Burns, Bellevue, Wash., and *Harry M.
Woods,* Seattle, gave me valuable information about Wellington, later called Tye, where both lived for many years.

I also gathered the following information about other
people affected by the disaster:

Alfred B. Hensel, retired from his work in the Postal
Service, lives in Spokane and spends winters in California.
His remembrances of the Wellington wreck appeared in
the Spokane *Spokesman-Review* on the Fortieth anniver-
sary of the disaster, in an article by his son-in-law, Keith
L. Yates.

Anna and John Gray are now dead but *Varden Gray*
still lives at Nooksack, Wash., where he is an evangelist
and is still known as "The Duke of Wellington." Andrew
Pascoe talked to him in 1956 but I was unable to get in
touch with him.

Lewis C. Jesseph died in Boise, Idaho, in May, 1957.
From his brother, Ward Jesseph, I obtained a verbatim

copy of a letter Lewis Jesseph wrote in 1952 giving details concerning the party with which he walked from Wellington to Scenic before the avalanche.

Division Superintendent James H O'Neill remained with the Great Northern Railway until his retirement, and is now dead.

NEWSPAPER FILES

Files of the Seattle *Post-Intelligencer,* Seattle *Star,* Seattle *Times,* Everett *Daily Herald,* Everett *Morning Tribune,* Spokane *Chronicle* and Spokane *Spokesman-Review* for February and March, 1910.

NEWSPAPER AND MAGAZINE ARTICLES

"Northwest Railroad Disaster," by Paul Hedrick, *Harper's Weekly,* March 19, 1910, page 27.

"Avalanche! Forty Years Ago in Deep Snow Disaster Struck in the Cascades," by Keith L. Yates and Alfred B. Hensel, Spokane *Spokesman-Review* magazine section, February 12, 1950.

"Washingtonia" column by Richard and Floss Lautzenhiser, Tacoma *News-Tribune,* April 8, 1951.

"State's Worst Railroad Disaster," by Bill Wood, Tacoma *News-Tribune* magazine section, March 4, 1956.

"West's Greatest Train Wreck," by Howard E. Jackson, Portland *Oregonian* magazine section, March 2, 1952.

"The Big Tunnel," Seattle *Post-Intelligencer,* January 29, 1897, page 8.

"Wreck on the Spokane Run," by Norman Carlisle, *Coronet,* December, 1955.

"Tunnels and Snowsheds in the Cascades, Great Northern Railway," *Engineering News,* June 4, 1914, p. 1225.

"Concrete and Timber Snowsheds on the Great Northern Railway," *Engineering News,* December 12, 1910, p. 951.

"Avalanches in the Cascades and Northern Rocky Mountains, 1909-10," by Edward A. Beals, *Monthly Weather Review,* Vol. 38, No. 6, p. 951.

BOOKS AND PAMPHLETS

Avalanche Handbook. U. S. Forest Service. (Government Printing Office, Washington, D. C., 1953) .

Avalanches and Forest Cover in the Northern Cascades, by Thornton T. Munger. (Forest Service Circular 173, U. S. Department of Agriculture, 1911) .

Electrical System of the Great Northern Railway (A paper presented at the 240th meeting of the American Institute of Electrical Engineers, New York, Nov. 12, 1909, by Cary T. Hutchinson. Copy in Seattle Public Library) .

A Condensed History of the Great Northern Railway, (Public Relations Dept. G. N. Ry., 1949) .

An Engineer's Recollections, by John Frank Stevens. (McGraw Hill, New York, 1936) .

Dedication and Opening of the New Cascade Tunnel, a Monument to James J. Hill. Addresses delivered at Scenic, Wash., Jan. 12, 1929.

Rails Through the Cascades, by Eva G. Anderson. (Wenatchee World Publishing Co. 1952) .

LEGAL AND PUBLIC DOCUMENTS

Topping vs. Great Northern Railway Company. No. 11949. Dept. Two. Aug. 11, 1914, (Washington Reports, Vol. 81, p. 166) . Also certified copy of trial testimony in this case, on file in the office of the Clerk of the Supreme Court of the State of Washington, Olympia, Wash.

Coroner's Death Record, 1909-1910, King County, Washington; includes "Verdict of Jury at Inquest." (King County Courthouse, Seattle, Wash) .

VICTIM LISTS—WELLINGTON AVALANCHE
PASSENGERS
The Dead

R. M. Barnhard, 40, attorney from Spokane. Survived by wife and small child.

G. L. Beck, 40, from Marcus, Wash.

Mrs. G. L. Beck, about 30.

Emma Beck, age 12.

Marian Beck, age 9.

Beck boy, about age 3.

R. H. Bethel, 44, contracting and consulting engineer of firm of Bethel & Downey, Seattle. Survived by wife.

Albert Boles, 34, from Moberly, Ontario, Canada. Survived by brother Edward W. Boles.

John Brockman, 45, rancher from Waterville, Wash. Survived by brother of the same name.

H. D. Chantrell, 50, customs officer at Blaine, Wash. Survived by brother, Spokane; son, Seattle.

Alex Chisholm, 60, Rossland, B C. Survived by wife.

Solomon Cohn, 50, Everett, Wash. Survived by wife and five children.

Mrs. M. A. (Sarah Jane) Covington, 69. Survived by husband and married children.

George F. Davis, 35, Seattle, motorman on Seattle, Renton & Southern line.

Thelma Davis, 3, daughter of George F. Davis.

Charles S. Eltinge, 50, treasurer of Pacific Coast Pipe Company, Seattle. Survived by wife and five children, Spokane.

George A. Heron, 26, from Ireland, working as sawmill hand in Moyie, B. C.

Mrs. M. L. (Libby) Latsch, 30, head of Northwestern Sales Company, Seattle. Survived by husband and small child.

Sam Lee, an American, age about 25. Identified by tattoos.

Edgar Lemman, 47, attorney from Hunters, Wash. Survived by daughter, Hunters, and parents, Ritzville, Wash.

Ada Lemman, 39, wife of Edgar Lemman.

John Mackie, 24, from Ireland. Friend and working companion of Heron and Monroe.

Nellie Sharp McGirl, 26, a writer. Survived by husband in California, father and sisters in Midwest.

James McNeny, 59, Seattle attorney and former judge. Survived by wife.

Albert G. Mahler, 55. Seattle real estate dealer. Survived by wife and thirteen-year-old son.

Bert Matthews, 37, traveling salesman from Cincinnati, Ohio.

William May, 54, Chemainus, B. C. Father of Mrs. Starrett.

James Monroe, 26, from Ireland. Friend and working companion of Heron and Mackie.

Catherine O'Reilly, 26, nurse from Sacred Heart Hospital, Spokane.

Lillian Starrett, age 9.

Francis Starrett, baby eight months old.

Benjamin G. Thompson, Rossland, B. C. Survived by wife.

Reverend J. M. Thomson, 57, Bellingham. Survived by wife and grown sons.

Edward W. Topping, 29, traveling representative for Safety Door Hanger Company, Ashland, Ohio. Survived by father and small son.

J. R. Vail, 60, sheepherder from Trinidad, Wash.

The Survivors

John Gray, from Nooksack, Wash. Broken right leg sustained in a prior accident. Rescued from snow. Leg rebroken and minor injuries.

Anna Gray, wife of John Gray. Rescued from snow. Fairly severe injuries.

Varden Gray, eighteen-month-old son of John and Anna Gray. Rescued from snow. Fairly severe injuries.

R. M. Laville, electrician from Missoula, Montana. Rescued. Minor injuries.

Mrs. William May, Chemainus, B. C. Rescued. Minor injuries. (Mother of Mrs. Starrett.)

Mrs. Ida Starrett. Rescued from snow after an eleven hour incarceration. Serious injuries.

Raymond Starrett, age 7. Fairly severe injuries.

Henry H. White, salesman American Paper Company. Fairly serious injuries.

PASSENGERS WHO WALKED TO SCENIC PRIOR TO AVALANCHE

Sunday, February 27, 1910

John Merritt, attorney, Spokane, Wash.

Lewis C. Jesseph, attorney, Colville, Wash.

Milton Horn, 18, Wenatchee, Wash.

Edward W. Rea.

George Loveberry, proprietor hay and feed store, Georgetown, Wash.

Monday, February 28, 1910

John Rogers, real estate man, Seattle.

E. A. Sperber, Spokane.

R. McKnight.

Charles Young.
Frank Ritter, 18, Bellingham.
E. W. Boles, brother of Albert Boles, killed in avalanche.
Samuel Field, from Alaska.
Included in this party on Monday were four railroad employes: Conductor J. L. Pettit, Everett; H. L. Mertz, Hillyard; Angus Van Larke, Seattle; and Guiseppe Dinatale, a laborer. Conductor Pettit returned to the train at Wellington and was killed in the avalanche.

TRAINMEN AND POSTAL EMPLOYEES

The Dead

Lee J. Ahern, age 25, mail weigher on Train No. 25. Survived by parents, Spokane, Wash.
Grover W. Begle, 24, express messenger on Train No. 25. Survived by wife, Seattle, Wash.
Earl Edgar Bennington, 29, fireman. From Kingston, Ontario, Canada.
John Bjart, about 40, laborer.
Arthur Reed Blackburn, 33, trainmaster. Survived by wife and week-old baby in Everett, Wash.
Richard C. Bogart, 36, mail clerk on Train No. 27. Survived by parents, brother and sister, Spokane.
Fred Bohn, 20, mail weigher Train No. 27. From Palouse, Wash.
William E. Bovee, 26, brakeman. Survived by father, Renton, Wash.
Peter Bruno, 40, Italian laborer.
Alex C. (Ed) Campbell, 28, rotary conductor. Perished in cabin. Survived by wife, Bellingham, Wash.
J. O. Carroll, engineer. Survived by wife, Everett.
G. Christy, laborer.
William Corcoran, 45, engine watchman.
William N. Dorety, brakeman.
Anthony John Dougherty, 27, brakeman. From Waverly, Minnesota.
H. J. Drehl, 40, express messenger Train No. 27. From West Alexandria, Ohio.
William A. Duncan, 45, colored porter. Survived by brother, Seattle.
Archie R. Dupy, 23, brakeman. Survived by family in Waynoka, Oklahoma.
Earl Fisher, 19, either a fireman or laborer. Home reported as Rossland, B. C.
John D. Fox, 42, mail clerk in charge of Train No. 27. Survived by wife and three children, Seattle.
Inigi Giammarusti, 45, Italian laborer. From Spokane.

Donald Cameron Gilman, 33, electrician. Killed in cabin. Survived by parents, Santa Barbara, Calif.
Mike Guglielmo, 23, Italian laborer. Survived by brother, Spokane.
Milton Hicks, 25, brakeman. Survived by father, Sedro-Woolley, Wash.
George Hoefer, 28, mail clerk Train No. 27. Survived by wife, Spokane.
Benjamin F. Jarnagan, 31, engineer. Survived by father, Seattle.
G. R. Jenks, fireman. Unmarried: lived in Everett.
Charles William Jennison, 28, brakeman. From Zimmerman, Minnesota.
Sidney S. Jones, 25, fireman. Survived by wife, Everett.
John Edward Kelly, 23, brakeman. Survived by father, Everett.
William Kenzal, 38, brakeman. Survived by brother, Rochester, New York.
Charles F. LaDu, 26, mail clerk Train No. 27. Survived by sister, Sidney, New York.
Gus Leibert, 25, laborer.
J. Liberati, laborer.
Steven E. (Ed) Lindsay, 33, rotary conductor. Survived by father and brother, Seattle.
Earl R. Longcoy, 19, secretary to Division Superintendent J. H. O'Neill. Survived by mother and sister, just arrived in Everett from Wisconsin.
Francis S. Martin, engineer Train No. 25. Survived by wife and children, Spokane.
Archibald McDonald, fireman. Body found in springtime.
Peter Nino, 37, engine watcher.
T. L. Osborne, engineer. Survived by family, Leavenworth, Wash.
Harry Otto Partridge, 35, fireman. Survived by mother, Biloxi, Mississippi.
John K. Parzybok, 24, rotary conductor. Survived by bride of six months, Everett.
J. L. Pettit, conductor Train No. 25. Survived by wife and children, Everett.
Antonio Porlowlino, 35, laborer.
William E. Raycroft, 31, brakeman. Survived by wife and mother, Everett.
L. Ross, 25, fireman. From Paintsville, Kentucky.
Carl Smith, 50, laborer.
Andrew Stohmier, 30, brakeman. Killed in cabin.
Vasily Suterin, about 35, Russian laborer.
Giovanni Tosti, 30, Italian laborer.
Hiram Towslee, 36, mail clerk in charge of mail car, Train No. 25. Survived by wife, Fort Steilacoom, Wash.

John C. Tucker, 37, mail clerk, Train No. 27. Survived by wife and father, Spokane.

Lewis George Walker, 53, steward O'Neill's private car. Survived by wife and grandmother, Everett.

Julian E. Wells, 19, brakeman. Lived in Seattle.

G. R. Yerks, 24, fireman. From Belding, Michigan.

Unidentified laborers, six in number.

The Survivors

Lucius Anderson, porter on sleeping car Winnipeg. Minor injuries.

Samuel A. Bates, fireman. Rescued after being trapped for six hours beneath an engine. Minor injuries.

Ira Clary, rotary conductor. Rescued from snow. Minor injuries.

E. S. Duncan, brakeman. Extricated from wreckage. Minor injuries.

Ray Forsyth, section laborer, sleeping on passenger car. Minor injuries.

William Harrington, trainmaster. Thrown clear of wreckage. Fairly severe injuries.

Alfred B. Hensel, mail clerk Train No. 27. Extricated himself from wreckage. Fairly severe injuries.

J. L. Kerlee, brakeman. Released by others from beneath an engine. Minor injuries.

George (Bat) Nelson, fireman. Minor injuries.

Homer E. Purcell, rotary conductor. Minor injuries. Thrown clear of wreckage.

Ross Phillips, brakeman. Rescued. Fairly severe injuries.

Adolph Smith, porter from sleeper Similkameen. Rescued. Minor injuries.

Irving Tegtmeier, master mechanic. Rescued. Fairly severe injuries.

M. O. White, rotary conductor. Rescued. Minor injuries.

APPENDIX II

1910 Fire

Bibliography and Sources

INTERVIEWS AND CORRESPONDENCE

I was able to locate a goodly number of residents of North Idaho and Western Montana who had personally experienced the ravages of the 1910 fires and whom I was able either to interview or to contact by letter.

Interviews—
Wallace, Idaho: Walter Hanson, H. E. Worstell, George Tabor, Mr. and Mrs Edwin B. Kribs, Mrs. Zoe Beswick Ferguson, Margaret Mallon, R. T. Strachan, Sister Joseph Antioch, Mr. and Mrs. Harry James, Mary M. Flohr, Roy Kingsbury, George Burden, Harry McLeod, Gus Ellars, Alice Jensen, James Nicholson, Mae Solem, Mrs Bertha Kottkey.
Mullan, Idaho: Thomas Powers, William Bean, Foster Gribble, Mr. and Mrs. Harvey S. Taft, Mr. and Mrs. George Wheatley, Helen E. Clubb (now living at Burien, Wash.).
Kellogg, Idaho: George Howard, Dr. T. R. Mason, Mr. and Mrs. C. A. McKinley, N. H. Brooke, Gertrude Lent Ham, Robert B. Lafferty, Lorna Foltz Meyer, O. M. Vang, Jack Nelson, F. H. Whiteman, C. M. (Jack) Shipman, George Thompson, Ted Anthony, Vance Corbeill, Helen McBride.
Avery, Idaho: Thomas Wurth, Al Ganyd, Franklin Theriault (now of Spokane).
Missoula, Montana: Joe B. Halm.

Correspondence—
Stalker Clubb, Mrs. F. W. Rolfs, Mullan. William G. Weigle, Pasadena, California; Sally Gyde Moffatt, Lewiston, New York; Robert C. Moffatt, Canon City, Colorado; O. W. Bass, Cape Fair, Missouri—all formerly of Wallace. E. C. Fous, Avery.
A. L. Pettygrew, Spokane; Asa M. Button, Spokane; E. R. Kirkwood, Moscow, Idaho; William J. Smith, Spokane; Mrs. A. H. Morgan, Walla Walla.
Montana: Mrs. Ed Albert, De Borgia. William F. Underhill, Ronan. A. J. Rock, Alberton. C. J. Coleman, Haugan. The Saltese experiences of Jennie Linn McKane, now of Oakland, California, were sent me by Hazel Corbeill, Kellogg.

NEWSPAPER FILES AND ARTICLES

Wallace, *Daily Idaho Press;* Wallace, *Miner;* Wardner, *News;* Spokane, *Chronicle* and *Spokesman Review;* Seattle, *Post-Intelligencer;* August, September, 1910. Copies of Murray, *Coeur d'Alene Sun* loaned by Robert Skeman, Kellogg.

Series of articles by Malcolm Glendenning, Spokane, *Spokesman-Review,* August 9, 16 and 30, 1953.

Mullan, *News,* August 23, 1951.

"Hero's Story of 1910 Fire as Told in His Own Words," Spokane, *Spokesman-Review,* June 6, 1955. (Ranger Ed Pulaski's experiences as recorded by his wife, Emma Pulaski.).

"The Courage of Ed Pulaski," by Alice Spencer Cook, Denver, *Post,* magazine section, Jan. 31, 1954.

MANUSCRIPTS AND RECORDED MATERIAL

"My Experiences as a Forest Ranger's Wife," by Emma Pulaski. (Ms. in possession of Elsie Pulaski Pabst, Wallace, Idaho).

"The Railroad that Refused to be Burned Out," ms. loaned by Public Relations Department, The Milwaukee Road, Chicago. (Engineer John G. McKedon's experiences).

A recording of the late Fred Foltz' reminiscences. (In possession of his daughter, Lorna Foltz Meyer, Kellogg, Idaho).

MAGAZINE ARTICLES

"A World Afire: Heroes in the Burning of the Northwestern Forests," by G. W. Ogden, *Everybody's Magazine,* Dec., 1910.

"Idaho's Thirty Days War," by E. B. Fussell, *Colliers,* Sept. 24, 1910.

"Our Latest Forest Fires," *Harper's Weekly,* Nov. 26, 1910.

"Loss in the National Forests in Montana and Idaho, 1910," *Outlook,* Nov. 19, 1910.

"Recent Forest Conflagrations," *Scientific American,"* Nov 5, 1910.

"The Bitter Root Range," by Edwin Swergal, *Milwaukee Magazine,* April and May, 1947.

"The Great Fire of 1910," by Joe B. Halm, *American Forests and Forest Life,* July, 1930.

"Surrounded by Forest Fires," by E. C. Pulaski, *American Forests,* August, 1923.

BOOKS

Burning an Empire, The Story of American Forest Fires, by Stewart H. Holbrook (Macmillan, New York, 1944), Chapter 11, "The Milestone Blaze."

The Big Blow-Up, by Betty Goodwin Spencer (Caxton Printers, Ltd., Caldwell, Idaho, 1956).

U. S. FOREST SERVICE MATERIAL

History of the 1910 Forest Fires in Idaho and Western Montana, by Elers Koch (U. S. Forest Service, District One, Missoula, Montana. Mimeographed, 25 pages).

Historic files, 1910 fire, U. S. Forest Service, District One, Headquarters Office, Missoula, Montana.
Report of the Forester, U. S. Forest Service, 1910 (in Annual Report of the Department of Agriculture, 1911). Contains list of names of fire fighters killed.
Annual Review, St. Joe National Forest, 1955, (mimeographed).
Map material from District One Headquarters Office, Missoula, and from the Coeur d'Alene and St. Joe national forests.
Forest Fires: Their Causes, Extent and Effect, with a Summary of Recorded Destruction and Loss, by Fred G. Plummer, 1912. (U. S. Forest Service Bulletin No. 117).

DEATH LIST — 1910 FIRE
FIRE FIGHTERS

Coeur d'Alene National Forest

PULASKI'S CREW (West Fork of Placer Creek).

William Learmouth, 22; had lived or worked in Winnipeg, Canada.
Joe Fern or Ferro, 24; friend of Learmouth, also from Winnipeg.
Harry Hanson, 30, from Racine, Wisconsin.
Richard Woods, 50, an old prospector.
August Berger, 26.
Louis Shoman.

BELL'S CREW (Middle Fork Big Creek, tributary to the St. Joe River).

Joseph Beauchamp, 55, homesteader. Survived by wife.
Roderick Ames, about 30, homesteader. Survived by brothers in Illinois.
Upton B. (Smitty) Smith, 24, from Mansfield, Ohio.
William J. Elliott, 25, also from Ohio.
George W. Cameron, 32, from Nova Scotia, Canada.
Tony Butcher, an Austrian.
Chris Omiso.
Jean Viettone, Italian.
Dominick Bruno, Italian.
C. Buck.

DANIELSON CREW (Stevens Peak).

Walter Beaman or Beamair, 26. Survived by father, Sunset, Wash.

TAYLOR CREW (Bullion Mine).

Aaron Benton, 30. Survived by wife in Wisconsin.
Louis Holmes, 40. Survived by mother in Birmingham, England.
Thomas Welch, 55, from Spokane, Wash.
S. D. Adams, 30; had friends in Chicago; mother in Persia.
Leslie Zellers, 18; survived by father, Gem, Idaho.
Val Nicholson, 17; survived by father, Gem, Idaho.
Larry Ryson, from Wallace, Idaho.
Ernest Elgin, 60.

DEBITT CREW (Setzer Creek, or more accurately, Storm Creek).

Identified dead

George Smith. Survived by father, Missoula, Montana.
George A. Blodgett, from New York.
James Kerr. Survived by wife, Lewiston, Idaho.
Harry Jackson, from Tacoma.
L. Ustlo, a Finn.
James Donahue. Believed to be a lumberjack from Havre, Montana.
Frank Sanders. Had worked in Ravalli County, Montana; probably from Midwest.
Patrick Grogan. Survived by daughter, Butte, Montana.
William Casey. Survived by wife, Great Falls, Montana.
Larry Levar, an Austrian.

Unidentified dead (names known from timekeeper's record)

M. Phweiser.
J. Rusick, Hungarian.
M. Dilo.
Jack Hill, probably from Seattle.
Oscar Berg (O. Bing in some lists).
Ed Murphy.
H. Siphers, from Utah.
Ralph Ekhoen.
Frank Skeychell.
Ed Dunn.
W. F. Norton.
L. Schwartz, probably from Germany.
W. H. Baker, from Minnesota.
Frank Masterson, probably from Wisconsin.
George McGurk.
O. Ellefson, from Midwest.
F. D. Swick.
W. Polk.

HOLLINGSHEAD CREW (West Fork Big Creek, tributary to St. Joe River).

Unidentified dead (names known from timekeeper's record)

Gus Johansen.
W. Flynn.
Chris Christianson.
Joe Denton.

Sam Hull.
L. Johnson.
Edward Frye.
John Hoss.
Harry Smith.
J. Stevens.
J. Harp.

James Denton.
(brothers from Pennsylvania).
Glenn Taylor.
K. Anderson.
E. Smith from Spokane
3 unindentified men, names unknown.

ROCK CREW (Setzer Creek).
Oscar Weigert.

Cabinet National Forest

ENGLE CREW (Swanp Creek).
George Strong.
George Fease.
E. Williams.
A. G. Bourette.

Pend Oreille National Forest

BRASHEAR CREW (DeFaut Gulch).
J. Harris.
J. Plant.

OTHERS

James G. Boyd, 66, Wallace, Idaho.
Unidentified man, Wallace.
Lumberjack from Taft, died at Saltese, Montana, name unknown.
Con Roberts, prospector, St. Joe River headwaters.
Mrs. Ernest Deinhardt, homesteader near Newport, Wash.
George R. Campbell, homesteader near Newport.
William Ziegler, homesteader near Newport.

Index